Berlitz®

Greek
phrase book

Berlitz Publishing
New York Munich Singapore

Contacting the Editors
Every effort has been made to provide accurate information in this publication, but changes are inevitable. The publisher cannot be responsible for any resulting loss, inconvenience or injury. We would appreciate it if readers would call our attention to any errors or outdated information by contacting Berlitz Publishing, 193 Morris Ave., Springfield, NJ 07081, USA. Fax: 1-908-206-1103, e-mail: comments@berlitzbooks.com

Printed in Singapore by Insight Print Services (Pte) Ltd., May 2007.

Developed and produced by: *G&W Publishing Services*, Oxfordshire, U.K.
Greek edition: Dr. Ioanna Psalti

Contents

Travel 65

Sightseeing 97

Leisure 108

Making Friends 118

Stores & Services 129

Health 161

English–Greek dictionary & index 169

Greek–English glossary 200

Reference 216

Pronunciation

This section is designed to make you familiar with the sounds of Greek using our simplified phonetic transcription. You'll find the pronunciation of the Greek letters and sounds explained below, together with their "imitated" equivalents. This system is used throughout the phrase book: simply read the pronunciation as if it were English, noting any special rules below.

The Greek language

Greek is a language with a long history. The language itself has developed over the centuries into the Modern Greek of today spoken by approximately 11 million people in Greece and Cyprus, as well as Greek-speaking communities within other countries.

It is a phonetic language – the sound of each letter does not usually change with its position. Although the characters may appear confusing at first, don't be put off by this. With a bit of practice most people can read Greek in just a few hours. Spelling, however, is a different matter, as certain sounds – such as the sound *i*, as in "l*i*t" – may be written in five different ways.

Stress

Stress, or emphasis on a word, is important in Greek, as often the meaning of the word changes depending upon which syllable is stressed. In written Greek, stress is indicated by a small mark (ʹ) on the syllable to be stressed. In the Greek phonetic transcription we indicate stress by underlining the stressed syllable, for example: πόσο *poso* (how much). If you do not stress a word properly, don't worry. Most people will still understand what you are trying to say – particularly if you point to the word or phrase in this book!

Note: Over the last 10 years, the Greek language has been greatly simplified with the number of stress and breathing marks reduced, although you will still see words written with the more elaborate stress marks.

Pronunciation of Greek letters

The pronunciation of many Greek letters is similar to their English equivalents. However, look out for the Greek letter ν, which is pronounced "n," and ρ, which is pronounced "r."

It is also worth paying some closer attention to the consonant and vowel combinations and to the diphthongs.

Consonants

Letter	Approximate pronunciation	Symbol	Example	Pron.
β	like *v* in *v*oice	*v*	βάζο	*vazo*
δ	voiced *th*, like *th* in *th*en	*TH*	δεν	*THen*
ζ	like *z* in *z*oo	*z*	ζω	*zo*
θ	unvoiced *th*, like *th* in *th*ing	*th*	θέλω	*thelo*
κ	like *k* in *k*ey	*k*	κότα	*kota*
λ	like *l* in *l*emon	*l*	λεμόνι	*lemonee*
μ	like *m* in *m*an	*m*	μαμά	*mama*
ν	like *n* in *n*et	*n*	νέο	*neo*
ξ	like *x* in fo*x*	*ks*	ξένος	*ksenos*
π	like *p* in *p*en	*p*	πένα	*pena*
ρ	trilled like a Scottish *r*	*r*	ώρα	*ora*
σ*	like *s* in *s*it	*s*	σε	*se*
τ	like *t* in *t*en	*t*	τι	*tee*
φ	like *f* in *f*un	*f*	φως	*fos*
χ	like *ch* in Scottish lo*ch*	*kh*	χαρά	*khara*
ψ	like *ps* in to*ps*	*ps*	ψάρι	*psaree*
γ	a combination of the *w* sound in *w*ere and the *y* sound in *y*ard	*gh*	γάλα	*ghala*

* if this character falls at the end of a word, it changes to ς

Consonant combinations

Although double consonants are typically pronounced in the same manner as each individual consonant, some two-consonant combinations produce a sound somewhere in the middle of the two individual consonants.

Letter	Approximate pronunciation	Symbol	Example	Pron.
γγ, γκ	like *g* in *go*, but in some cases a more nasal *ng* as in a*ng*ling	*g*	γκαρσόν	*garson*
μπ	like *b* in *b*ath, but in some cases more like *mp* as in la*mp*	*b*	μπαρ	*bar*
ντ	like *d* in *do*, but in some cases more like *nd* as in e*nd*	*d*	ντομάτα	*domata*
τζ	like *j* in *jazz*	*tz*	τζατζίκι	*tzatzeekee*
τσ	like *ts* in le*ts*	*ts*	τσάντα	*tsanda*

Vowels

Letter	Approximate pronunciation	Symbol	Example	Pron.
α	like *a* in t*a*p	*a*	μα	*ma*
ε	like *e* in t*e*n	*e*	θέλω	*thelo*
η, ι, υ	like *i* in t*i*n	*ee*	πίνω	*peeno*
ο, ω	like *o* in t*o*p	*o*	πότε	*pote*

Diphthongs

Two vowels are often found next to each other and may be pronounced as separate sounds or as one combined sound. If they are to be pronounced separately either the first vowel bears the stress mark or the second vowel bears the ¨ symbol, similar to the German *umlaut*. For example: ρολόι – *roloee*, μαϊμού – *maeemoo*.

Letter	Approximate pronunciation	Symbol	Example	Pron.
αι	like *e* in t*e*n	*e*	μπαίνω	*beno*
οι, ει, υι	like *i* in t*i*n	*ee*	πλοίο	*pleeo*
αυ	*av* or *af*	*av/af*	αυτός	*aftos*
ευ	*ev* or *ef*	*ev/ef*	λευκός	*lefkos*
ου	like *oo* in z*oo*	*oo*	ούζο	*oozo*

Other combinations

Below are other two and three letter combinations. Notice that more than one combination can produce the same sound. For example, the combinations γι, γυ, and γη all produce the sound **ee**.

Letter	Approximate pronunciation	Symbol	Example	Pron.
για, γεια	like *ya* in *ya*k	*ya*	για	*ya*
γε, γιε	like *ye* in *ye*n	*ye*	γερὸ	*yero*
ειο, γιο	like *yo* in *yo*yo	*yo*	γιος	*yos*
γι, γυ, γη	like *yea* in *yea*st	*yee*	γὺρω	*yeero*
ια, οια	like *ia* in p*ia*no	*ia*	ποια	*pia*

The Greek alphabet

Α α	*alfa*	Ν ν	*nee*
Β β	*veeta*	Ξ ξ	*ksee*
Γ γ	*ghama*	Ο ο	*omeekron*
Δ δ	*THelta*	Π π	*pee*
Ε ε	*epseelon*	Ρ ρ	*ro*
Ζ ζ	*zeeta*	Σ σ, ς	*seeghma*
Η η	*eeta*	Τ τ	*taf*
Θ θ	*theeta*	Υ υ	*eepseelon*
Ι ι	*yota*	Φ φ	*fee*
Κ κ	*kapa*	Χ χ	*khee*
Λ λ	*lamTHa*	Ψ ψ	*psee*
Μ μ	*mee*	Ω ω	*omegha*

Basic Expressions

ESSENTIAL

Yes.	Ναί./Μάλιστα. *ne/maleesta*
No.	Όχι. *okhee*
Okay.	Εντάξει. *endaksee*
Please.	Παρακαλώ. *parakalo*
Thank you (very much).	Ευχαριστώ (πολύ). *efkhareesto (polee)*

Greetings/Apologies
Χαιρετισμοί/ζητώντας συγγνώμη

Hello./Hi!	Χαίρετε./Γειά σας! *kherete/ya sas*
Good morning.	Καλημέρα. *kaleemera*
Good afternoon/evening.	Καλησπέρα. *kaleespera*
Good night.	Καληνύχτα. *kaleeneekhta*
Good-bye.	Αντίο. *andeeo*
Excuse me! (getting attention)	Παρακαλώ! *parakalo*
Excuse me. (May I get past?)	Συγγνώμη. *seeghnomee*
Excuse me!/Sorry!	Συγγνώμη! *seeghnomee*
It was an accident.	Ήταν κατά λάθος. *eetan kata lathos*
Don't mention it.	Παρακαλώ, τίποτα. *parakalo, teepota*
Never mind.	Δεν πειράζει. *THen peerazee*

INTRODUCTIONS ➤ 118

Communication difficulties
Δυσκολίες επικοινωνίας

Do you speak English?	Μιλάτε Αγγλικά; *meelate angleeka*
Does anyone here speak English?	Μιλάει κανείς εδώ Αγγλικά; *meelaee kanees eTHo angleeka*
I don't speak (much) Greek.	Δεν μιλώ (πολλά) Ελληνικά. *THen meelo (pola) eleeneeka*
Could you speak more slowly?	Μπορείτε να μιλάτε πιο αργά; *boreete na meelate peeo argha*
Could you repeat that?	Μπορείτε να το επαναλάβετε; *boreete na to epanalavete*
Excuse me? [Pardon?]	Συγγνώμη, δεν άκουσα καλά. *seeghnomee, THen akoosa kala*
Please write it down.	Μπορείτε να μου το γράψετε; *boreete na moo to ghrapsete*
Can you translate this for me?	Μπορείτε να μου μεταφράσετε αυτό; *boreete na moo metafrasete afto*
What does this/that mean?	Τι σημαίνει αυτό/εκείνο; *tee seemenee afto/ekeeno*
What do you call this/ that in Greek?	Πώς λέγεται αυτό/εκείνο στα Ελληνικά; *pos leghete afto/ekeeno sta eleeneeka*
How do you pronounce that?	Πώς το προφέρετε αυτό; *pos to proferete afto*
Please point to the phrase in the book.	Παρακαλώ δείξτε μου την φράση στο βιβλίο. *parakalo THeekste moo tee frasee sto veevleeo*
I understand.	Καταλαβαίνω. *katalaveno*
I don't understand.	Δεν καταλαβαίνω. *THen katalaveno*
Do you understand?	Καταλαβαίνετε; *katalavenete*

– *kanee saranda evro.*
– THen katalaveno.
– *kanee saranda evro.*
– boreete na moo to ghrapsete? ... Ah!
"40 euros." ... Oreeste.

Questions Ερωτήσεις

GRAMMAR

Questions in Greek are formed by simply raising the intonation of your voice. However, the Greek script uses a semicolon in place of a question mark:

Πού πηγαίνετε; Where are you going?

Where? Πού;

Where is it?	Πού είναι; *poo eene*
Where are you going?	Πού πηγαίνετε; *poo peeghenete*
at the meeting place [point]	στο σημείο συνάντησης *sto seemeeo seenandeesees*
here (to here)	εδώ (ως εδώ) *eTHo (os eTHo)*
in the car	μέσα στο αυτοκίνητο *mesa sto aftokeeneeto*
in Greece	στην Ελλάδα *steen elaTHa*
inside	μέσα *mesa*
from the U.S.	από τις Ηνωμένες Πολιτείες *apo tees eenomenes poleetee-es*
near the bank	κοντά στη Τράπεζα *konda steen trapeza*
next to the apples	δίπλα στα μήλα *THeepla sta meela*
opposite the market	απέναντι από την αγορά *apenandee apo teen aghora*
on the left/right	στα αριστερά/δεξιά *sta areestera/THekseea*
over the road	απέναντι *apenandee*
there (to there)	εκεί (ως εκεί) *ekee (os ekee)*
to the hotel	στο ξενοδοχείο *sto ksenoTHokheeo*
towards Athens	προς την Αθήνα *pros teen atheena*
outside the café	έξω από το καφενείο *ekso apo to kafeneeo*
upstairs	επάνω *epano*

When? Πότε;

When does the museum open?	Πότε ανοίγει το μουσείο; *pote aneeyee to mooseeo*
When does the train arrive?	Πότε φτάνει το τραίνο; *pote ftanee to treno*
after lunch	μετά το μεσημεριανό *meta to meseemereeano*
around midnight	γύρω στα μεσάνυχτα *yeero sta mesaneekhta*
at 7 o'clock	στις εφτά *stees efta*
10 minutes ago	πριν από δέκα λεπτά *preen apo THeka lepta*
before Friday	πριν την Παρασκευή *preen teen paraskevee*
by tomorrow	μέχρι αύριο *mekhree avreeo*
always	πάντα *panda*
daily	καθημερινά *katheemereena*
every week	κάθε εβδομάδα *kathe evTHomaTHa*
for 2 hours	για δύο ώρες *ya THeeo ores*
frequently	συχνά *seekhna*
from 9 a.m. to 6 p.m.	από τις εννέα π.μ. ως τις έξι μ.μ. *apo tees enea pro meseemvreeas os tees eksee meta meseemvreeas*
immediately	αμέσως *amesos*
in 20 minutes	σε είκοσι λεπτά *se eekosee lepta*
never	ποτέ *pote*
now	τώρα *tora*
often	συχνά *seekhna*
on March 8	στις οχτώ Μαρτίου *stees okhto marteeoo*
on weekdays	τις καθημερινές *tees katheemereenes*
sometimes	μερικές φορές *mereekhes fores*
soon	σύντομα *seendoma*
then	τότε *tote*

What sort of ...? Τί είδους ...;

I'd like something ...	Θα ήθελα κάτι ... *tha eethela katee*
It's ...	Είναι ... *eene*
beautiful/ugly	ωραίο/άσχημο *oreo/askheemo*
better/worse	καλύτερο/χειρότερο *kaleetero/kheerotero*
big/small	μεγάλο/μικρό *meghalo/meekro*
cheap/expensive	φτηνό/ακριβό *fteeno/akreevo*
clean/dirty	καθαρό/βρώμικο *katharo/vromeeko*
dark/light	σκούρο/ανοιχτό *skooro/aneekhto*
delicious/revolting	νόστιμο/αηδιαστικό *nosteemo/aeeTHeeasteeko*
early/late	νωρίς/αργά *norees/argha*
easy/difficult	εύκολο/δύσκολο *efkolo/THeeskolo*
empty/full	άδειο/γεμάτο *aTHyo/yemato*
fresh/stale	φρέσκο/μπαγιάτικο *fresko/bayateeko*
good/bad	καλό/κακό *kalo/kako*
heavy/light	βαρύ/ελαφρύ *varee/elafree*
hot/warm/cold	ζεστό/χλιαρό/κρύο *zesto/khleearo/kreeo*
modern/old-fashioned	μοντέρνο/ντεμοντέ *monderno/demonde*
narrow/wide	στενό/φαρδύ *steno/farTHee*
old/new	παλιό/καινούργιο *paleeo/kenooryo*
open/shut	ανοιχτό/κλειστό *aneekhto/kleesto*
pleasant, nice/unpleasant	ευχάριστο/δυσάρεστο *efkhareesto/THeesaresto*
quick/slow	γρήγορο/αργό *ghreeghoro/argho*
quiet/noisy	ήσυχο/θορυβώδες *eeseekho/thoreevoTHes*
right/wrong	σωστό/λάθος *sosto/lathos*
tall/short	ψηλό/κοντό *pseelo/kondo*
thick/thin	χοντρό/λεπτό *khondro/lepto*
vacant/occupied	ελεύθερο/κατειλημένο *elefthero/kateeleemeno*
young/old	νέος/γέρος *neos/yeros*

GRAMMAR

Nouns in Greek are one of three genders: masculine, feminine, or neuter. (The masculine is used here for general expressions.) Nouns also change their endings according to where they are in a sentence (➤ 169 for more explanation).

How much/many? Πόσο; /Πόσοι;

How much is that?	Πόσο κάνει αυτό; *poso kanee afto*
How many are there?	Πόσοι υπάρχουν; *posee eeparkhoon*
1/2/3	ένας/δύο/τρεις *enas/THeeo/trees*
4/5	τέσσερις/πέντε *teserees/pende*
none	κανένας *kanenas*
about 30 euros	πρίπου 30 ευρώ *pereepoo treeanda evro*
a little	λίγο *leegho*
a lot of traffic	πολύ κίνηση *polee keeneesee*
no more	πια/όχι *pia/okhee*
enough	αρκετό *arketo*
few/a few of them	λίγα/λίγα απ' αυτά *leegha/leegha ap afta*
many people	πολύς κόσμος *polees kozmos*
more than that	περισσότερο απ' αυτό *pereesotero ap afto*
less than that	λιγότερο απ' αυτό *leeghotero ap afto*
much more	πολύ περισσότερο *polee pereesotero*
nothing else	τίποτε άλλο *teepote alo*
too much	πάρα πολύ *para polee*

Why? Γιατί;

Why is that?	Για ποιό λόγο; *ya peeo logho*
Why not?	Γιατί όχι; *yatee okhee*
because of the weather	λόγω του καιρού *logho too keroo*
because I'm in a hurry	επειδή βιάζομαι *epeeTHee veeazome*
I don't know why.	δεν ξέρω γιατί *THen ksero yatee*

Who? / Which (one)?

Ποιός; /Ποιό (απ' όλα);

Which one do you want?	Ποιό απ' όλα θέλετε; *peeo ap ola thelete*
Who is it for?	Γιά ποιόν είναι; *ya peeon eene*
him / her	αυτόν/αυτήν *afton/afteen*
me	εμένα *emena*
you *(formal)* / you *(informal)*	εσάς/εσένα *esas/esena*
them	αυτούς *aftoos*
none	κανένα *kanena*
no one	κανέναν/καμμία/κανένα *kanenan/kameea/kanena*
one like that	ένα σαν αυτό *ena san afto*
that / this one	αυτό/εκείνο *afto/ekeeno*

Whose? Ποιανού/-ής;

Whose is that?	Ποιανού/-ής είναι αυτό; *peeanoo/-ees eene afto*
It's ...	Είναι ... *eene*
mine / ours	δικό μου/δικό μας *THeeko moo/THeeko mas*
yours *(formal)* / yours *(informal)*	δικό σας/δικό σου *THeeko sas/THeeko soo*
his / hers / theirs	δικό του/δικό της/δικό τους *THeeko too/THeeko tees/THeeko toos*

GRAMMAR

The possessive adjectives are:

my	**moo**	our	**mas**
your	**soo**	your	**sas**
his / its	**too**	their	**toos**
her	**tees**		

They follow the word (with its article) with which they are associated:

my name	**to onoma moo**	our aunt	**ee theea mas**
your name	**to onoma sou**	your aunt	**ee theea sas**
his name	**to onoma too**	their house	**to speetee toos**
her friend	**o feelos tees**		

How? Πώς;

How would you like to pay?	Πώς θέλετε να πληρώσετε; *pos thelete na pleerosete*
by credit card	με πιστωτική κάρτα *me peestoteekee karta*
How are you getting here?	Πώς θα έρθετε εδώ; *pos tha erthete etho*
by car	με το αυτοκίνητο *me to aftokeeneeto*
on foot	με τα πόδια *me ta poTHya*
quickly	γρήγορα *ghreeghora*
slowly	αργά *argha*
too fast	πολύ γρήγορα *polee ghreeghora*
totally	τελείως *teleeos*
by chance	συμπτωματικά *seemptomateeka*
equally	εξίσου *ekseesoo*
extremely	υπερβολικά *eepervoleeka*
very	πολύ *polee*
with a friend	με έναν φίλο *me enan feelo*
without a passport	χωρίς διαβατήριο *khorees THeeavateereeo*

Is it ...?/Is there ...? Είναι ...;/Υπάρχει ...;

Is it free (of charge)?	Είναι δωρεάν; *eene THorean*
It isn't ready.	Δεν είναι έτοιμο. *THen eene eteemo*
Is there a bus into town?	Υπάρχει λεωφορείο για την πόλη; *eeparkhee leoforeeo ya teen polee*
There are showers in the rooms.	Υπάρχουν ντουζ στα δωμάτια. *eeparkhoon dooz sta THomateea*
There isn't any hot water.	Δεν υπάρχει ζεστό νερό. *THen eeparkhee zesto nero*
Here it is/they are.	Νάτο./Νάτα. *nato/nata*
There it is/they are.	Εκεί είναι. *ekee eene*

Can/May? Μπορώ;

Can I have ...?	Μπορώ να έχω ... ; *boro na ekho*
May we have ...?	Μπορούμε να έχουμε ... ; *boroome na ekhoome*
Can you show me ...?	Μπορείτε να μου δείξετε ... ; *boreete na moo THeeksete*
I can't.	Δεν μπορώ. *THen boro*
Can you tell me ...?	Μπορείτε να μου πείτε ... ; *boreete na moo peete*
Can you help me?	Μπορείτε να με βοηθήσετε; *boreete na me voeetheesete*
Can I help you?	Μπορώ να σας βοηθήσω; *boro na sas voeetheeso*
Can you direct me to ...?	Μπορείτε να με κατευθύνετε προς ... ; *boreete na me kateftheenete pros*

What do you want? Τι θέλετε;

I'd like ...	Θα ήθελα ... *tha eethela*
Could I have ...?	Μπορώ να έχω ... ; *boro na ekho*
We'd like ...	Θα θέλαμε ... *tha thelame*
Give me ...	Δώστε μου ... *THoste moo*
I'm looking for ...	Ψάχνω για ... *psakhno ya*
I need to ...	Χρειάζομαι να... *khreeazome na*
go ...	πάω ... *pao*
find ...	βρω ... *vro*
see ...	δω ... *THo*
speak to ...	μιλήσω με τον/την ... *meeleeso me ton/teen*

– seeghnomee.
– ne?
– boro?
– ne, veveos.
– efkhareesto.
– parakalo.

Other useful words
Άλλες χρήσιμες λέξεις

fortunately	ευτυχώς *efteekhos*
hopefully	ελπίζω να ... *elpeezo na*
of course	βεβαίως *veveos*
perhaps	ίσως *eesos*
unfortunately	δυστυχώς *THeesteekhos*
also	επίσης *epeesees*
and	και *ke*
but	αλλά *ala*
or	ή *ee*

Exclamations Επιφωνήματα

and so on	και λοιπά *ke leepa*
At last!	Επιτέλους! *epeeteloos*
Go on.	Συνεχίστε. *seenekheeste*
Nonsense.	Βλακείες. *vlakee-es*
Really?	Αλήθεια; *aleetheea*
You're joking!	Αστειεύεσαι! *astee-evese*
How are things?	Πώς πάνε τα πράγματα; *pos pane ta praghmata*
great/terrific	θαυμάσια *thavmaseea*
very good	πολύ καλά *polee kala*
fine	μια χαρά *mia khara*
not bad	καλά *kala*
okay	εντάξει *endaksee*
not good	όχι πολύ καλά *okhee polee kala*
pretty bad	μάλλον άσχημα *malon askheema*
terrible	χάλια *khaleea*

Accommodations

If you don't have a place to stay when you arrive in Greece, the tourist police (**tooreesteekee asteenomeea**) or the Greek National Tourist Organisation, EOT (**eleeneekos organeezmos tooreezmoo** or **eot**), will provide you with a list of hotels and telephone numbers. However, they will not book rooms for you. If you would like to make a reservation before you leave, contact the Hellenic Chamber of Hotels in Athens (☎ 01-3310022-6).

The main types of accommodation are:

Ξενοδοχεία *ksenodokheea*

Hotels. Depending on the facilities offered, hotels are classed as deluxe, A' (**protees kateeghoreeas**), B' (**THefterees kateeghoreeas**), Γ' (**treetees**), Δ' (**tetartees**), and E' (**pemptees**). Some hotels also have bungalows (**bangalo-oo**).

During the summer season (July-August), several hotels rent roof space for sleeping at a nominal price.

Διαμερίσματα *THeeamereezmata*

Furnished self-catering appartments.

Δωμάτια *THomateea*

Furnished rooms, with or without a private bath (**me baneeo/khorees baneeo**). You may be approached by several people offering you **THomateea**. Haggle for the price, especially during the low season.

Ξενία *kseneea*

Hotels operated by EOT, with strictly controlled standards.
They are usually good value.

Παραδοσιακά δωμάτια *paraTHoseeaka THomateea*

Traditional apartments in renovated, traditional old houses. Usually well equipped for self-catering and modernized inside, while retaining some original features. Ask EOT for prices, telephone numbers, and locations.

Ξενώνας νεότητας *ksenonas neoteetas*

Youth hostels. Several operate mainly in Athens and large cities. You can stay for a maximum of three nights, especially during the high season.

Reservations Κρατήσεις

In advance Εμπρός

Can you recommend a hotel in ...?	Μπορείτε να μου συστήσετε ένα ξενοδοχείο στο/στη ...; *boreete na moo seesteesete ena ksenoTHokheeo sto/stee*
Is it near the center of town?	Είναι κοντά στο κέντρο της πόλης; *eene konda sto kendro tees polees*
How much is it per night?	Πόσο κοστίζει τη βραδιά; *poso kosteezee tee vraTHya*
Is there anything cheaper?	Υπάρχει κάτι φτηνότερο; *eeparkhee katee fteenotero*
Could you reserve me a room there, please?	Μπορείτε να μου κλείσετε ένα δωμάτιο εκεί, παρακαλώ; *boreete na moo kleesete ena THomateeo ekee parakalo*
How do I get there?	Πώς πάω εκεί; *pos pao ekee*

At the hotel Στο ξενοδοχείο

Do you have any vacancies?	Έχετε ελεύθερα δωμάτια; *ekhete elefthera THomateea*
I'm sorry, we're full.	Λυπάμαι, είμαστε γεμάτοι. *leepame eemaste yematee*
Is there another hotel nearby?	Υπάρχει άλλο ξενοδοχείο εδώ κοντά; *eeparkhee alo ksenoTHokheeo eTHo konda*
I'd like a single/double room.	Θα ήθελα ένα μονό/διπλό δωμάτιο. *tha eethela ena mono/ THeeplo THomateeo*
A room with ...	Ένα δωμάτιο με ... *ena THomateeo me*
twin beds	δύο κρεββάτια *THeeo krevateea*
a double bed	διπλό κρεββάτι *THeeplo krevatee*
a bath/shower	μπάνιο/ντουζ *baneeo/dooz*

– ekhete elefthera THOmateea?
– leepame, eemaste yematee.
– eeparkhee alo ksenoTHOkheeo eTHO konda?
– Ne. THokeemaste to "Ambassador" apenandee.

Reception Στη ρεσεψιόν

I have a reservation. My name is ...	Έχω κλείσει δωμάτιο. Λέγομαι ... *ekho kleesee THomateeo. leghome*
We've reserved a double and a single room.	Έχουμε κλείσει ένα διπλό και ένα μονό δωμάτιο. *ekhoome kleesee enah THeeplo ke ena mono THomateeo*
I confirmed my reservation by mail.	Έχω επιβεβαιώσει την κράτησή μου με επιστολή. *ekho epeeveveosee teen krateesee moo me epeestolee*
Could we have adjoining rooms?	Μπορούμε να έχουμε επικοινωνούντα δωμάτια; *boroome na ekhoome epeekeenonoonda THomateea*

Amenities and facilities
Διευκολύνσεις και εξυπηρέτηση

Is there (a) ... in the room?	Υπάρχει ... στο δωμάτιο; *eeparkhee ... sto THomateeo*
air conditioning	κλιματισμός *kleemateezmos*
TV/telephone	τηλεόραση/τηλέφωνο *teeleorasee/teelefono*
Does the hotel have (a) ...?	Έχει το ξενοδοχείο ...; *ekhee to ksenoTHokheeo*
fax facilities	υπηρεσία φαξ *eepeereseea "fax"*
laundry service	υπηρεσία πλυντηρίου *eepeereseea pleendeereeoo*
satellite TV	δορυφορική τηλεόραση *THoreeforeekee teeleorasee*
swimming pool	πισίνα *peeseena*
Could you put ... in the room?	Μπορείτε να βάλετε ... στο δωμάτιο; *boreete na valete ... sto THomateeo*
an extra bed	άλλο ένα κρεββάτι *alo ena krevatee*
a crib [cot]?	ένα παιδικό κρεββάτι *ena peTHeeko krevatee*
Do you have facilities for the disabled?	Έχετε διευκολύνσεις για άτομα με ειδικές ανάγκες; *ekhete THee-efkoleensees ya atoma me eeTHeekes ananges*
children	παιδιά *pedya*

How long will you be staying?
Πόσο καιρό θα μείνετε;

We'll be staying ...	Θα μείνουμε ... *tha meenoome*
overnight only	μόνο για ένα βράδυ *mono ya ena vraTHee*
a few days	για λίγες ημέρες *ya leeyes eemeres*
a week (at least)	μια εβδομάδα (τουλάχιστον) *mia evTHomaTHa (toolakheeston)*
I'd like to stay an extra night.	Θα ήθελα να μείνω άλλο ένα βράδυ. *tha eethela na meeno alo ena vraTHee*

– ekho kleesee THomateeo. To onoma moo eene John Newton.

– A, kherete keeree-e Newton. Ya na THoome. Poso tha meenete?

– ekho kleesee ya THeeo vraTHya, ala tha eethela na meeno alo ena vraTHee.

– ne, endaksee. Parakalo eepoghrapste eTHO.

Μπορώ να δω το διαβατήριό σας, παρακαλώ;	May I see your passport, please?
Παρακαλώ συμπληρώστε αυτό το έντυπο/υπογράψτε εδώ.	Please fill in this form/ sign here.
Τι σημαίνει αυτό;	What does this mean?

ΜΕ ΠΡΩΙΝΟ	breakfast included
ΣΕΡΒΙΡΟΝΤΑΙ ΓΕΥΜΑΤΑ	meals available
ΟΝΟΜΑΤΕΠΩΝΥΜΟ/ ΟΝΟΜΑ/ΕΠΩΝΥΜΟ	full name/ first name/surname
ΔΙΕΥΘΥΝΣΗ ΚΑΤΟΙΚΙΑΣ/ ΟΔΟΣ/ΑΡΙΘΜΟΣ	home address/ street/number
ΥΠΗΚΟΟΤΗΤΑ/ΕΠΑΓΓΕΛΜΑ	nationality/profession
ΗΜΕΡΟΜΗΝΙΑ/ΤΟΠΟΣ ΓΕΝΝΗΣΕΩΣ	date/place of birth
ΑΡΙΘΜΟΣ ΔΙΑΒΑΤΗΡΙΟΥ	passport number
ΑΡΙΘΜΟΣ ΚΥΚΛΟΦΟΡΙΑΣ	car registration number
ΤΟΠΟΣ/ΗΜΕΡΟΜΗΝΙΑ	place/date
ΥΠΟΓΡΑΦΗ	signature

Price Τιμή

How much is it ...?	Πόσο κάνει ...; *poso kanee*
per night/week	τη βραδιά/την εβδομάδα *tee vraTHya/teen evTHomaTHa*
for bed and breakfast	για διαμονή και πρωινό *ya THeeamonee ke proeeno*
excluding meals	χωρίς γεύματα *khorees yevmata*
for full board [American Plan (A.P.)]	με πλήρη διατροφή *me pleeree THeeatrofee*
for half board [Modified American Plan (M.A.P.)]	με ημιδιατροφή *me eemeeTHeeatrofee*
Does the price include ...?	Η τιμή συμπεριλαμβάνει ...; *ee teemee seembereelamvanee*
breakfast	πρωινό *proeeno*
service	το σέρβις *to servees*
sales tax [VAT]	ΦΠΑ *fee-pee-a*
Do I have to pay a deposit?	Πρέπει να πληρώσω προκαταβολή; *prepee na pleeroso prokatavolee*
Is there a reduction for children?	Υπάρχει έκπτωση για τα παιδιά; *eeparkhee ekptosee ya ta peTHya*

Decision Απόφαση

May I see the room?	Μπορώ να δω το δωμάτιο; *boro na THo to THomateeo*
That's fine. I'll take it.	Εντάξει. Θα το πάρω. *endaksee. tha to paro*
It's too ...	Είναι πολύ ... *eene polee*
dark/small	σκοτεινό/μικρό *skoteeno/meekro*
noisy	θορυβώδες *thoreevoTHes*
Do you have anything ...?	Έχετε τίποτα ... ; *ekhete teepota*
bigger/cheaper	μεγαλύτερο/φτηνότερο *meghaleetero/fteenotero*
quieter/warmer	πιό ήσυχο/πιό ζεστό *peeo eeseekho/peeo zesto*
No, I won't take it.	Όχι, δεν θα το πάρω. *okhee, THen tha to paro*

Problems Προβλήματα

The ... doesn't work.	... δεν δουλεύει. *THen THoolevee*
air conditioning	Ο κλιματισμός *o kleemateezmos*
fan	Ο ανεμιστήρας *o anemeesteeras*
light	Το φως *to fos*
radio	Το ραδιόφωνο *to raTHeeofono*
television	Η τηλεόραση *ee teeleorasee*
I can't turn the heat [heating] on/off.	Δεν μπορώ να ανάψω/σβήσω τη θέρμανση. *THen boro na anapso/ sveeso tee thermansee*
There is no hot water/ toilet paper.	Δεν υπάρχει ζεστό νερό/χαρτί υγείας. *THen eeparkhee zesto nero/ khartee eeyeeas*
The faucet [tap] is dripping.	Η βρύση στάζει. *ee vreesee stazee*
The sink/toilet is blocked.	Έχει βουλώσει ο νιπτήρας/η τουαλέττα. *ekhee voolosee o neepteeras/ee tooaleta*
The window/door is jammed.	Έχει σφηνώσει το παράθυρο/η πόρτα. *ekhee sfeenosee to paratheero/ee porta*
My room has not been made up.	Δεν έχουν καθαρίσει το δωμάτιο μου. *THen ekhoon kathareesee to THomateeo moo*
The ... is/are broken.	... έχει/έχουν σπάσει. *ekhee/ekhoon spasee*
blinds/shutter	Οι περσίδες/Το παραθυρόφυλλο *ee perseeTHes/to paratheerofeelo*
lock	Η κλειδαριά *ee kleeTHarya*

Action Ενέργεια

Could you have that seen to?	Μπορείτε να μας το φτιάξετε; *boreete na mas to fteeaksete*
I'd like to move to another room.	Θα ήθελα να μετακομίσω σε άλλο δωμάτιο. *tha eethela na metakomeeso se alo THomateeo*
I'd like to speak to the manager.	Θα ήθελα να μιλήσω στο διευθυντή. *tha eethela na meeleeso sto THee-eftheendee*

Requirements Ανάγκες

In Greece the electricity supply is 220 V, with standard continental 2-pin or 3-pin plugs. A multi-adapter is recommended.

About the hotel Για το ξενοδοχείο

Where's the ...?	Πού είναι ...; *poo eene*
bar	το μπαρ *to bar*
bathroom [toilet]	η τουαλέττα *ee tooaleta*
dining room	η τραπεζαρία *ee trapezareea*
elevator [lift]	το ασανσέρ *to asanser*
parking lot [car park]	το πάρκινγκ *to "parking"*
shower	το ντουζ *to dooz*
swimming pool	η πισίνα *ee peeseena*
Does the hotel have a garage?	Το ξενοδοχείο έχει γκαράζ; *to ksenoTHokheeo ekhee garaz*
Can I use this adapter here?	Μπορώ να χρησιμοποιήσω αυτόν τον προσαρμοστή εδώ; *boro na khreeseemopee-eeso afton ton prosarmostee eTHo*
What time is breakfast served?	Τί ώρα σερβίρεται το πρωινό; *tee ora serveerete to proeeno*
Is there room service?	Υπάρχει υπηρεσία δωματίου; *eeparkhee eepeereseea domateeoo*

ΠΡΙΖΑ ΞΥΡΙΣΜΑΤΟΣ	razors [shavers] only
ΕΞΟΔΟΣ ΚΙΝΔΥΝΟΥ	emergency exit
ΜΗΝ ΕΝΟΧΛΕΙΤΕ	do not disturb
ΑΠΑΓΟΡΕΥΕΤΑΙ ΤΟ ΦΑΓΗΤΟ ΣΤΑ ΔΩΜΑΤΙΑ	no food in the room
ΠΑΡΤΕ ... ΓΙΑ ΕΞΩΤΕΡΙΚΗ ΓΡΑΜΜΗ	dial ... for an outside line
ΠΑΡΤΕ ... ΓΙΑ ΤΗΝ ΡΕΣΕΨΙΟΝ	dial ... for reception

Personal needs Προσωπικές ανάγκες

The key to room ..., please.	Το κλειδί για το δωμάτιο ..., παρακαλώ *to kleeTHee ya to THomateeo parakalo*
I've lost my key.	Έχασα το κλειδί μου. *ekhasa to kleeTHee moo*
I've locked myself out of my room.	Κλειδώθηκα έξω από το δωμάτιό μου. *kleeTHotheeka ekso apo to THomateeo moo*
Could you wake me at ...?	Μπορείτε να με ξυπνήσετε στις ...; *boreete na me kseepneesete stees*
I'd like breakfast in my room.	Θα ήθελα πρωινό στο δωμάτιό μου. *tha eethela proeeno sto THomateeo moo*
Can I leave this in the safe?	Μπορώ να αφήσω αυτό στη θυρίδα; *boro na afeeso afto stee theereeTHa*
Could I have my things from the safe?	Μπορώ να έχω τα πράγματά μου από τη θυρίδα; *boro na ekho ta praghmata moo apo tee theereeTHa*
Where can I find a ...?	Πού μπορώ να βρω ...; *poo boro na vro*
maid	μια καμαριέρα *mia kamary-era*
porter	έναν πορτιέρη *enan portee-eree*
May I have a/some ...?	Μπορώ να έχω ...; *boro na ekho*
bath towel	μια πετσέτα του μπάνιου *mia petseta too baneeoo*
blanket	μια κουβέρτα *mia kooverta*
hangers	λιγες κρεμαστρες *leeyes kremastres*
pillow	ένα μαξιλάρι *ena makseelaree*
soap	σαπούνι *sapoonee*
Is there any mail for me?	Υπάρχει αλληλογραφία/γράμμα για μένα; *eeparkhee aleeloghrafeea/ghrama ya mena*
Are there any messages for me?	Υπάρχει κανένα μήνυμα για μένα; *eeparkhee kanena meeneema ya mena*

BREAKFAST ➤ 43; CHANGING MONEY ➤ 138

Renting Ενοικιάζοντας

We've reserved an apartment in the name of ...	Έχουμε κλείσει ένα διαμέρισμα στο όνομα ... *ekhoome kleesee ena THeeameree˙ma sto onoma*
Where do we pick up the keys?	Από πού παίρνουμε τα κλειδιά; *apo poo pernoome ta kleeTHya*
Where is the...?	Πού είναι ...; *poo eene*
electricity meter	το ρολόι του ηλεκτρικού ρεύματος *to roloee too eelektreekoo revmatos*
fuse box	το κουτί με τις ασφάλειες *to kootee me tees asfalee-es*
valve [stopcock]	κεντρικός διακόπτης νερού *kendreekos THeeakoptees neroo*
water heater	θερμοσίφωνας *thermoseefonas*
Are there any spare ...?	Υπάρχουν επιπλέον ...; *eeparkhoon epeepleon*
fuses	ασφάλειες *asfalee-es*
sheets	σεντόνια *sendoneea*
Which day does the maid come?	Ποιά ημέρα έρχεται η καθαρίστρια; *pia eemera erkhete ee kathareestreea*
When do I put out the trash [rubbish]?	πότε να βγάλω έξω τα σκουπίδια; *pote na vghalo ekso ta skoopeeTHya*

Problems Προβλήματα

Where can I contact you?	Πώς μπορούμε να επικοινωνήσουμε; *pos boroome na epeekeenoneesoome*
How does the stove [cooker]/ water heater work?	Πώς δουλεύει η κουζίνα/ο θερμοσίφωνας; *pos THoolevee ee koozeena/ o thermoseefonas*
The ... is/are dirty.	Ο/η/το ... είναι βρώμικ-ος/-η/-ο. *o/ee/to ... eene vromeek-os/-ee/-o*
The ... has broken down.	Ο/η/το ... χάλασε. *o/ee/to ... khalase*
We accidentally broke/lost ...	Σπάσαμε/χάσαμε κατά λάθος τον/την/το ... *spasame/khasame kata lathos ton/teen/to*
That was already damaged when we arrived.	Αυτό ήταν ήδη χαλασμένο όταν φτάσαμε. *afto eetan eeTHee khalazmeno otan ftasame*

HOUSEHOLD ARTICLES ➤ 148

Useful terms Χρήσιμοι όροι

boiler	θερμοσίφωνας *thermoseefonas*
crockery	πιατικά *piateeka*
cutlery	μαχαιροπήρουνα *makheropeeroona*
freezer	κατάψυξη *katapseeksee*
frying pan	τηγάνι *teeghanee*
lamp	λάμπα *lamba*
refrigerator	ψυγείο *pseeyeeo*
saucepan	κατσαρόλα *katsarola*
stove [cooker]	κουζίνα *koozeena*
toilet paper	χαρτί υγείας *khartee eeyeeas*
washing machine	πλυντήριο *pleendeereeo*

Room Δωμάτιο

balcony	μπαλκόνι *balkonee*
bathroom	μπάνιο *baneeo*
bedroom	υπνοδωμάτιο *eepnoTHomateeo*
dining room	τραπεζαρία *trapezareea*
kitchen	κουζίνα *koozeena*
living room	σαλόνι *salonee*
toilet	τουαλέτα *tooaleta*

Youth hostel Ξενώνας νεότητας

Is there a youth hostel near here?	Υπάρχει ξενώνας νεότητας εδώ κοντά; *eeparkhee ksenonas neoteetas eTHo konda*
Do you have any places left for tonight?	Έχετε θέση για απόψε; *ekhete thesee ya apopse*
Do you rent out bedding?	Νοικιάζετε σεντόνια; *neekeeazete sendoneea*
What time are the doors locked?	Τί ώρα κλειδώνετε; *tee ora kleeTHonete*
I have an International Student Card.	Έχω διεθνή φοιτητική κάρτα. *ekho THee-ethnee feeteeteekee karta*

REQUIREMENTS ➤ 26; CAMPING ➤ 30

Camping
Κατασκήνωση/κάμπινγκ

Camping is allowed in designated areas only, and strictly forbidden elsewhere. EOT can provide a list of campsites and facilities. Most campsites have showers, a laundry area, electricity, a bar with snacks and drinks, and an eating area. Arrive early during July and August if you want to find a shady spot to camp.

Reservations Κρατήσεις

Is there a campsite near here?	Υπάρχει χώρος κάμπινγκ εδώ κοντά; *eeparkhee khoros "camping" eTHo konda*
What is the charge ...?	Ποιό είναι το κόστος για ...; *peeo eene to kostos ya*
per day/week	την ημέρα/την εβδομάδα *teen eemera/teen evTHomaTHa*
for a tent/car	μια σκηνή/ένα αυτοκίνητο *mia skeenee/ena aftokeeneeto*
for a trailer [caravan]	ένα τροχόσπιτο *ena trokhospeeto*

Facilities Διευκολύνσεις

Are there cooking facilities on site?	Υπάρχει ειδικός χώρος για μαγείρεμα; *eeparkhee eeTHeekos khoros ya mayeerema*
Are there any electrical outlets [power points]?	Υπάρχουν πρίζες; *eeparkhoon preezes*
Where is/are the ...?	Πού είναι ...; *poo eene*
drinking water	το πόσιμο νερό *to poseemo nero*
trashcans [dustbins]	οι τενεκέδες *ee tenekeTHes*
laundry facilities	ο χώρος για πλύσιμο *o khoros ya pleeseemo*
showers	τα ντους *ta dooz*
Where can I get some butane gas?	Πού μπορώ να βρω υγραέριο; *poo boro na vro eeghraereeo*

ΑΠΑΓΟΡΕΥΕΤΑΙ Η ΚΑΤΑΣΚΗΝΩΣΗ	no camping
ΠΟΣΙΜΟ ΝΕΡΟ	drinking water
ΜΗΝ ΑΝΑΒΕΤΕ ΦΩΤΙΑ	no fires/barbeques

Complaints Παράπονα

It's too sunny/shady/crowded here. — Έχει πολύ ήλιο/σκιά/κόσμο εδώ. *ekhee polee eeleeo/skeea/kozmo eTHo*

The ground's too hard/uneven. — Το έδαφος είναι πολύ σκληρό/ανώμαλο. *to eTHafos eene polee skleero/anomalo*

Do you have a more level spot? — Έχετε μια πιο ομαλή θέση; *ekhete mia peeo omalee thesee*

You can't camp here. — Δεν μπορείτε να κατασκηνώσετε εδώ. *THen boreete na kataskeenosete eTHo*

Camping equipment Εξοπλισμός κάμπινγκ

butane gas	το υγραέριο *to eeghraereeo*
campbed	το κρεββάτι εκστρατείας *to krevatee ekstrateeas*
charcoal	το κάρβουνο *to karvoono*
cooler [coolbox]	το φορητό ψυγείο *to foreeto pseeyeeo*
compass	η πυξίδα *ee peekseeTHa*
flashlight [torch]	ο φακός *o fakos*
groundcloth [groundsheet]	ο μουσαμάς για το έδαφος *o moosamas ya to eTHafos*
guy rope	το σκοινί της τέντας *to skeenee tees tendas*
hammer	το σφυρί *to sfeeree*
kerosene stove	το καμινέτο *to kameeneto*
knapsack	ο σάκκος *o sakos*
mallet	ο κόπανος *o kopanos*
matches	τα σπίρτα *ta speerta*
(air) mattress	το στρώμα (αέρος) *to stroma (aeros)*
paraffin	το παραφινέλαιο *to parafeeneleo*
sleeping bag	ο υπνόσακκος *o eepnosakos*
tent	η σκηνή *ee skeenee*
tent pegs	το παλούκι *to palookee*
tent pole	ο στύλος της σκηνής *o steelos tees skeenees*

Checking out Αναχώρηση

What time do we need to vacate the room?	Τί ώρα πρέπει να αδειάσουμε το δωμάτιο; *tee ora prepee na aTHyasoome to THomateeo*
Could we leave our baggage here until ...?	Μπορούμε να αφήσουμε τα πράγματά μας εδώ ως τις ...; *boroome na afeesoome ta praghmata mas eTHo os tees ...*
I'm leaving now.	Φεύγω τώρα. *fevgho tora*
Could you order me a taxi, please?	Μπορείτε να μου καλέσετε ένα ταξί; *boreete na moo kalesete ena taksee*
It's been a very enjoyable stay.	Η διαμονή μου ήταν πολύ ευχάριστη. *ee THeeamonee moo eetan polee efkhareestee*

Paying Πληρωμή

Tipping depends largely on what class hotel you are staying at – the higher the class, the more generous the tip. As a guideline, €1 per suitcase to the porter and €1–1.50 per night to the chamber maid (more in a deluxe hotel) are recommended.

May I have my bill, please?	Μπορώ να έχω το λογαριασμό, παρακαλώ; *boro na ekho to logharyazmo parakalo*
How much is my telephone bill?	Πόσο είναι ο λογαριασμός τηλεφώνου; *poso eene o logharyazmos teelefonoo*
I think there's a mistake in this bill.	Νομίζω ότι έγινε ένα λάθος στο λογαριασμό. *nomeezo otee eyeene ena lathos sto logharyazmo*
I've made ... telephone calls.	Έχω κάνει ... τηλεφωνήματα. *ekho kanee ... teelefoneemata*
I've taken ... from the mini-bar.	Έχω πάρει ... από το μίνι-μπαρ. *ekho paree ... apo to "mini-bar"*
Can I have an itemized bill?	Μπορώ να έχω έναν αναλυτικό λογαριασμό; *boro na ekho enan analeeteeko logharyazmo*
Could I have a receipt, please?	Μπορώ να έχω μια απόδειξη, παρακαλώ; *boro na ekho mia apoTHeeksee parakalo*

TIME ➤ 220

Eating Out

Restaurants Εστιατόρια

Eating out or at home is a social occasion in Greece. Children get used to eating out in restaurants from a very young age, and you will see them with their families even late at night. Restaurants that display tourist menus, or fixed price menus, will usually provide good value meals. But if you wish to sample truly Greek food you should try to seek out more ethnic restaurants. Here you can often select your meal, particularly fish, from a display in the kitchen and even talk to the chef about how you want it cooked.

The following are the most common types of restaurant:

Ταβέρνα *taverna*

The taverna is the most common eating place you will find. Prices are reasonable, and you will find a good selection of **mezeTHes** (appetizers) and **mayeerefta** (baked or stewed snacks), as well as **tees oras** (meat and fish).

Εστιατόριο *esteeatoreeo*

A more general term for restaurant. These tend to be more expensive than tavernas. Most offer a selection of Greek and foreign food.

Ψαροταβέρνα *psarotaverna*

A fish taverna, usually found on the islands and in coastal areas. These specialize in fish (**psaree**) and seafood (**thalaseena**). If you can't decide what to eat, ask to see the fish in the kitchen (sometimes still alive!). Point to the one you want – and you will soon be enjoying it cooked on your plate!

Ψησταριά *pseestareea*

Like a taverna but specializes in grilled meat (always cooked **sta karvoona**, charcoal grilled), which gives it a very distinctive flavor. Apart from meat, the usual choice of salads and **mezeTHes** can be found, but no **mayeerefta** or a very limited choice.

Μεζεδοπωλείο *mezeTHopoleeo*

Specializes in **mezeTHes**, which can be incredibly substantial and filling. These are served with wine, beer, or **oozo** (ouzo, an anise-flavored aperitif).

Ουζερί *oozeree*

A traditional establishment, nowadays popular with young people, where you can enjoy an ouzo with a few **mezeTHes** – traditionally, **khtapoTHee** (octopus), **elee-es** (olives), **antzooyes** (anchovies), and **feta** (feta cheese).

Σουβλατζίδικο *soovlatzeeTHeeko*

The Greek answer to fast food, these shops, often mere stalls, serve grilled skewered meat (**soovlakee**) or **yeeros** (gyros) in pita bread (**peeta**) with tomatoes, onions, and **tzatzeekee** (tzatziki).

Those who prefer something more familiar will feel at home in a McDonald's orWendy's, or their Greek equivalents, Goodies and Hambo.

Meal times Τα φαγητά

Breakfast Πρωινό *proeeno*

Greeks rarely eat breakfast. They usually have a strong sweet cup of coffee (**varee ghleeko**) in the morning, followed by another one at work between 10 and 11 a.m., maybe with a pastry. At summer resorts, however, you will typically have a wider choice of English or continental breakfast ➤ 43

Lunch μεσημεριανό *meseemeryano*

The main meal, although because of the summer heat some Greeks eat lighter at lunchtime and have their main meal in the evening. Lunch is usually eaten from 2 to 3 p.m., but most restaurants will serve it until 4 p.m.

Dinner βραδυνό *vraTHeeno*

This is often eaten late – normally at 9 or 10 p.m., and it is not unusual to find restaurants serving food until midnight or later. Snacks can be bought at **soovlatzeeTHeeka** (souvlaki stalls) or **snak bar** (snack bars) until the early hours of the morning.

Greek cuisine η Ελληνική κουζίνα

Greek cuisine has a tradition almost as long as Greek history itself. The emphasis is on fresh meat, fish, vegetables, and fruit, flavored with a delicate combination of herbs and spices found in abundance in the Greek mountains. Some of the food you can taste today in the Greek islands probably does not differ much from what the ancient Greeks enjoyed 2,500 years ago, albeit with Turkish and Italian influences .

ESSENTIAL

A table for ..., please.	Ένα τραπέζι για ..., παρακαλώ. *ena trapezee ya ..., parakalo*
1/2/3/4	έναν (μια)/δύο/τρεις/τέσσερις *enan/THeeo/trees/teserees*
Thank you.	Ευχαριστώ. *efkhareesto*
I'd like to pay.	Θα ήθελα να πληρώσω. *tha eethela na pleeroso*

Finding a place to eat
Βρίσκοντας ένα μέρος για φαγητό

Can you recommend a good restaurant?	Μπορείτε να μας συστήσετε ένα καλό εστιατόριο; *boreete na mas seesteesete ena kalo esteeatoreeo*
Is there a(n) ... near here?	Υπάρχει ... εδώ κοντά; *eeparkhee...eTHo konda*
traditional local restaurant	ένα τοπικό παραδοσιακό εστιατόριο *ena topeeko paraTHoseeako esteeatoreeo*
fish restaurant	μια ψαροταβέρνα *mia psarotaverna*
Greek restaurant	ένα ελληνικό εστιατόριο *ena eleeneeko esteeatoreeo*
Italian restaurant	ένα ιταλικό εστιατόριο *ena eetaleeko esteeatoreeo*
inexpensive restaurant	ένα φτηνό εστιατόριο *ena fteeno esteeatoreeo*
Where can I find a(n) ...?	Πού μπορώ να βρώ ...; *poo boro na vro*
souvlaki/gyros stand	ένα σουβλατζίδικο *ena soovlatzeeTHeeko*
café	μια καφετέρια *mia kafeteria*
fast food restaurant	ένα φαστ φουντ *ena "fast food"*
pizzeria	πιτσαρία *peetsareea*
pastry shop	ένα ζαχαροπλαστείο *ena zakharoplasteeo*

DIRECTIONS ➤ 94

Reservations Κρατήσεις

I'd like to reserve a table for 2 this evening at ...	Θα ήθελα να κλείσω ένα τραπέζι για δύο απόψε στις ... *tha eethela na kleeso ena trapezee ya THeeo apopse stees*
We'll come at 11:00.	Θα έρθουμε στις έντεκα. *tha erthoome stees endeka*
A table for 2, please.	Ένα τραπέζι για δύο, παρακαλώ. *ena trapezee ya THeeo, parakalo*
We have a reservation.	Έχουμε κλείσει τραπέζι. *ekhoome kleesee trapezee*

Τό όνομα, παρακαλώ;	What's the name, please?
Λυπάμαι, είμαστε γεμάτοι.	I'm sorry. We're very busy/full up.
Θα έχουμε ένα ελεύθερο τραπέζι σε ... λεπτά.	We'll have a free table in ... minutes.
Ελάτε σε ... λεπτά.	You'll have to come back in ... minutes.

Where to sit Πού να καθήσετε

Could we sit ...?	Μπορούμε να καθήσουμε ...; *boroome na katheesoome*
over there/outside	εκεί/έξω *ekee/ekso*
in a non-smoking area	σε μια περιοχή για μη καπνίζοντες *se mia pereeokhee ya mee kapneezondes*
by the window	κοντά στο παράθυρο *konda sto paratheero*
Smoking or non-smoking?	Καπνίζοντες ή μη καπνίζοντες; *kapneezondes ee mee kapneezondes*

- tha eethela na kleeso ena trapezee ya apopse.
- *ya posa atoma?*
- ya tesera.
- *tee ora tha erthete?*
- tha erthoome stees okhto.
- *ke to onoma, parakalo?*
- Smith.
- *endaksee. Tha sas THoome stees okhto.*

TIME ➤ 220; NUMBERS ➤ 216

Ordering Παραγγέλνοντας

Waiter! / Waitress!	Γκαρσόν!/Δεσποινίς! *garson/THespeenees*
May I see the wine list, please?	Μπορώ να δω τον κατάλογο κρασιών, παρακαλώ; *boro na THo ton katalogho kraseeon, parakalo*
Do you have a set menu?	Υπάρχει μενού α λα κάρτ; *eeparkhee menoo a la kart*
Can you recommend some typical local dishes?	Μπορείτε να μας συστήσετε τυπικά παραδοσιακά πιάτα; *boreete na mas seesteesete teepeeka paraTHoseeaka piata*
Could you tell me what ... is?	Μπορείτε να μου πείτε τί είναι το ...; *boreete na moo peete tee eene to*
What's in it?	Τί έχει μέσα; *tee ekhee mesa*
What kind of ... do you have?	Τί είδους ... έχετε; *tee eeTHoos ... ekhete*
I'll have ...	Θα πάρω ... *tha paro*
a bottle / glass / carafe of ...	ένα μπουκάλι/ένα ποτήρι/μια καράφα ... *ena bookalee/ena poteeree/ mia karafa*

Είσαστε έτοιμοι να παραγγείλετε;	Are you ready to order?
Τι θα πάρετε;	What would you like?
Σας συστηνω ...	I recommend ...
Δεν έχουμε ...	We don't have ...
Θα πάρει ... λεπτά.	That will take ... minutes.
Καλή όρεξη.	Enjoy your meal.

- eeste eteemee na parangeelete?
- *boreete na seesteesete katee teepeeka eleeneeko?*
- nc. sas seesteeno ...
- *endaksee, tha paro afto ke mia saluta, parakalo.*
- veveos. Ke tee tha thelate na pee-eete?
- *mia karafa kokeeno krasee.*

DRINKS ➤ 50; MENU READER ➤ 52

Accompaniments Συνοδεία φαγητού

Could I have ... without ...?	Μπορώ να έχω ... χωρίς ...; *boro na ekho ... khorees*
Could I have a salad instead of vegetables, please?	Μπορώ να πάρω σαλάτα αντί λαχανικά, παρακαλώ; *boro na paro salata andee lakhaneeka, parakalo*
Does the meal come with vegetables/potatoes?	Το φαγητό σερβίρεται με λαχανικά/πατάτες; *to fayeeto serveerete me lakhaneeka/patates*
Do you have any sauces?	Έχετε σάλτσες; *ekhete saltses*
Would you like ... with that?	Θέλετε ... με αυτό; *thelete ... me afto*
vegetables/a salad	λαχανικά/σαλάτα *lakhaneeka/salata*
potatoes/fries	πατάτες/πατάτες τηγανητές *patates/patates teeghaneetes*
sauce	σάλτσα *saltsa*
ice	πάγο *pagho*
May I have some ...?	Μπορώ να έχω λίγο ...; *boro na ekho leegho*
bread	ψωμί *psomee*
butter	βούτυρο *vooteero*
lemon	λεμόνι *lemonee*
mustard	μουστάρδα *moostarTHa*
pepper	πιπέρι *peeperee*
salt	αλάτι *alatee*
seasoning	αλατοπίπερο *alatopeepero*
sugar	ζάχαρη *zakharee*
artificial sweetener	ζακχαρίνη *zak-khareenee*
vinaigrette [French dressing]	λαδόξιδο *laTHokseeTHo*
olive oil	ελαιόλαδο *eleolaTHo*

MENU READER ➤ 52

General questions Γενικές ερωτήσεις

Could I/we have a(n) (clean) ..., please?	Μπορώ να έχω/μπορούμε να έχουμε ένα/μια (καθαρό/καθαρή) ... παρακαλώ; *boro na ekho/boroome na ekhoome ena/mia (katharo/ katharee) ... parakalo*
ashtray	σταχτοδοχείο *stakhtoTHokheeo*
cup/glass	φλυτζάνι/ποτήρι *fleetzanee/poteeree*
fork/knife	πηρούνι/μαχαίρι *peeroonee/makheree*
napkin [serviette]	πετσέτα *petseta*
plate/spoon	πιάτο/ένα κουτάλι *piato/kootalee*
I'd like some more ..., please.	Θα ήθελα λίγο ακόμη ..., παρακαλώ. *tha eethela leegho akomee ..., parakalo*
Nothing more, thanks.	Τίποτε άλλο, ευχαριστώ. *teepote alo, efkhareesto*

Special requirements Ειδικές ανάγκες

I mustn't eat food containing ...	Δεν πρέπει να φάω φαγητό που περιέχει ... *THen prepee na fao fayeeto poo peree-ekhee*
flour/fat	αλεύρι/λίπος *alevree/leepos*
salt/sugar	αλάτι/ζάχαρη *alatee/zakharee*
Do you have meals for diabetics?	Έχετε φαγητά/ποτά για διαβητικούς; *ekhete fayeeta ya THeeaveeteekoos*
Do you have vegetarian meals?	Έχετε φαγητά για χορτοφάγους; *ekhete fayeeta ya khortofaghoos*

For the children Για τα παιδιά

Could we have a child's seat, please?	Μπορούμε να έχουμε ένα παιδικό κάθισμα; *boroome na ekhoome ena peTHeeko katheezma*
Where can I feed/ change the baby?	Πού μπορώ να ταΐσω/αλλάξω το μωρό; *poo boro na taeeso/alakso to moro*

CHILDREN ➤ 113

Café / Fast food
Καφετέρια/Φαστ φουντ

Something to drink Κάτι να πιείτε

I'd like ...	Θα ήθελα ... *tha eethela ...*
beer	μια μπύρα *mia beera*
(hot) chocolate	μια ζεστή σοκολάτα *mia zestee sokolata*
coffee / tea	ένα καφέ/ένα τσάι *ena kafe/ena tsaee*
black / with milk	σκέτο/με γάλα *sketo/me ghala*
fruit juice	ένα χυμό φρούτων *ena kheemo frooton*
mineral water	ένα εμφιαλωμένο νερό *ena emfeealomeno nero*
red / white wine	άσπρο/κόκκινο κρασί *aspro/ kokeeno krasee*

And to eat Και να φάτε

A piece of ..., please.	Ένα κομμάτι ..., παρακαλώ. *ena komatee ..., parakalo*
I'd like two of those.	Θα ήθελα δύο από αυτά. *tha eethela THeeo apo afta*
burger / cake	το χάμπουργκερ/το κέηκ *to khamboorger/to "cake"*
fries / omelet	οι τηγανητές πατάτες/η ομελέττα *ee teeghaneetes patates/ee omeleta*
sandwich / sausage	το σάντουιτς/το λουκάνικο *to "sandwich"/to lookaneeko*
A ... ice cream, please.	Ένα παγωτό ..., παρακαλώ. *ena paghoto ..., parakalo*
vanilla / chocolate	βανίλλια/σοκολάτα *vaneeleea/sokolata*
A ... portion, please.	Μια ... μερίδα, παρακαλώ. *mia ... mereeTHa, parakalo*
small / medium / large	μικρή/κανονική/μεγάλη *meekree/kanoneekee/meghalee*
It's to go [take away].	Είναι για να το πάρω (σπίτι). *eene ya na to paro (speetee)*

DRINKS ➤ 50

– tee tha parete?

– THeeo kafeTHes, parakalo.

– sketee ee me ghala?

– me ghala, parakalo.

– THa fate teepota?

– ne, THeeo komatya "cake," parakalo.

– teepota alo?

– okhee, efkhareesto.

Complaints Παράπονα

I have no knife/fork/spoon.	Δεν έχω μαχαίρι/πηρούνι/κουτάλι. *THen ekho makheree/ peeroonee/kootalee*
There must be some mistake.	Πρέπει να έγινε κάποιο λάθος. *prepee na eyeene kapeeo lathos*
That's not what I ordered.	Δεν παρήγγειλα αυτό. *THen pareengeela afto*
I asked for ...	Ζήτησα ... *zeeteesa*
The meat is ...	Το κρέας είναι ... *to kreas eene ...*
overdone	πολύ ψημένο *polee pseemeno*
underdone	όχι καλά ψημένο *okhee kala pseemeno*
too tough	πολύ σκληρό *polee skleero*
This is too ...	Αυτό είναι πολύ ... *afto eene polee ...*
bitter/sour/salty	πικρό/ξυνό/αλμυρό *peekro/kseeno/almeero*
The food is cold.	Το φαγητό είναι κρύο. *to fayeeto eene kreeo*
This isn't fresh.	Αυτό δεν είναι φρέσκο. *afto THen eene fresko*
How much longer will our food be?	Πόση ώρα ακόμη θα κάνει το φαγητό; *posee ora akomee tha kanee to fayeeto*
Have you forgotten our drinks?	Ξεχάσατε τα ποτά μας; *ksekhasate ta pota mas*
This isn't clean.	Αυτό δεν είναι καθαρό. *afto THen eene katharo*
I'd like to speak to the head waiter/manager.	Θα ήθελα να μιλήσω στον αρχισερβιτόρο/μάνατζερ. *tha eethela na meeleeso ston arkheeserveetoro/ "manager"*

Paying Πληρωμή

In Greek restaurants the service charge is included in the price. However, it is still customary to leave a little extra if you are satisfied with the service.

I'd like to pay.	Θα ήθελα να πληρώσω. *tha eethela na pleeroso*
We'd like to pay separately.	Θα πληρώσουμε ξεχωριστά. *tha pleerosoome ksekhoreesta*
It's all together.	Όλοι μαζί. *olee mazee*
I think there's a mistake in this bill.	Νομίζω ότι έχει γίνει λάθος στο λογαριασμό. *nomeezo otee ekhee yeenee lathos sto logharyazmo*
What is this amount for?	Τι είναι αυτό το ποσό; *tee eene afto to poso*
I didn't have that. I had ...	Δεν πήρα αυτό. Πήρα ... *THen peera afto. peera*
Is service included?	Συμπεριλαμβάνεται και η υπηρεσία; *seembereelamvanete ke ee eepeereseea*
Can I pay with this credit card?	Μπορώ να πληρώσω με αυτήν την πιστωτική κάρτα; *boro na pleeroso me afteen teen peestoteekee karta*
I've forgotten my wallet.	Ξέχασα το πορτοφόλι μου. *ksekhasa to portofolee moo*
I don't have enough money.	Δεν έχω αρκετά χρήματα. *THen ekho arketa khreemata*
Could I have a tax [VAT] receipt, please?	Μπορώ να έχω απόδειξη με ΦΠΑ, παρακαλώ; *boro na ekho apoTHeeksee me fee-pee-a, parakalo*
That was a delicious meal.	Ήταν ένα πολύ νόστιμο γεύμα. *eetan ena polee nosteemo yevma*

- garson! to logharyazmo, parakalo.
- *veveos. oreeste.*
- seembereelamvanete ee eepeereseea?
- *ne.*
- boro na pleeroso me afteen teen peestoteekee karta?
- *veveos.*
- efkhareesto. eetan ena polee nosteemo yevma.

NUMBERS ➤ 216

Course by course Κατά πιάτο

Breakfast Πρωινό

Breakfast is not an important meal in Greece (➤ 34). Hotels that cater for tourists will probably offer a contintental style breakfast, and maybe also eggs (➤ 44).

I'd like …	Θα ήθελα … *tha eethela*
fruit juice	ένα χυμό φρούτων *ena kheemo frooton*
jam	μαρμελάδα *marmelaTHa*
yogurt (with honey)	γιαούρτι (με μέλι) *yaoortee (me melee)*
bread	ψωμί *psomee*
butter	βούτυρο *vooteero*
milk	γάλα *ghala*
rolls	ψωμάκια *psomakeea*

Appetizers [Starters] Ορεκτικά

ελιές (γεμιστές)	*elee-es (yemeestes)*	(stuffed) olives
κρύο κρέας	*kreeo kreas*	cold meat
πατέ	*pate*	pâté
πεπόνι	*peponee*	melon
ποικιλία ορεκτικών	*peekeeleea orekteekon*	assorted appetizers
ρέγγα (καπνιστή)	*renga (kapneestee)*	(smoked) herring
καλαμαράκια	*kalamarakeea*	baby squid fried in batter
μαρίδα τηγανητή	*mareeTHa teeghaneetee*	whitebait fried in batter

Ντολμαδάκια *dolmaTHakeea*

Vine leaves stuffed with rice and onions and flavored with dill.

Ταραμοσαλάτα *taramosalata*

Dip made from fish roe blended with bread, olive oil, lemons, and onions.

Τζατζίκι *tzatzeekee*

A dip of yogurt, garlic, cucumber and olive oil.

Σπανακόπιττα *spanakopeeta*

Filo pastry pies filled with spinach, feta cheese, and eggs.

Κεφτεδάκια *kefteTHakeea*

Fried mincemeat balls containing onions, bread crumbs, and herbs.

Soups Σούπες

κοτόσουπα	*kotosoopa*	clear chicken soup
ρεβύθια	*reveetheea*	chickpea soup
σούπα αυγολέμονο	*soopa avgholemono*	soup with rice, eggs, and lemon juice
πατσάς	*patsas*	tripe soup
σούπα φακές	*soopa fakes*	lentil soup
τοματόσουπα	*tomatosoopa*	tomato soup
ταχινόσουπα	*takheenosoopa*	"tahini" (sesame seed) soup
φασολάδα	*fasolaTHa*	bean soup with tomatoes and parsley
χορτόσουπα	*khortosoopa*	vegetable soup
κακαβιά	*kakavya*	fish stew with tomatoes

Κρεατόσουπα *kreatosoopa*

Meat soup, sometimes thickened with egg and lemon.

Ψαρόσουπα *psarosoopa*

Fish soup thickened with egg and lemon, and often also with white rice.

Τραχανάς *trakhanas*

Cracked wheat soup. Varies by region. Eaten plain for breakfast (like porridge) in winter, or with chopped tomatoes and grated cheese as a more substantial meal. Typically eaten without the cheese during fasting periods.

Egg dishes/Omelets Πιάτα αυγών/Ομελέτες

I'd like an omelet.	Θα ήθελα μια ομελέττα. *tha eethela mia omeleta*
eggs	αυγά *avgha*
soft-boiled	μελάτα *melata*
hard-boiled	σφικτά *sfeekhta*
fried	τηγανητά (μάτια) *teeghaneeta (mateea)*
poached	ποσέ *pose*
cheese omelet	ομελέττα με τυρί *omeleta me teeree*
ham omelet	ομελέττα με ζαμπόν *omeleta me zambon*

Fish and seafood Ψάρι και θαλασσινά

Fresh fish and seafood are always available in Greece, and fish products are widely consumed. Don't miss the boiled fish (scorpion fish, grouper, and blackfish are the best). A soup made from fish broth and thickened with egg and lemon (**afgholemono**) is eaten first, followed by the fish itself and vegetables with mayonnaise. Smaller fish are eaten fried in olive oil (**teeghaneeta**) or grilled over charcoal (**pseeta**).

αντζούγιες	*antzooyes*	anchovies
αστακός	*astakos*	lobster
γαρίδες	*ghareeTHes*	shrimp [prawns]
γλώσσα	*ghlosa*	sole
καβούρι	*kavooree*	crab
καλαμάρι	*kalamaree*	squid
κέφαλος	*kefalos*	mullet
μπακαλιάρος	*bakalee-aros*	fresh cod
μπακαλιάρος παστός	*bakaleearos pastos*	salted cod
μπαρμπούνι	*barboonee*	red mullet
μύδια	*meeTHya*	mussels
ξιφίας	*kseefeeas*	swordfish
σαρδέλλα	*sarTHela*	sardines
σουπιά	*soopia*	cuttlefish
στρείδια	*streeTHya*	oysters
σφυρίδα	*sfeereeTHa*	grouper
τόνος	*tonos*	tuna
χέλι	*khelee*	eel
χταπόδι	*khtapoTHee*	octopus

Αστακός *astakos*
Lobster, often served with oil and lemon sauce or garlic mayonnaise.

Γαρίδες με φέτα/σαγανάκι *ghareeTHes me feta/saghanakee*
Shrimp [prawns] with onions, tomatoes, and seasonings, baked with feta.

Χταπόδι κρασάτο *khtapoTHee krasato*
Octopus stewed in wine sauce.

Ψάρι μαρινάτο *psaree mareenato*
Mullet, sole, or mackerel, fried and served with a wine sauce.

Meat and poultry Κρέας και πουλερικά

βοδινό	*voTHeeno*	beef
χοιρινό	*kheereeno*	pork
μοσχάρι	*moskharee*	veal
αρνί	*arnee*	lamb
ζαμπόν	*zambon*	ham
κατσικάκι	*katseekakee*	goat
κοτολέτες	*kotoletes*	cutlets
λουκάνικα	*lookaneeka*	sausages
μπριζόλα βοδινή/χοιρινή	*breezola voTHeenee/heereenee*	beef/pork steak
μυαλό	*mialo*	brains
νεφρά	*nefra*	kidneys
συκώτι	*seekotee*	liver
φιλέτο	*feeleto*	fillet
γαλοπούλα	*ghalopoola*	turkey
κοτόπουλο	*kotopoolo*	chicken
κουνέλι	*koonelee*	rabbit
πάπια	*papia*	duck
φασιανός	*faseeanos*	pheasant
χήνα	*kheena*	goose

Αρνάκι εξοχικό *arnakee eksokheeko*
Spiced lamb and potatoes baked in parchment (sometimes in filo pastry).

Γιουβέτσι *yoovetsee*
Meat (usually lamb) with Greek pasta baked in the oven with tomatoes.

Κοντοσούβλι *kondosoovlee*
Skewered pork or lamb, well seasoned and cooked over charcoal.

Μελιτζανάτο *meleetzanato*
Beef or veal stewed with tomatoes and eggplant [aubergine].

Μουσακάς *moosakas*
Layers of eggplant [aubergine] and minced meat topped with bechamel sauce.

Μπιφτέκι *beeftekee*
A Greek "beefburger" – mincemeat burger with breadcrumbs, onions, and herbs grilled over charcoal, sometimes topped with grilled cheese or egg.

Vegetables and pulses

Λαχανικά και όσπρια

Vegetables (**lakhaneeka**) and beans (**ospreea**) often tend to be mixed or cooked with meat or fish. Vegetarians should ask for **ena fayeeto poo na meen ekhee kre-as** ("a dish that has no meat").

αγγούρι	*angooree*	cucumber
αγκινάρες	*angeenares*	artichokes
αρακάς	*arakas*	peas
καρότα	*karota*	carrots
κολοκύθια	*kolokeetheea*	zucchini [courgettes]
κουνουπίδι	*koonoopeeTHee*	cauliflower
κουκιά	*kookeea*	broad beans
κρεμμύδια	*kremeeTHya*	onions
λάχανο	*lakhano*	cabbage
κόκκινο λάχανο	*kokeeno lakhano*	red cabbage
μανιτάρια	*maneetarya*	mushrooms
μαρούλι	*maroolee*	(cos) lettuce
μελιτζάνες	*meleetzanes*	eggplant [aubergine]
μπάμιες	*bamee-es*	okra
ντομάτες	*domates*	tomatoes
πατάτες	*patates*	potatoes
πιπεριές	*peeperyes*	peppers
πιπεριές πράσινες	*peeperyes praseenes*	green peppers
πράσα	*prasa*	leeks
ρύζι	*reezee*	rice
σέλινο	*seleeno*	celery
σπαράγγια	*sparangeea*	asparagus
σπανάκι	*spanakee*	spinach
φασολάκια φρέσκα	*fasolakeea freska*	green beans
ρεβύθια	*reveetheea*	chickpeas
φακές	*fakes*	lentils
φασόλια γίγαντες	*fasoleea yeeghandes*	butter beans

Herbs and spices Βότανα και μπαχαρικά

άνηθος	*aneethos*	dill
βασιλικός	*vaseeleekos*	basil
δάφνη	*THafnee*	bay leaf
δεντρολίβανο	*THendroleevano*	rosemary
δυόσμος	*THeeozmos*	mint
θυμάρι	*theemaree*	thyme
κανέλλα	*kanela*	cinnamon
μαϊντανός	*maeeTHanos*	parsley
μαστίχα	*masteekha*	mastic
ρίγανη	*reeghanee*	oregano
σκόρδο	*skorTHo*	garlic
φασκόμηλο	*faskomeelo*	sage

Fruit Φρούτα

ανανάς	*ananas*	pineapple
αχλάδι	*akhlaTHee*	pear
βερύκοκο	*vereekoko*	apricot
δαμάσκηνο	*THamaskeeno*	plum
γκρέιπφρουτ	*"grapefruit"*	grapefruit
καρπούζι	*karpoozee*	watermelon
κεράσι	*kerasee*	cherry
λεμόνι	*lemonee*	lemon
μήλο	*meelo*	apple
μπανάνα	*banana*	banana
πεπόνι	*peponee*	melon
πορτοκάλι	*portokalee*	orange
μανταρίνι	*mantareenee*	tangerine
ροδάκινο	*roTHakeeno*	peach
σταφύλι	*stafeelee*	grape
σύκο	*seeko*	fig
χουρμάς	*khoormas*	date

Cheese Τυρί

Cheese is eaten by itself and also frequently used in cooking. These are some of the wide variety of white and hard cheeses:

φέτα *feta*
Crumbly salted white cheese made from goat's milk. This is the most popular cheese and varies in texture and saltiness by region.

γραβιέρα *ghravy-era*
A Swiss-style cheese. The best varieties are made in Crete and Dodoni (Ipiros).

κασέρι *kaseree*
Light, yellow cheese, rich in cream with a soft texture.

κασκαβάλι *kaskavalee*
Yellow cheese, very creamy and rich.

μανούρι *manooree*
Similar to cottage cheese; makes a tasty dessert when mixed with honey.

Desserts / Pastries Επιδόρπια/Γλυκά

Greeks rarely eat dessert after their meal. Sweets are usually eaten after the afternoon siesta and accompanied by a strong cup of coffee.

γρανίτα	*ghraneeta*	sherbet [water-ice]
καραμέλες	*karameles*	candy [sweets]
καρυδόπιτα	*kareeтнopeeta*	walnut cake
κρέμα καραμελέ	*krema karamele*	caramel custard
μηλόπιτα	*meelopeeta*	apple pie
παγωτό	*paghoto*	ice cream
ρυζόγαλο	*reezoghalo*	rice pudding
φρουτοσαλάτα	*frootosalata*	fruit salad
λουκούμι	*lookoomee*	Turkish delight

γαλακτομπούρεκο *ghalaktobooreko*
Flaky pastry filled with custard and steeped in syrup.

καταΐφι *kata-eefee*
Shredded pastry roll filled with nuts and steeped in syrup.

κοπεγχάγη *kopenkhaghee*
Filo pastry filled with a mixture of almonds, orange juice, and cinnamon.

μπακλαβάς *baklavas*
Baklava; a flaky pastry with a nut filling.

χαλβάς *khalvas*
Halva; sesame seed paste and sugar.

Alcoholic drinks Οινοπνευματώδη

Aperitifs Απεριτίφ

The usual aperitif is ouzo (**oozo**), a fairly strong anise-flavored drink served either neat (**sketo**) or with water. As Greeks rarely drink alcohol without food, your drink will be served with a few savory **mezeTHes**, such as octopus, pieces of cheese, and olives.

I'd like an ouzo.	Θα ήθελα ένα ούζο. *tha eethela ena oozo*

Beer Μπύρα

The Greeks used to make their own Bavarian-style lager, but this is no longer the case. However, you will find a range of imported beers.

Do you have ... beer?	Έχετε ... μπύρα; *ekhete ... beera*
bottled	εμφιαλωμένη *emfee-alomenee*
draft	βαρελίσια *vareleeseea*
light / dark	ξανθή/μαύρη *ksanthee/mavree*

Wine Κρασί

The quality of wine that you will encounter is likely to vary. Greece produces some wines good enough to rival some of the French names, but unfortunately in tiny quantities not sufficient for export. Among the top rated are the red wines from the Averof vineyards and the Athos Peninsula. Porto Carras in Chalkidiki and Achaea Clauss in northwest Peloponnisos produce excellent wines at affordable prices. Also well known is the sweet muscat from Samos and Mavrodaphni. A type of typically Greek wine that takes some getting used to is retsina, essentially a white wine containing pine resin.

Wine is usually produced very locally: it is often the case that a restaurant owner will bring you a carafe of his very own wine, made from grapes from his few square meters of vineyard, if you ask for house wine (**krasee vareleeseeo**).

I'd like a a bottle of red / blush [rosé] / white wine.	Θα ήθελα ένα μπουκάλι κόκκινο/ροζέ/ άσπρο κρασί. *tha eethela ena bookalee kokeeno/roze/aspro krasee*
a carafe	μια καράφα *mia karafa*
a liter	ένα λίτρο *ena leetro*
dry / sweet	ξηρό/γλυκό *kseero/ghleeko*
light / full-bodied	ελαφρύ/δυνατό *elafree/THeenato*
chilled	παγωμένο *paghomeno*

Other alcoholic drinks
Άλλα οινοπνευματώδη ποτά

Bars serve a variety of cocktails and the usual range of spirits . Note that brandy is **koneeak** and rum is **roomee** – other spirits are known by their English names (whisky, vodka, gin, etc.).

straight [neat]	σκέτο *sketo*
on the rocks	με πάγο *me pagho*
and soda	και σόδα *ke soTHa*
glass	ένα ποτήρι *ena poteree*
bottle	ένα μπουκάλι *ena bookalee*

κίτρο *keetro*

A sweet liqueur, with a citrus flavor; found on the island of Naxos.

Μεταξά *metaksa*

A Greek brandy (from three to seven stars, indicating quality).

κουμ-κουάτ *koom-kooat*

Orange-colored brandy made from tiny oranges (*Corfu*).

Nonalcoholic drinks
Μη οινοπνευματώδη ποτά

The most popular drink in the summer is **frape** – iced coffee shaken with or without milk and sugar – found at most coffee shops and bars. Freshly squeezed juices are also widely consumed. Tap water is drinkable almost everywhere, but if you prefer you can get bottled water (**emfeealomeno**).

coffee	ένα καφέ *ena kafe*
instant	ένα Νεσκαφέ *ena neskafe*
Greek	ελληνικό *eleeneeko*
black	σκέτο *sketo*
with cream/milk	με κρέμα/γάλα *me krema/ghala*
tea	ένα τσάι *ena tsaee*
with milk/lemon	με γάλα/με λεμόνι *me ghala/me lemonee*
iced tea	ένα παγωμένο τσάι *ena paghomeno tsaee*
fruit juice	ένα χυμό φρούτων *ena kheemo frooton*
mineral water	ένα μεταλλικό νερό *ena metaleeko nero*
cabonated [fizzy]/still	αεριούχο/χωρίς ανθρακικό *aereeookho/khorees anthrakeeko*

Menu Reader

This Menu Reader gives listings of common food types and dishes. The Greek words are shown in large type to help you identify the basic ingredients making up a dish from a menu that has no English. Note that tavernas rarely have menus, but you could ask the waiter to write down the dish if you don't understand what's on offer.

Meat and poultry

κρέας	*kreas*	meat (general)
βοδινό	*voTHeeno*	beef
χοιρινό	*kheereeno*	pork
κουνέλι	*koonelee*	rabbit
αρνί	*arnee*	lamb
κοτόπουλο	*kotopoolo*	chicken
πάπια	*papia*	duck
κιμάς	*keemas*	minced meat
αρνάκι γάλακτος	*arnakee ghalaktos*	baby lamb
περιστέρι	*pereesteree*	pigeon
μυαλό	*mialo*	brains
κατσικάκι	*katseekakee*	goat
χήνα	*kheena*	goose

Fish

ψάρι	psaree	fish (general)
θαλασσινά	thalaseena	seafood (general)
αντζούγιες	antzooyes	anchovies
μπακαλιάρος	bakaleearos	cod
καβούρι	kavooree	crab
αστακός	astakos	lobster
κέφαλος	kefalos	mullet
λιθρίνι	leethreenee	gray mullet
μύδια	meeTHya	mussels
χταπόδι	khtapoTHee	octopus
στρείδια	streeTHya	oysters
γαρίδες	ghareeTHes	shrimp [prawns]
σαρδέλλα	sarTHela	sardine
καλαμάρι	kalamaree	squid
τόννος	tonos	tuna

Vegetables

λαχανικά	*lakhaneeka*	vegetables (general)
αγκινάρες	*ageenares*	artichokes
μελιτζάνες	*meleetzanes*	eggplant [aubergine]
λάχανο	*lakhano*	cabbage
αγγούρι	*agooree*	cucumber
χωριάτικη σαλάτα	*khoryateekee salata*	Greek salad *made of olives, tomatoes, cucumber, onions, green peppers, and feta*
καρότα	*karota*	carrots
σέλινο	*seleeno*	celery
κολοκύθι	*kolokeethee*	zucchini [courgette]
μπάμιες	*bamee-es*	okra
κρεμμύδια	*kremeeTHya*	onions
αρακάς	*arakas*	peas
πατάτες	*patates*	potatoes
σαλάτα	*salata*	salad
σπανάκι	*spanakee*	spinach
ντομάτα	*domata*	tomato

Fruit

φρούτα	*froota*	fruit (general)
μήλο	*meelo*	apple
βερύκοκο	*vereekoko*	apricot
μπανάνα	*banana*	banana
χουρμάς	*khoormas*	date
σύκο	*seeko*	fig
σταφύλι	*stafeelee*	grape
γκρέιπφρουτ	*"grapefruit"*	grapefruit
λεμόνι	*lemonee*	lemon
πεπόνι	*peponee*	melon
πορτοκάλι	*portokalee*	orange
ροδάκινο	*roTHakeeno*	peach
αχλάδι	*akhlaTHee*	pear
ανανάς	*ananas*	pineapple
δαμάσκηνο	*THamaskeeno*	plum
φράουλα	*fraoola*	strawberry

Staples, beans, and bread

ψωμί	psomee	bread
ρεβύθια	reveetheea	chickpeas
φακές	fakes	lentils
ζυμαρικά	zeemareeka	pasta
ρύζι	reezee	rice
ψωμάκι	psomakee	bread roll
ζάχαρη	zakharee	sugar
ταχινόσουπα	takheenosoopa	tahini (sesame seed) soup
ψωμί φρυγανιά	psomee freeghaneea	toast
λαγάνα	laghana	unleavened bread

Cooking methods

του φούρνου	*too foornoo*	baked
της σχάρας	*tees skharas*	barbecued, grilled
βραστός	*vrastos*	boiled
λαδερό	*laTHero*	cooked in olive oil
τηγανητός	*teeghaneetos*	fried
μαρινάτος	*mareenatos*	marinated
ποσέ	*pose*	poached
ψητό	*pseeto*	roasted, baked
παστός	*pastos*	salted
μαγειρευτό	*mayeerefto*	stewed
γιαχνί	*yakhnee*	stewed in tomato sauce
κρασάτο	*krasato*	stewed in wine
γεμιστό	*yemeesto*	stuffed

Classic dishes

μελιτζανοσαλάτα	meleetzanosalata	*a dip of baked eggplant mashed with garlic, lemon, and olive oil*
τζατζίκι	tzatzeekee	tzatziki *a dip of yogurt, garlic, cucumber, and olive oil*
ταραμοσαλάτα	taramosalata	taramasalata *cod roe dip*
κεφτεδάκια	kefteTHakeea	*fried mincemeat balls containing onions, bread crumbs, and herbs*
σπανακόπιτα	spanakopeeta	*filo pastry pies filled with spinach, feta cheese, and eggs*
μουσακάς	moosakas	moussaka *oven-baked layers of sliced eggplant and minced meat (lamb or beef) topped with bechamel sauce*
ντολμαδάκια	dolmaTHakeea	*vine leaves stuffed with rice and onions and flavored with herbs (sometimes also contain mince-meat)*

Drinks

νερό	*nero*	water
μεταλλικό νερό	*metaleeko nero*	mineral water
τσάι	*tsaee*	tea
καφέ	*kafe*	coffee (instant)
Ελληνικό καφέ	*eleeneeko kafe*	Greek coffee
Μεταξά	*metaksa*	Metaxa *a Greek brandy (from two to seven stars* ➤ 51)
μπύρα	*beera*	beer
ούζο	*oozo*	ouzo
κρασί	*krasee*	wine
χυμό φρούτων	*kheemo frooton*	fruit juice
χυμό πορτοκάλι	*kheemo portokalee*	orange juice
χυμό λεμόνι	*kheemo lemonee*	lemon juice
λεμονάδα	*lemonaTHa*	lemonade

Snacks

σάντουιτς	*"sandwitch"*	sandwich
ελιές (γεμιστές)	*elee-es (yemeestes)*	(stuffed) olives
μπιφτέκι	*beeftekee*	*a Greek "beefburger": minced meat burger with breadcrumbs, onions, and herbs grilled over charcoal, sometimes topped with cheese or egg*
τσιπς	*"chips"*	chips [crisps]
πατάτες τηγανητές	*patates teeghaneetes*	french fries [chips]
λουκάνικα	*lookaneeka*	sausages
μπισκότα	*beeskota*	cookies [biscuits]
κέικ	*"cake"*	cake
τυροπιττάκια	*teeropeetakia*	*baked triangular pastries containing feta and another hard cheese*

Dairy products

αυγά	*avgha*	eggs
γιαούρτι	*yaoortee*	yogurt
κρέμα	*krema*	cream
βούτυρο	*vooteero*	butter
γάλα	*ghala*	milk
τυρί	*teeree*	cheese
φέτα	*feta*	feta *crumbly salted white cheese made from goat's milk. Varies regionally in texture and saltiness.*
μυζήθρα	*meezeethra*	*salted white soft cheese made from ewe's milk*
μανούρι	*manooree*	*similar to cottage cheese, makes a tasty dessert when mixed with honey*

Herbs and spices

βασιλικός	vaseeleekos	basil
κανέλλα	kanela	cinnamon
γαρύφαλλο	ghareefalo	cloves
άνηθος	aneethos	dill
σκόρδο	skorTHo	garlic
δυόσμος	THeeozmos	mint
μουστάρδα	moostarTHa	mustard
ρίγανη	reeghanee	oregano
μαϊντανός	maeeTHanos	parsley
πιπέρι	peeperee	pepper
δεντρολίβανο	THendroleevano	rosemary
σαφράνη	safranee	saffron
αλάτι	alatee	salt
θυμάρι	theemaree	thyme

Desserts

τούρτα αμυγδάλου	*toorta ameeghTHaloo*	almond cake
ρεβανί	*revanee*	*almond sponge cake with syrup*
μπακλαβάς	*baklavas*	baklava *a flaky pastry with a nut filling*
κρέμα καραμελέ	*krema karamele*	caramel custard
δίπλες	*THeeples*	*crispy fried dough sprinkled with nuts and sweetened with honey*
φρουτοσαλάτα	*frootosalata*	fruit salad
χαλβάς	*khalvas*	halva *sesame seed paste and sugar, sometimes flavored with pistachio nuts*
μέλι	*melee*	honey

Desserts, continued

μαντολάτο	mandolato	nougat *best on the island of Zakinthos*
παγωτό	paghoto	ice cream
ρυζόγαλο	reezoghalo	rice pudding
πάστα	pasta	cake (general)
τάρτα	tarta	fruit tart
πίτα	peeta	pie
λουκουμάδες	lookoomaTHes	fritters *round fritters, served with honey and cinnamon*
μελομακάρονα	melomakarona	*traditional small Christmas cakes, containing walnuts and cinnamon*
τσουρέκι	tsoorekee	*similar to the Italian Panattone. Traditionally made at Easter but now eaten all year.*

Travel

ESSENTIAL

A ticket to …	Ένα εισιτήριο για … *ena eeseeteereeo ya*
How much …?	Πόσο κάνει …; *poso kanee*
When?	Πότε; *pote*
When will … arrive/leave?	Πότε θα φτάσει/φύγει ο/η/το …; *pote tha ftasee/feeyee o/ee/to*

How you get around will depend mainly on which part of Greece you would like to visit. If you plan on visiting the islands there are regular ferry links from Piraeus, Athens' main port.

The most efficient way of traveling on the mainland, unless you have your own car, is by bus. The train offers a picturesque view but takes longer.

Safety Ασφάλεια

Would you accompany me to the bus stop?	Μπορείτε να με συνοδεύσετε ως τη στάση του λεωφορείου; *boreete na me seenoTHefsete os tee stasee too leoforeeoo*
I don't want to … on my own.	Δεν θέλω να … μόνος (μόνη) μου. *THen thelo na … monos (monee) moo*
stay here	μείνω εδώ *meeno eTHo*
walk home	περπατήσω σπίτι *perpateeso speetee*
I don't feel safe here.	Δεν αισθάνομαι ασφαλής εδώ. *THen esthanome asfalees eTHo*

POLICE ➤ 152; EMERGENCY ➤ 224

Arrival Άφιξη

If you are an EU citizen, there are minimal arrival formalities – either a valid passport, a visitor's passport, or an ID card are acceptable. A visa is not required for nationals of the U.S., Canada, Australia, and New Zealand for a three-month stay. If you are coming from an EU country and have nothing to declare, go through the blue channel (**ble eksoTHos**); from a non-EU country with nothing to declare go through the green channel (**praseenee eksoTHos**); otherwise through the red channel (**kokeenee eksoTHos**). Be advised: some random checks are carried out in both green and blue channels, mainly for drugs.

Passport control Έλεγχος διαβατηρίων

Μπορώ να δω το διαβατήριό σας, παρακαλώ;	May I see your passport, please?
Ποιός είναι ο σκοπός του ταξιδιού σας;	What's the purpose of your visit?
Με ποιόν είστε εδώ;	Who are you here with?

We have a joint passport.	Έχουμε κοινό διαβατήριο. *ekhoome keeno THeeavateereeo*
The children are on this passport.	Τα παιδιά είναι σε αυτό το διαβατήριο. *ta peTHya eene se afto to THeeavateereeo*
I'm here on vacation [holiday]/ business.	Είμαι εδώ για διακοπές/δουλειά. *eeme eTHo ya THeeakopes/THooleea*
I'm just passing through.	Απλώς περνώ από εδώ. *aplos perno apo eTHo*
I'm going to …	Θα … *tha*
I won't be working here.	Δεν θα δουλέψω εδώ. *THen tha THoolepso eTHo.*
I'm …	Είμαι … *eeme*
on my own	μόνος (μόνη) μου *monos (monee) moo*
with my family	με την οικογένειά μου *me teen eekoyeneea moo*
with a group	με γκρουπ *me "group"*

WHO ARE YOU WITH? ➤ 120

Customs Τελωνείο

I have only the normal allowances.	Έχω μόνο τα επιτρεπόμενα όρια. *ekho mono ta epeetrepomena oreea*
It's a gift/for my personal use.	Είναι για δώρο/για προσωπική μου χρήση. *eene ya THoro/ya prosopeekee moo khreesee*

Έχετε τίποτα να δηλώσετε;	Do you have anything to declare?
Πρέπει να πληρώσετε φόρο γι αυτό.	You must pay duty on this.
Από πού το αγοράσατε;	Where did you buy this?
Παρακαλώ ανοίξτε αυτή τη τσάντα.	Please open this bag.
Έχετε άλλες αποσκευές;	Do you have any more baggage?

I would like to declare …	Θα ήθελα να δηλώσω … *tha eethela na THeeloso*
I don't understand.	Δεν καταλαβαίνω. *THen katalaveno*
Does anyone here speak English?	Μιλάει κανείς εδώ Αγγλικά; *meelaee kanees eTHo angleeka*

ΕΛΕΓΧΟΣ ΔΙΑΒΑΤΗΡΙΩΝ	passport control
ΣΥΝΟΡΑ	border crossing
ΤΕΛΩΝΕΙΑ	customs
ΤΙΠΟΤΑ ΓΙΑ ΔΗΛΩΣΗ	nothing to declare
ΕΙΔΗ ΓΙΑ ΔΗΛΩΣΗ	goods to declare
ΑΣΤΥΝΟΜΙΑ	police
ΑΦΟΡΟΛΟΓΗΤΑ ΕΙΔΗ	duty-free goods

Duty-free shopping Αγορά αφορολόγητων ειδών

What currency is this in?	Σε ποιό νόμισμα είναι αυτό; *se peeo nomeezma eene afto*
Can I pay in …	Μπορώ να πληρώσω σε …; *boro na pleeroso se*
dollars/euros/pounds	δολλάρια/ευρώ/λίρες Αγγλίας *THolareea/evro/leeres angleeas*

COMMUNICATION DIFFICULTIES ➤ 11

Plane Αεροπλάνο

The national airline of Greece is Olympic Airways (**oleembeeakee aeroporeea**) and it offers both international and domestic flights. Airports exist in all main towns and most of the larger islands.

A bus connects the airport to downtown Athens – Sintagma square and Omonia. Domestic flights get very full during July and August, and you might not find a seat unless you have reserved in advance.

Tickets and reservations Εισιτήρια και κρατήσεις

When is the … flight to Athens?	Πότε είναι η … πτήση για Αθήνα; *pote eene ee … pteesee ya athena*
first/next/last	πρώτη/επόμενη/τελευταία *protee/epomenee/teleftea*
I'd like 2 … tickets to …	Θα ήθελα δύο … εισιτήρια για … *tha eethela THeeo … eeseeteereea ya*
one-way [single]	απλό *aplo*
round-trip [return]	με επιστροφή *me epeestrofee*
first class	πρώτη θέση *protee thesee*
business class	μπίζνες *"busines"*
economy class	τουριστική *tooreesteekee*
How much is a flight to …?	Πόσο κάνει η πτήση για …; *poso kanee ee pteesee ya*
I'd like to … my reservation for flight number …	Θα ήθελα να … την κράτησή μου για τον αριθμό πτήσεως … *tha eethela na … teen krateesee moo ya ton areethmo pteeseos*
cancel	ακυρώσω *akeeroso*
change	αλλάξω *alakso*
confirm	επιβεβαιώσω *epeeveveoso*

Inquiries about the flight Πληροφορίες για την πτήση

How long is the flight?	Πόσο διαρκεί η πτήση; *poso THeearkee ee pteesee*
What time does the plane leave?	Τι ώρα φεύγει το αεροπλάνο; *tee ora fevyee to aeroplano*
What time will we arrive?	Τι ώρα θα φτάσουμε; *tee ora tha ftasoome*

NUMBERS ➤ 216; TIME ➤ 220

Checking in Έλεγχος αποσκευών

Where is the check-in desk for flight …?	Πού είναι το γραφείο ελέγχου αποσκευών για την πτήση …; *poo eene to ghrafeeo elenkhoo aposkevon ya teen pteesee*
I have …	Έχω … *ekho*
3 cases to check in	τρεις βαλίτσες να ελέγξω *trees valeetses na elenkso*
2 pieces of hand baggage	δύο τεμάχια αποσκευών χειρός *THeeo temakheea aposkevon kheeros*
How much baggage is allowed free?	Πόσο είναι επιτρεπόμενο βάρος; *poso eene to epeetrepomeno varos*

Το εισιτήριο/διαβατήριο σας, παρακαλώ.	Your ticket/passport, please.
Θέλετε παράθυρο ή διάδρομο;	Would you like a window or an aisle seat?
Καπνίζοντες ή μη καπνίζοντες;	Smoking or non-smoking?
Παρακαλώ, προχωρήστε στην αίθουσα αναχωρήσεων.	Please go through to the departure lounge.
Πόσες αποσκευές έχετε;	How many pieces of baggage do you have?
Έχετε υπέρβαρο.	You have excess baggage.
Θα πρέπει να πληρώσετε … ευρώ για κάθε κιλό υπέρβαρου.	You'll have to pay a supplement of … euros per kilo of excess baggage.
Αυτό είναι πολύ βαρύ/μεγάλο για αποσκευή χειρός.	That's too heavy/large for hand baggage.
Φτιάξατε τις βαλίτσες σας μόνος σας/μόνη σας;	Did you pack these bags yourself?
Περιέχουν αιχμηρά ή ηλεκτρικά αντικείμενα;	Do they contain any sharp or electronic items?

ΑΦΙΞΕΙΣ	arrivals
ΑΝΑΧΩΡΗΣΕΙΣ	departures
ΕΛΕΓΧΟΣ ΑΣΦΑΛΕΙΑΣ	security check
ΜΗΝ ΑΦΗΝΕΤΕ ΤΙΣ ΑΠΟΣΚΕΥΕΣ ΣΑΣ ΑΣΥΝΟΔΕΥΤΕΣ.	Do not leave bags unattended.

BAGGAGE ➤ 71

Information Πληροφορίες

Is flight … delayed?	Υπάρχει καθυστέρηση στην πτήση …; *eeparkhee katheestereesee steen pteesee*
How late will it be?	Πόσο θα αργήσει; *poso tha argheesee*
Has the flight from … landed?	Προσγειώθηκε η πτήση από … *prozyeeotheeke ee pteesee apo*
Which gate does flight … leave from?	Από ποιά έξοδο φεύγει η πτήση …; *apo pia eksoTHo fevyee ee pteesee*

Boarding/In-flight Επιβίβαση/Στην πτήση

Your boarding card, please.	Το δελτίο επιβιβάσεως, παρακαλώ. *teen karta epeeveevaseos, parakalo*
Could I have a drink/something to eat, please?	Μπορώ να έχω ένα ποτό/κάτι να φάω; *boro na ekho ena poto/katee na fao*
Please wake me for the meal.	Παρακαλώ, ξυπνήστε με για το γεύμα. *parakalo, kseepneeste me ya to yevma*
What time will we arrive?	Τι ώρα θα φτάσουμε; *tee ora tha ftasoome*
An air sickness bag, please.	Μια σακούλα ναυτίας, παρακαλώ. *mia sakoola nafteeas, parakalo*

Arrival Άφιξη

Where is/are the …?	Πού είναι …; *poo eene*
currency exchange	συναλλάγματος *seenalaghmatos*
buses	τα λεωφορεία *ta leoforeea*
car rental [hire]	το γραφείο ενοικιάσεως αυτοκινήτων *to ghrafeeo eneekeeaseos aftokeeneeton*
exit	η έξοδος *ee eksoTHos*
taxis	τα ταξί *ta taksee*
telephone	το τηλέφωνο *to teelefono*
Is there a bus into town?	Υπάρχει λεωφορείο για το κέντρο της πόλης; *eeparkhee leoforeeo ya to kendro tees polees*
How do I get to the … Hotel?	Πώς πάω στο ξενοδοχείο …; *pos pao sto ksenoTHokheeo*

BAGGAGE ➤ 71; CUSTOMS ➤ 67

Baggage Αποσκευές

Porter! Excuse me!	Αχθοφόρε! Παρακαλώ! *akhthofore! parakalo!*
Could you take my baggage to …?	Μπορείτε να πάτε τις αποσκευές μου …; *boreete na pate tees aposkeves moo …*
a taxi/bus	στο ταξί/στο λεωφορείο *sto taksee/sto leoforeeo*
Where is/are …?	Πού είναι …; *poo eene …*
baggage carts [trolleys]	τα καροτσάκια αποσκευών *ta karotsakeea aposkevon*
baggage lockers	οι θυρίδες *ee theereeTHes*
baggage check [left-luggage office]	η φύλαξη αποσκευών *ee feelaksee aposkevon*
Where is the baggage from flight …?	Πού είναι οι αποσκευές από την πτήση …; *poo eene ee aposkeves apo teen pteesee*

Loss, damage, and theft Απώλεια, ζημιά και κλοπή

My baggage has been lost/stolen.	Οι αποσκευές μου χάθηκαν/κλάπηκαν. *ee aposkeves moo khatheekan/klapeekan*
My suitcase was damaged in transit.	Η βαλίτσα μου χάλασε στη μεταφορά. *ee valeetsa moo khalase stee metafora*
Our baggage has not arrived.	Οι αποσκευές μας δεν έφτασαν. *ee aposkeves mas THen eftasan*
Do you have a claim form in English?	Έχετε αίτηση αποζημίωσης στα Αγγλικά; *ekhete eteesee apozeemeeosees sta angleeka*

Πώς είναι οι αποσκευές σας;	What does your baggage look like?
Έχετε την ετικέττα παραλαβής αποσκευών;	Do you have the claim check [reclaim tag]?
Οι αποσκευές σας …	Your baggage …
ίσως στάλθηκαν στο/στη …	may have been sent to …
ίσως φτάσουν αργότερα σήμερα	may arrive later today
Παρακαλώ, ελάτε πάλι αύριο.	Please come back tomorrow.
Καλέστε αυτόν τον αριθμό για να δείτε αν έφτασαν οι αποσκευές σας.	Call this number to check if your baggage has arrived.

POLICE ➤ 152; COLORS ➤ 143

Train Τραίνο

The Greek rail system is operated by OSE (ΟΣΕ, **osse** or **orghaneezmos seeTHeeroTHromon elaTHos**). The network is quite limited: a main line connects Athens with Kalamata via Patras; Athens with Tripolis; and Athens with Thessaloniki, stopping at the main towns in between. There are connections to Kalavrita, Trikkala, Volos, and Kalampaka within Greece; and Sofia and Istanbul via Thessaloniki.

The train journey is usually quite slow but scenic, and is cheaper than the bus. It is not recommended if you are short of time.

The Intercity (**eepertakheea**, abbreviated I/C) makes fewer stops, but you have to pay an extra charge of around €3–4 each way on this train. Interail and Eurorail passes are accepted on all trains but you have to reserve in advance.

All trains have bars and a sleeping car for longer journeys.

There are cheap rates for children under 12 (50% off) and groups over 10 people (30% off), but there are no season tickets available.

In summer, reservations are recommended at least three days in advance. However, there will not be a ticket on the seat to show it has been reserved, so you may have to fight for your right to sit in your reserved place!

Tourist season tickets are available and are valid for a defined period for an unlimited number of trips on all routes.

You can normally leave your baggage in a locker at larger stations, or at the baggage check [left-luggage office] – look for the sign ΦΥΛΑΞΗ ΑΠΟΣΚΕΥΩΝ **feelaksee aposkevon**.

ΕΙΣΟΔΟΣ	entrance
ΕΞΟΔΟΣ	exit
ΠΡΟΣ ΑΠΟΒΑΘΡΕΣ	to the platforms
ΠΛΗΡΟΦΟΡΙΕΣ	information
ΚΡΑΤΗΣΕΙΣ	reservations
ΑΦΙΞΕΙΣ	arrivals
ΑΝΑΧΩΡΗΣΕΙΣ	departures

To the station Προς το σταθμό

How do I get to the (main) train station?	Πώς πάνε στον (κεντρικό) σιδηροδρομικό σταθμό; *pos pane ston (kendreeko) seeTHeeroTHromeeko stathmo*
Do trains to … leave from … Station?	Αναχωρούν τραίνα για … από το σταθμό …; *anakhoroon trena ya … apo to stathmo*
How far is it?	Πόσο απέχει; *poso apekhee*
Can I leave my car there?	Μπορώ να αφήσω το αυτοκίνητό μου εδώ; *boro na afeeso to aftokeeneeto moo eTHo*

At the station Στο σταθμό

Where is/are the …?	Πού είναι …; *poo eene*
information desk	το γραφείο πληροφοριών *to ghrafeeo pleeroforeeon*
baggage check [left-luggage office]	η φύλαξη αποσκευών *ee feelaksee aposkevon*
lost and found [lost property office]	το γραφείο απωλεσθέντων αντικειμένων *to ghrafeeo apolesthendon andeekeemenon*
platform	η αποβάθρα *ee apovathra*
snack bar	το κυλικείο *to keeleekeeo*
telephones	τα τηλέφωνα *ta teelefona*
ticket office	το γραφείο εισιτηρίων *to ghrafeeo eeseeteereeon*
toilets	οι τουαλέττες *ee tooaletes*
waiting room	η αίθουσα αναμονής *ee ethoosa anamonees*

DIRECTIONS ➤ 94

Tickets Εισιτήρια

I'd like a …	Θα ήθελα ένα … *tha eethela ena*
one-way [single] ticket	απλό εισιτήριο *aplo eeseteereeo*
round-trip [return] ticket	εισιτήριο με επιστροφή *eeseeteereeo me epeestrofee*
first/second class	πρώτη/δεύτερη θέση *protee/THefteree thesee*
concessionary	μειωμένο *meeomeno*
I'd like to reserve a seat.	Θα ήθελα να κλείσω μια θέση. *tha eethela na kleeso mia thesee*
aisle seat	μια θέση στο διάδρομο *mia thesee sto THeeaTHromo*
window seat	μια θέση στο παράθυρο *mia thesee sto paratheero*
berth	μια κουκέτα *mia kooketa*
Is there a sleeper?	Υπάρχει βαγόνι με κουκέτες; *eeparkhee vaghonee me kooketes*
I'd like a … berth.	Θα ήθελα μια … κουκέτα. *tha eethela mia … kooketa*
upper/lower	πάνω/κάτω *pano/kato*
Can I buy a ticket on board?	Μπορώ να αγοράσω εισιτήριο μέσα στο τραίνο; *boro na aghoraso eeseeteereeo sto treno*

Price Τιμή

How much is that?	Πόσο κάνει αυτό; *poso kanee afto*
Is there a discount for …?	Υπάρχει μειωμένο εισιτήριο για … *eeparkhee meeomeno eeseeteereeo ya*
children/families	παιδιά/οικογένειες *peTHya/eekoyenee-es*
senior citizens	συνταξιούχους *seendakseeookhoos*
students	φοιτητές *feeteetes*
Do you offer a cheap same-day round-trip [return] fare?	Υπάρχει έκπτωση για επιστροφή αυθημερόν; *eeparkhee ekptosee ya epeestrofee aftheemeron*
There is a supplement of …	Υπάρχει επιβάρυνση των … *eeparkhee epeevareensee ton*

NUMBERS ➤ 216; DAYS OF THE WEEK ➤ 218

Queries Ερωτήσεις

Do I have to change trains?	Χρειάζεται να αλλάξω τραίνο; *khreeazete na alakso treno*
It's a direct train.	Είναι κατευθείαν τραίνο. *eene kateftheean treno*
You have to change at …	Πρέπει να αλλάξετε στο/στη … *prepee na alaksete sto/stee*
How long is this ticket valid for?	Για πόσο ισχύει αυτό το εισιτήριο … *ya poso eeskhee-ee afto to eeseeteereeo*
Can I return on the same ticket?	Μπορώ να επιστρέψω με το ίδιο εισιτήριο; *boro na epeestrepso me to eeTHyo eeseeteereeo*
In which car [coach] is my seat?	Σε ποιά αμαξοστοιχία είναι η κουκέτα μου; *se pia amaksosteekheea eene ee kooketa moo*
Is there a dining car on the train?	Υπάρχει εστιατόριο στο τραίνο; *eeparkhee esteeatoreeo sto treno*

– tha eethela ena eeseeteereeo ya teen Kavala, parakalo.
– *aplo ee me epeestrofee?*
– me epeestrofee.
– *kanee 13 evro ke 20 lepta (THekatreea evro ke eekosee lepta).*
– khreeazete na alakso treno?
– *ne, prepee na alaksete stee Thessaloneekee.*
– efkhareesto. kherete.

Train times Δρομολόγιο τραίνου

Could I have a timetable, please?	Μπορώ να έχω ένα δρομολόγιο, παρακαλώ; *boro na ekho ena THromoloyeeo, parakalo*
When is the … train to …?	Πότε είναι το … τραίνο για …; *pote eene to … treno ya*
first/next/last	πρώτο/επόμενο/τελευταίο *proto/epomeno/telefteo*
There's a train to … at …	Υπάρχει τραίνο για … στις … *eeparkhee treno ya … stees*

BASIC EXPRESSIONS ➤ 12–19

How frequent are the trains to …?	Πόσο συχνά είναι τα τραίνα για …; *poso seekhna eene ta trena ya*
once/twice a day	μια φορά/δύο φορές την ημέρα *mia fora/THeeo fores teen eemera*
5 times a day	πέντε φορές την ημέρα *pende fores teen eemera*
every hour	μια φορά την ώρα *mia fora teen ora*
What time do they leave?	Τί ώρα φεύγουν; *tee ora fevghoon*
on the hour	στην ώρα *steen ora*
20 minutes past the hour	20 λεπτά μετά την ώρα *eekosee lepta meta teen ora*
What time does the train stop/arrive in …?	Τί ώρα σταματάει/φτάνει το τραίνο στο/στη …; *tee ora stamataee/ftanee to treno sto/stee*
How long is the trip [journey]?	Πόση ώρα διαρκεί το ταξίδι; *posee ora THeearkee to takseeTHee*
Is the train on time?	Είναι το τραίνο στην ώρα του; *eene to treno steen ora too*

Departures Αναχώρηση

Which platform does the train to … leave from?	Από ποιά αποβάθρα φεύγει το τραίνο για …; *apo pia apovathra fevyee to treno ya*
Where is platform 4?	Πού είναι η αποβάθρα τέσσερα; *poo eene ee apovathra tesera*
over there	εκεί *ekee*
on the left/right	στα αριστερά/δεξιά *sta areestera/THekseea*
through the underpass	κάτω από την υπόγεια διάβαση *kato apo teen eepoyeea THeeavasee*
over the bridge	από την άλλη μεριά της γέφυρας *apo teen alee merya tees yefeeras*
Where do I change for …?	Πού αλλάζω για …; *poo alazo ya*
How long will I have to wait for a connection?	Πόση ώρα πρέπει να περιμένω για ανταπόκριση; *posee ora prepee na pereemeno ya andapokreesee*

TIME ➤ 220; DIRECTIONS ➤ 94

Boarding Επιβίβαση

Is this the right platform for the train to …?	Αυτή είναι η σωστή αποβάθρα για το τραίνο για …; *aftee eene ee sostee apovathra ya to treno ya*
Is this the train to …?	Αυτό είναι το τραίνο για …; *afto eene to treno ya*
Is this seat taken?	Αυτή η θέση είναι πιασμένη; *aftee ee thesee eene piazmenee*
I think that's my seat.	Νομίζω αυτή είναι η θέση μου. *nomeezo aftee eene ee thesee moo*
Here's my reservation.	Αυτή είναι η κράτησή μου. *aftee eene ee krateesee moo*
Are there any seats/berths available?	Υπάρχουν ελεύθερες θέσεις/κουκέτες; *eeparkhoon eleftheres thesees/kooketes*
Do you mind …?	Σας πειράζει …; *sas peerazee*
if I sit here	να καθήσω εδώ *na katheeso eTHo*
if I open the window	να ανοίξω το παράθυρο *na aneekso to paratheero*

On the journey Στο ταξίδι

How long are we stopping here for?	Για πόσο θα σταματήσουμε εδώ; *ya poso tha stamateesoome eTHo*
When do we get to …?	Πότε θα φτάσουμε στο/στη …; *pote tha ftasoome sto/stee*
Have we passed …?	Έχουμε περάσει τον/την/το … ; *ekhoome perasee ton/teen/to*
Where is the dining/sleeping car?	Πού είναι το εστιατόριο/το βαγκόν-λι; *poo eene to esteeatoreeo/to vagon-lee*
Where is my berth?	Πού είναι η κουκέτα μου; *poo eene ee kooketa moo*
I've lost my ticket.	Έχασα το εισιτήριό μου. *ekhasa to eeseeteereeo moo*

ΦΡΕΝΟ ΚΙΝΔΥΝΟΥ	emergency brake
ΑΥΤΟΜΑΤΕΣ ΠΟΡΤΕΣ	automatic doors

TIME ➤ 220

Long-distance bus [Coach] Υπεραστικό λεωφορείο

KTEL (ΚΤΕΛ) runs a very efficient and reliable service linking most major towns. Reserving a seat is advisable. The main bus station in Athens is at Kifissos. To find your seat look for the number after the word θέση (**thesee**) on your ticket. There is no food or beverage service on long-distance buses, but the driver will stop every three hours or so at a café.

Where is the bus [coach] station?	Πού είναι ο σταθμός ΚΤΕΛ; *poo eene o stathmos ktel*
When's the next bus [coach] to …?	Πότε είναι το επόμενο λεωφορείο για …; *pote eene to epomeno leoforeeo ya·*
Where does it leave from?	Από πού φεύγει; *apo poo fevyee*
Does the bus [coach] stop at …?	Το λεωφορείο σταματάει στο/στη …; *to leoforeeo stamataee sto/stee*
How long does the trip [journey] take?	Πόση ώρα διαρκεί το ταξίδι; *posee ora THeearkee to takseeTHee*

Bus/Trolley [Tram] Λεωφορείο-Τρόλλεϋ

Before boarding a bus you need to buy a ticket at the special kiosks marked ΕΙΣΙΤΗΡΙΑ (**eeseeteereea**). There's only one fare whatever the distance. You validate your ticket by placing it in the special orange machine on the bus. You can also get around Athens by trolley [tram] (**trole-ee**). Blue and yellow signs mark bus and trolley [tram] stops respectively, and tickets are interchangeable.

Where can I get a bus/ trolley [tram] to …?	Από πού μπορώ να πάρω ένα λεωφορείο/τρόλλεϋ για τον/την/το …; *apo poo boro na paro ena leoforeeo/trole-ee ya ton/teen/to*
What time is the next bus to …?	Τι ώρα είναι το επόμενο λεωφορείο για τον/την/το …; *tee ora eene to epomeno leoforeeo ya ton/teen/ton …*

Θέλετε το λεωφορείο αριθμός …	You want bus number …
Πρέπει να αλλάξετε λεωφορείο στο/στη …	You must change buses at …

ΣΤΑΣΗ ΛΕΩΦΟΡΕΙΩΝ	bus stop
ΕΞΟΔΟΣ (ΚΙΝΔΥΝΟΥ)	(emergency) exit

DIRECTIONS ➤ 94; TIME ➤ 220

Buying tickets Αγοράζοντας εισιτήρια

Where can I buy tickets?	Από πού μπορώ να αγοράσω εισιτήρια; *apo poo boro na aghoraso eeseeteereea*
A … ticket to …, please.	Ένα … εισιτήριο για τον/τη/το …, παρακαλώ. *ena … eeseeteereeo ya ton/teen/to …, parakalo*
one-way [single]	απλό εισιτήριο *aplo eeseeteereeo*
round-trip [return]	εισιτήριο με επιστροφή *eeseeteereeo me epeestrofee*
multi-trip	εισιτήριο πολλαπλών διαδρομών *eeseeteereeo polaplon THeeaTHromon*
A booklet of tickets, please.	Μια δεσμίδα εισιτηρίων, παρακαλώ. *mia THezmeeTHa eeseeteereeon, parakalo*
How much is the fare to …?	Πόσο κάνει το εισιτήριο για τον/την/το …; *poso kanee to eeseeteereeo ya ton/teen/to*

Traveling Ταξιδεύοντας

Is this the right bus/ trolley [tram] to …?	Αυτό είναι το σωστό λεωφορείο/τρόλλεϋ για …; *afto eene to sosto leoforeeo/ trole-ee ya*
Could you tell me when to get off?	Μπορείτε να μου πείτε πού να κατεβώ; *boreete na moo peete poo na katevo*
Do I have to change buses?	Χρειάζεται να αλλάξω λεωφορείο; *khreeazete na alakso leoforeeo*
Next stop, please!	Η επόμενη στάση, παρακαλώ. *ee epomenee stasee, parakalo*

ΑΚΥΡΩΣΤΕ ΤΟ ΕΙΣΙΤΗΡΙΟ ΣΑΣ validate your ticket

– seeghnomee. afto eene to sosto leoforeeo ya to leemanee?
– okhee. thelete to okto. nato, ekee eene.
– ena eeseeteereeo ya to leemanee, parakalo.
– kanee 45 (sarandapende) lepta.
– boreete na moo peete poo na katevo?
– se teserees stasees apo eTHo.

NUMBERS ➤ 216; DIRECTIONS ➤ 94

Subway [Metro] Μετρό

Athens is the only Greek city currently served by a subway, or underground, system, known as the "metro." Subway (metro) tickets are different from bus tickets and can be purchased at the ticket desk or machines at each station. Tickets must be validated by punching them in the special machines by the platform.

General inquiries Γενικές πληροφορίες

Where's the nearest subway [metro] station?	Πού είναι ο κοντινότερος σταθμός μετρό; *poo eene o kondeenoteros stathmos metro*
Where do I buy a ticket?	Από πού αγοράζω εισιτήριο; *apo poo aghorazo eeseeteereeo*
Could I have a map of the subway [metro]?	Μπορώ να έχω ένα χάρτη του μετρό; *boro na ekho ena khartee too metro*

Traveling Ταξιδεύοντας

Which line should I take for ...?	Ποιά γραμμή πρέπει να πάρω για το ...; *pia ghramee prepee na paro ya to*
Is this the right train for ...?	Αυτό είναι το σωστό τραίνο για ...; *afto eene to sosto treno ya*
Which stop is it for ...?	Ποιά στάση είναι για ...; *pia stasee eene ya*
How many stops is it to ...?	Πόσες στάσεις είναι για ...; *poses stasees eene ya*
Is the next stop ...?	Η επόμενη στάση είναι ο/η/το ...; *ee epomenee stasee eene o/ee/to*
Where are we?	Πού είμαστε; *poo eemaste*
Where do I change for ...?	Πού αλλάζω για τον/την/το ...; *poo alazo ya ton/teen/to*
What time is the last train to ...?	Πότε είναι το τελευταίο τραίνο για τον/την/το ...; *pote eene to telefteo treno ya ton/teen/to*

ΑΝΤΑΠΟΚΡΙΣΗ ΜΕ ΑΛΛΕΣ ΓΡΑΜΜΕΣ	to other lines/transfer

NUMBERS ➤ 216; BUYING TICKETS ➤ 74, 79

Ferry / Boat Φέρρυ-μπωτ/Πλοίο

It is likely that after your arrival in Athens, you will be heading straight for the port of Piraeus to catch a ferry. The harborfront is lined with ticket agents – and ferry prices are fixed. So as long as you go to an approved agent the price is the same everywhere. Each agent tends to sell tickets for one company serving a particular route. A window display (usually in Greek and English) will tell you exactly what islands that ferry goes to. Eurorail and Interail ticket holders can travel deck class for free on the Brindisi-Patras route on Adriatica and HNL liners. Sleeping on the deck is allowed, but take a sleeping bag and wear warm clothes, even in July!

Once on an island you may decide to go on an island tour. Several converted fishing boats run daily trips and stop at the nicer spots for a quick dive in the sea. However, throwing anything into the sea off a boat deck is an offense in Greece, and you will be fined if caught.

When is the … car ferry to …?	Πότε είναι το … φέρρυ-μπωτ για …; *pote eene to feree-bot ya*
first/next/last	πρώτο/επόμενο/τελευταίο *proto/epomeno/telefteo*
A round-trip [return] ticket for …	Ένα εισιτήριο με επιστροφή για … *ena eeseeteereeo me epeestrofee ya*
1 car and 1 trailer [caravan]	ένα αυτοκίνητο και ένα τροχόσπιτο *ena aftokeeneeto ke ena trokhospeeto*
2 adults and 3 children	δύο ενήλικες και τρία παιδιά *THeeo eneeleekes ke treea peTHya*
I want to reserve a … cabin.	Θέλω να κλείσω μια … καμπίνα. *thelo na kleeso mia … kambeena*
single/double	μονή/διπλή *monee/THeeplee*

ΣΩΣΙΒΙΟ	life preserver [life belt]
ΝΑΥΑΓΟΣΩΣΤΙΚΗ ΛΕΜΒΟΣ	life boat
ΑΠΑΓΟΡΕΥΕΤΑΙ Η ΠΡΟΣΒΑΣΗ ΣΤΑ ΓΚΑΡΑΖ	no access to car decks

Boat trips Ταξίδια με το βαπόρι

Is there a boat trip?	Υπάρχει ένα ταξίδι με πλοίο; *eeparkhee ena takseeTHee me pleeo*
What time does it leave/return?	Τι ώρα ξεκινάει/επιστρέφει; *tee ora ksekeenaee/epeestrefee*

TIME ➤ 220; BUYING TICKETS ➤ 74, 79

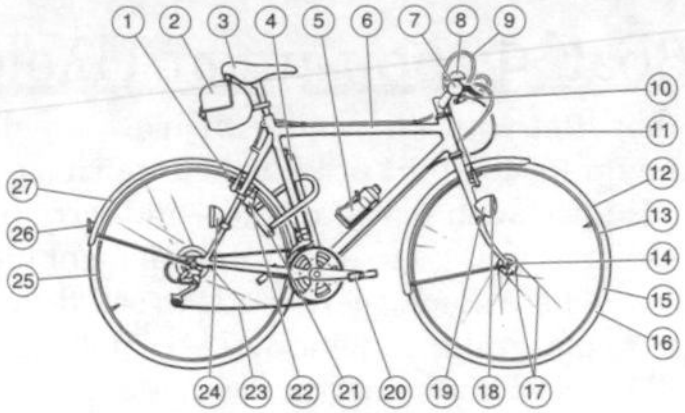

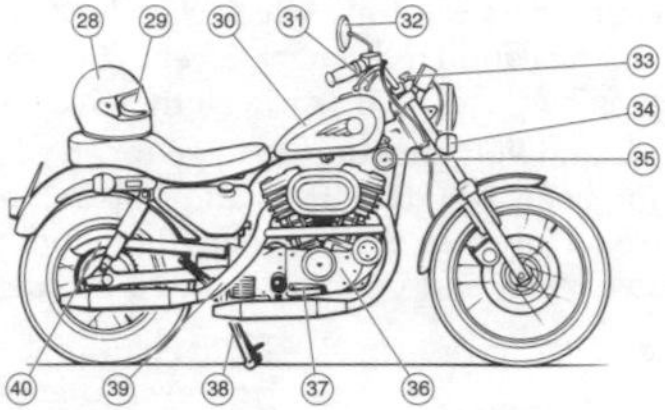

1 brake pad το τακάκι φρένου *to takakee frenoo*
2 bicycle bag το σακκίδιο *to sakeeTHeeo*
3 saddle η σέλα *ee sela*
4 pump η αεραντλία *ee aerandleea*
5 water bottle η φιάλη νερού *ee feealee neroo*
6 frame το πλαίσιο *to pleseeo*
7 handlebars οι χειρολαβές *ee kheerolaves*
8 bell το κουδούνι *to kooTHoonee*
9 brake cable το σύρμα φρένων *to seerma frenon*
10 gear shift [lever] ο μοχλός ταχυτήτων *o mokhlos takheeteeton*
11 gear/control cable το σύρμα ταχυτήτων *to seerma takheeteeton*
12 inner tube η σαμπρέλλα *ee sambrela*
13 front/back wheel ο μπροστινός/πίσω τροχός *o brosteenos/peeso trokhos*
14 axle ο άξονας τροχού *o aksonas trokhoo*
15 tire [tyre] το λάστιχο *to lasteekho*
16 wheel η ρόδα *ee roTHa*
17 spokes οι ακτίνες τροχού *ee akteenes trokhoo*
18 bulb ο λαμπτήρας *o lambteeras*
19 headlight το μπροστινό φως *to brosteeno fos*
20 pedal το πετάλι *to petalee*
21 lock η κλειδαριά *ee kleeTHarya*
22 generator [dynamo] το δυναμό *to THeenamo*
23 chain η αλυσίδα *ee aleeseeTHa*
24 rear light το πίσω φως *to peeso fos*
25 rim η στεφάνη τροχού *ee stefanee trokhoo*
26 reflector οι ανταυγαστήρες *ee andafghasteeres*
27 fender [mudguard] ο λασπωτήρας *o laspoteeras*
28 helmet το κράνος *to kranos*
29 visor το γυαλί του κρανίου *to yalee too kraneeoo*
30 fuel tank το ντεπόζιτο καυσίμων *to depozeeto kafseemon*
31 clutch lever ο μοχλός συμπλέκτη *o mokhlos seemblektee*
32 mirror ο καθρέπτης *o kathreptees*
33 ignition switch η ανάφλεξη *ee anafleksee*
34 turn signal [indicator] το φλας *to flas*
35 horn η κόρνα *ee korna*
36 engine η μηχανή *ee meekhanee*
37 gear shift [stick] ο μοχλός ταχυτήτων *o mokhlos takheeteeton*
38 kick [main] stand το σταντ *to stand*
39 exhaust pipe η εξάτμιση *ee eksatmeesee*
40 chain guard ο εκτροχιαστής αλυσίδας *o ektrokheeastees aleeseeTHas*

REPAIRS ➤ *89*

Bicycle / Motorbike Ποδήλατο/μοτοσυκλέτα

Motorbikes, or usually mopeds, and bicycles are widely available for hire on the islands, but not so common on the mainland. Despite what you might see, crash helmets are compulsory and riding a motorbike is forbidden during the siesta hours (2–5 p.m.) and after midnight, although the latter rule is rarely enforced in most tourist resorts.

I'd like to rent [hire] a …	Θα ήθελα να νοικιάσω ένα … *tha eethela na neekeeaso ena*
3-/10-speed bicycle	ποδήλατο τριών/δέκα ταχυτήτων *poTHeelato treeon/THeka takheeteeton*
moped	μοτοποδήλατο *motopoTHeelato*
motorbike	μοτοσυκλέτα *motoseekleta*
How much does it cost per day / week?	Πόσο κοστίζει την ημέρα/την εβδομάδα *poso kosteezee teen eemera/teen evTHomaTHa*
The brakes don't work.	Τα φρένα δεν δουλεύουν. *ta frena THen THoolevoon*
There is / are no …	Δεν υπάρχει/υπάρχουν … *THen eeparkhee/eeparkhoon …*
lights	φώτα *fota*
pump	τρόμπα/αεραντλία *trompa/aerandleea*
The front / rear tire [tyre] has a flat [puncture].	Μού τρύπησε το μπροστινό/πίσω λάστιχο. *moo treepeese to brosteeno/peeso lasteekho*

Hitchhiking Ώτο-στοπ

Hitchhiking is reasonably wide-spread and usually safe, but it's better for women to travel together. If you decide to hitchhike, toll booth areas on roads are a good spot to wait for a ride.

Where are you heading?	Προς τα πού πηγαίνετε; *pros ta poo peeyenete*
Can you give me / us a lift?	Μπορείτε να μας πάρετε; *boreete na mas parete*
Could you drop me off here?	Μπορείτε να με αφήσετε εδώ; *boreete na me afeesete eTHo*
Thanks for the lift.	Σας ευχαριστώ για το ταξίδι. *sas efkhareesto ya to takseeTHee*

DIRECTIONS ➤ 94; NUMBERS ➤ 216

Taxi Ταξί

Licensed taxis are yellow with a blue stripe in Athens, although private companies and radio cabs may have their own colors. Within Athens and in all major cities, fares are fixed. For longer distances you should agree to a fare before the trip. Tipping is not compulsory, but it is common to round the amount to the nearest 30 cents.

Where can I get a taxi?	Πού μπορώ να βρω ταξί; *poo boro na vro taksee*
Do you have the number for a taxi?	Έχετε το τηλέφωνο κάποιου ταξί; *ekhete to teelefono kapeeoo taksee*
I'd like a taxi …	Θα ήθελα ένα ταξί … *tha eethela ena taksee …*
now	τώρα *tora*
in an hour	σε μια ώρα *se mia ora*
for tomorrow at 9 a.m.	για αύριο στις εννέα *ya avreeo stees enea*

ΕΛΕΥΘΕΡΟΣ for hire

Please take me to …	Παρακαλώ πηγαίνετέ με … *parakalo peeyenete me*
the airport	στο αεροδρόμιο *sto aeroTHromeeo*
the train station	στο σιδηροδρομικό σταθμό *sto seeTHeeroTHromeeko stathmo*
this address	σε αυτή τη διεύθυνση *se aftee tee THee-eftheensee*
How much will it cost?	Πόσο θα κοστίσει; *poso tha kosteesee*
Is it far?	Είναι μακριά; *eene makreea*
You said … euros.	Είπατε … ευρώ. *eepate … evro*
Keep the change.	Κρατήστε τα ρέστα. *krateeste ta resta*

– boreete na me pate sto stathmo, parakalo?
– veveos.
– posee ora tha mas paree?
– THeka lepta …
– ftasame.
– efkhareesto. poso kanee?
– enameesee evro, parakalo.
– krateeste ta resta.

NUMBERS ➤ 216; DIRECTIONS ➤ 94

Car/Automobile Αυτοκίνητο

In Greece you drive on the right, but in Cyprus you drive on the left. Seat belts are officially compulsory, although you will see many people without them. There are car ferries to and from most Mediterranean ports or you can drive overland (depending on the prevailing conditions in neighboring countries). Make sure you have an international license and comprehensive insurance. Greece is part of the EU and so the *Green Card* is valid.

While in Greece you will need to adapt to the more forceful style of driving. Flashing headlights and horns are more often a signal or greeting than a rebuke and could mean anything from "I'm about to pass you," to "The police are speed-checking just ahead of us."

Conversion chart

km	1	10	20	30	40	50	60	70	80	90	100	110	120	130
miles	0.62	6	12	19	25	31	37	44	50	56	62	68	74	81

Road network

A highway links Thessaloniki to Athens, although in the more mountainous areas this is limited to one lane per side plus a narrow lane for passing. Another highway links Athens to Patras, and this is being extended. Most highways are tolled although some are free. Other roads linking main towns tend to be one lane each way, with perhaps a passing lane in the middle. Roads linking smaller towns and villages range from asphalt to mud-track. Cars are not allowed on a few of the islands, so check before you go.

Road signs giving directions, town and street names are usually in both Greek and English characters, so you will have little problem reading them. However, names may vary a little from what you have on your map, for example Piraeus could be written as "Pireas" or "Pirefs," Athens or "Athine" or "Athina."

Cars are now restricted in central Athens. No car can enter without a catalytic converter, and Greek-registered cars can only enter on even or odd days of the month, depending on the last number of the car registration. Much of historic Athens and the main shopping area are closed completely to traffic.

Honking your horn during siesta hours (2–5 p.m.) and between 12–7 a.m. is prohibited in residential areas.

Gas [petrol] stations are widespread, apart from the more remote areas and smaller islands. In villages they can be part of the local coffee shop. Lead-free and diesel fuel, as well as regular leaded, are widely available. Most stations are not self-service, and it is customary to tip the attendant, who will probably also clean your windshield [windscreen].

Car rental Ενοικίαση αυτοκινήτου

Most international car rental companies have branches in Greece. However, renting a car can be expensive, and there is usually a large deposit required and additional charges for mileage above 100km/day or for delivering the car to a different office. Fire and third-party insurance is included in the cost but not collision damage, which is extra. A special permit is needed for taking rental cars outside of Greece or on a ferry.

Where can I rent a car?	Πού μπορώ να νοικιάσω ένα αυτοκίνητο; *poo boro na neekeeaso ena aftokeeneeto*
I'd like to rent a car.	Θα ήθελα να νοικιάσω ένα αυτοκίνητο. *tha eethela na neekeeaso ena aftokeeneeto*
2-/4-door car	δίπορτο/τετράπορτο *THeeporto/tetraporto*
an automatic	αυτόματο *aftomato*
with 4-wheel drive	τετρακινητήριο *tetrakeeneeteereeo*
with air conditioning	με κλιματισμό *me kleemateezmo*
with a child seat	με παιδικό κάθισμα *me peTHeeko katheezma*
I'd like it for a day/week.	Θα το ήθελα για μια μέρα/μια εβδομάδα *tha to eethela ya mia mera/ mia evTHomaTHa*
How much does it cost per day/week?	Πόσο κάνει την ημέρα/εβδομάδα; *poso kanee teen eemera/teen evTHomaTHa*
Is mileage/insurance included?	Συμπεριλαμβάνονται τα χιλιόμετρα/ συμπεριλαμβάνεται η ασφάλεια; *sembereelamvanonde ta kheeleeometra/ seembereelamvanete ee asfaleea*
Can I leave the car at your office in …?	Μπορώ να αφήσω το αυτοκίνητό στο γραφείο σας στο/στη …; *boro na afeeso to aftokeeneeto sto ghrafeeo sas sto/stee*
What sort of fuel does it take?	Τί είδους καύσιμα παίρνει; *tee eeTHoos kafseema pernee*
Where's the high [full]/low [dipped] beam?	Πού είναι τα φώτα πόλεως/φώτα πορείας; *poo eene ta fota poleos/fota poreeas*
Could I have full insurance, please?	Μπορώ να έχω ολική ασφάλεια, παρακαλώ; *boro na ekho oleekee asfaleea, parakalo*

DAYS OF THE WEEK ➤ *218*

Gas [Petrol] station Βενζινάδικο

Where's the next gas [petrol] station, please?	Πού είναι το επόμενο βενζινάδικο, παρακαλώ; *poo eene to epomeno venzeenaTHeeko, parakalo*
Is it self-service?	Είναι σελφ-σέρβις; *eene "self-service"*
Fill it up, please.	Γεμίστε το, παρακαλώ. *yemeeste to, parakalo*
… liters of gasoline [petrol], please.	… λίτρα βενζίνη, παρακαλώ. *leetra venzenee, parakalo*
regular	απλή *aplee*
lead-free	αμόλυβδη *amoleevTHee*
diesel	ντήζελ *"diesel"*
Where is the air pump/water?	Πού είναι η αντλία αέρος/νερού …; *poo eene ee andleea aeroos/neroo*

ΤΙΜΗ ΑΝΑ ΛΙΤΡΟ	price per liter

Parking Πάρκινγκ

Parking in large cities, particularly Athens, can be a problem as parking spaces are limited. Often you will need to buy a parking ticket from a roadside machine and attach it to your car. If you break a parking rule you will get a ticket which you'll need to take to the traffic police station to pay. More serious offenses (causing an obstruction, parking on a double-yellow line, etc.) can lead to the removal of your registration plates, which you will have to pay to reclaim at the traffic police station.

Is there a parking lot [car park] nearby?	Υπάρχει χώρος στάθμευσης εδώ κοντά; *eeparkhee khoros stathmefsees eTHo konda*
What's the charge per hour/day?	Πόσο κοστίζει την ώρα/ημέρα; *poso kosteezee teen ora/eemera*
Do you have some change for the parking meter?	Έχετε ψιλά για το παρκόμετρο; *ekhete pseela ya to parkometro*
They have taken my registration plates. Who do I call?	Μου πήραν τις πινακίδες. Ποιόν να καλέσω; *moo peeran tees peenakeeTHes. peeon na kaleso*

NUMBERS ➤ 216; DIRECTIONS ➤ 94

Breakdown Βλάβη

There are a number of automobile rescue organizations in Greece. The most well known is ELPA (☎ 104), but Express Service, Hellas Service, and SOS Service are also fine. These organizations often have links with other international services. Additionally, there are regular emergency phones, marked SOS on most highways.

Where is the nearest garage?	Πού είναι το κοντινότερο συνεργείο; *poo eene to kondeenotero seeneryeeo*
My car broke down.	Έπαθα βλάβη. *epatha vlavee*
Can you send a mechanic/ tow [breakdown] truck?	Μπορείτε να στείλετε ένα μηχανικό/οδικό συνεργείο; *boreete na steelete ena meekhaneeko/oTHeeko seeneryeeo*
I belong to … recovery service.	Ανήκω στην εταιρία … οδικής βοήθειας. *aneeko steen etereea … oTHeekees voeetheeas*
My registration number is …	Ο αριθμός κυκλοφορίας μου είναι … *o areethmos keekloforeeas moo eene*
The car is …	Το αυτοκίνητο είναι … *to aftokeeneeto eene*
on the highway [motorway]	στον αυτοκινητόδρομο *ston aftokeeneetoTHromo*
2 km from …	δύο χιλιόμετρα από … *THeeo kheeleeometra apo*
How long will you be?	Πόση ώρα θα κάνετε; *posee ora tha kanete*

What is wrong? Τί πρόβλημα έχει;

I don't know what's wrong.	Δεν ξέρω τί πρόβλημα έχει. *THen ksero tee provleema ekhee*
My car won't start.	Η μηχανή δεν παίρνει μπρος. *ee meekhanee THen pernee bros*
I've run out of gas [petrol].	Έχω μείνει από βενζίνη. *ekho meenee apo venzeenee*
I have a flat [puncture].	Μου έσκασε το λάστιχο. *moo eskase to lasteekho*
There is something wrong with …	Υπάρχει κάποιο πρόβλημα με … *eeparkhee kapeeo provleema me*
I've locked the keys in the car.	Κλείδωσα τα κλειδιά στο αυτοκίνητο. *kleeTHosa ta kleeTHya sto aftokeeneeto*

TELEPHONING ➤ 127; CAR PARTS ➤ 90–91

Repairs Επισκευές

Do you do repairs?	Κάνετε επισκευές; *kanete epeeskeves*
Could you take a look at my car?	Μπορείτε να ρίξετε μια ματιά στο αυτοκίνητό μου; *boreete na reeksete mia mateea sto aftokeeneeto moo*
Can you repair it (temporarily)?	Μπορείτε να το διορθώσετε (προσωρινά); *boreete na to THeeorthosete (prosoreena)*
Please make only essential repairs.	Παρακαλώ κάνετε μόνο τις αναγκαίες επισκευές. *parakalo kanete mono tees anange-es epeeskeves*
Can I wait for it?	Μπορώ να περιμένω; *boro na pereemeno*
Can you repair it today?	Μπορείτε να το επισκευάσετε σήμερα; *boreete na to epeeskevasete seemera*
When will it be ready?	Πότε θα είναι έτοιμο; *pote tha eene eteemo*
How much will it cost?	Πόσο θα κοστίσει; *poso tha kosteesee*
That's outrageous!	Αυτό είναι εξωφρενικό ποσό! *afto eene eksofreneeko poso*
Can I have a receipt for my insurance?	Μπορώ να έχω μια απόδειξη για την ασφάλεια; *boro na ekho mia apoTHeeksee ya teen asfaleea*

Ο/η/το … δεν δουλεύει	The … isn't working.
Δεν έχω τα απαραίτητα ανταλλακτικά.	I don't have the necessary parts.
Πρέπει να παραγγείλω τα ανταλλακτικά.	I will have to order the parts.
Μπορώ να το επισκευάσω μόνο προσωρινά.	I can only repair it temporarily.
Δεν μπορεί να επισκευαστεί.	It can't be repaired.
Θα είναι έτοιμο …	It will be ready …
αργότερα σήμερα	later today
αύριο	tomorrow
σε … ημέρες	in … days

DAYS OF THE WEEK ➤ 218; NUMBERS ➤ 216

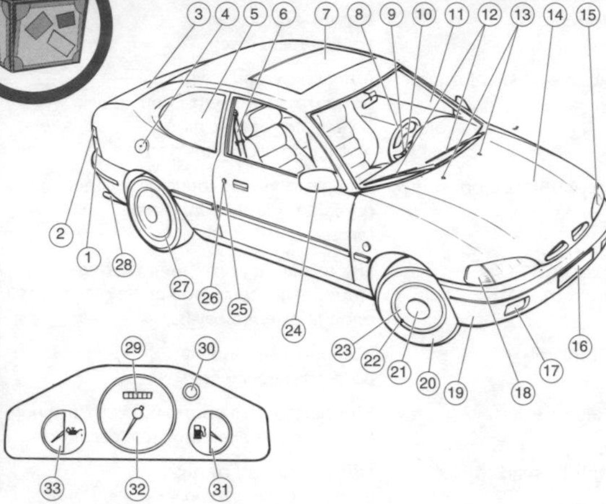

1 tail lights [back lights] πίσω φώτα πορείας *peeso fota poreeas*
2 brakelights τα φώτα φρένων *ta fota frenon*
3 trunk [boot] το πόρτ-μπαγκάζ *to port-bagaz*
4 gas tank door [petrol cap] η τάπα βενζίνης *ee tapa venzeenees*
5 window το παράθυρο *to paratheero*
6 seat belt η ζώνη ασφαλείας *ee zonee asfaleeas*
7 sunroof η ηλιοροφή *ee eeleeorofee*
8 steering wheel το τιμόνι *to teemonee*
9 ignition η ανάφλεξη *ee anafleksee*
10 ignition key κλειδί ανάφλεξης *kleeTHee anafleksees*
11 windshield [windscreen] το παρμπρίζ *to parbreez*
12 windshield [windscreen] wipers οι υαλοκαθαριστήρες *ee eealokathareesteeres*
13 windshield [windscreen] washer ο καθαριστήρας παρμπρίζ *o kathareesteeras parbreez*
14 hood [bonnet] το καπό *to kapo*
15 headlights τα φώτα πορείας *ta fota poreeas*
16 licence [number] plates οι πινακίδες κυκλοφορίας *ee peenakeeTHes keekloforeeas*
17 fog lamp τα φώτα ομίχλης *ta fota omeekhlees*
18 turn signals [indicators] το φλας *to flas*
19 bumper ο προφυλακτήρας *o profeelakteeras*
20 tires [tyres] τα λάστιχα *ta lasteekha*
21 hubcap το τάσι *to tasee*
22 valve η βαλβίδα *ee valveeTHa*
23 wheels οι ρόδες *ee roTHes*
24 outside [wing] mirror ο εξωτερικός καθρέπτης *o eksotereekos kathreptees*
25 central locking το κεντρικό κλείδωμα *to kendreeko kleeTHoma*
26 lock η κλειδαριά *ee kleeTHarya*
27 wheel rim η ζάντα *ee zanda*
28 exhaust pipe η εξάτμιση *ee eksatmeesee*
29 odometer [milometer] ο χιλιομετρυτης *o kheeleeometreetees*
30 warning light τα προειδοποιητικά φώτα *ta proeeTHopee-eeteeka fota*
31 fuel gauge ο δείκτης καυσίμων *o THeektees kafseemon*

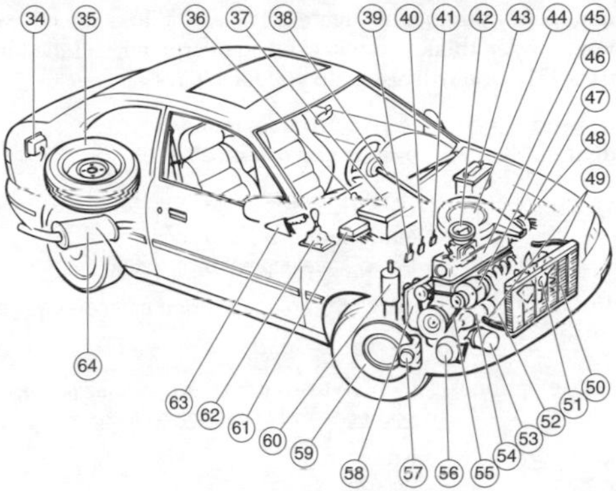

32 speedometer το κοντέρ *to konder*
33 oil gauge ο δείκτης λαδιού *o THeektees laTHyoo*
34 backup [reversing] lights φώτα όπισθεν *fota opeesthen*
35 spare tire η ρεζέρβα *ee rezerva*
36 choke το τσοκ *to tsok*
37 heater το καλοριφέρ *to kaloreefer*
38 steering column η βάση τιμονιού *ee vasee teemoneeoo*
39 accelerator το γκάζι *to gazee*
40 pedal το πετάλι *to petalee*
41 clutch ο συμπλέκτης *o seemblektees*
42 carburetor το καρμπυρατέρ *to karbeerater*
43 battery η μπαταρία *ee batareea*
44 alternator ο εναλλακτής *o enalaktees*
45 camshaft ο (εκκεντροφόρος) άξονας *o (ekendrofor os) aksonas*
46 air filter το φίλτρο αέρα *to feeltro aera*
47 distributor ο διανομέας *o THeeanomeas*
48 points οι πλατίνες *ee plateenes*
49 radiator hose (top/bottom) ο αγωγός θέρμανσης *o aghoghos thermansees*
50 radiator το καλοριφέρ *to kaloreefer*
51 fan ο ανεμιστήρας *o anemeesteeras*
52 engine η μηχανή *ee meekhanee*
53 oil filter το φίλτρο λαδιού *to feel-tro laTHyoo*
54 starter η μίζα *ee meeza*
55 fan belt ο ιμάντας ανεμιστήρα *[illegible]mandas anemeesteera*
56 horn η κόρνα *ee korna*
57 brake pads τα τακάκια φρένων *ta takakeea frenon*
58 transmission [gearbox] το κιβώτιο ταχυτήτων *to keevoteeo takheeteeton*
59 brakes τα φρένα *ta frena*
60 shock absorbers τα αμορτισέρ *ta amorteeser*
61 fuses οι ασφάλειες *ee asfalee-es*
62 shift [gear lever] ο μοχλός ταχυτήτων *o mokhlos takheeteeton*
63 handbrake το χειρόφρενο *to kheerofreno*
64 muffler [silencer] ο σιγαστήρας *o seeghasteeras*

REPAIRS ➤ 89

Accidents Ατυχήματα

The emergency number in Greece is 100, and it links directly with the police. If you think you will need an interpreter, call the tourist police (☎ 171) who will also help you fill in Greek forms.

There has been an accident.	Έγινε ένα ατύχημα. *eyeene ena ateekheema*
It's …	Είναι … *eene*
2 km from …	δύο χιλιόμετρα από εδώ. *THeeo kheeleeometra apo eTHo*
on the highway [motorway]	στον εθνικό δρόμο *ston ethneeko THromo*
near …	κοντά … *konda*
Where's the nearest telephone?	Πού είναι το κοντινότερο τηλέφωνο; *poo eene to kondeenotero teelefono*
Call …	Καλέστε … *kaleste*
the police	την αστυνομία *teen asteenomeea*
an ambulance	ένα ασθενοφόρο *ena asthenoforo*
a doctor	ένα γιατρό *ena yatro*
the fire department [brigade]	την πυροσβεστική *teen peerozvesteekee*
Can you help me please?	Μπορείτε να με βοηθήσετε; *boreete na me voeetheesete*

Injuries Τραυματισμοί

There are people injured.	Υπάρχουν τραυματίες. *eeparkhoon travmatee-es*
No one is hurt.	Δεν υπάρχουν τραυματίες. *THen eeparkhoon travmatee-es*
He is seriously injured/bleeding.	Είναι σοβαρά τραυματισμένος/αιμορραγεί. *eene sovara travmateezmenos/emorayee*
She's unconscious.	Είναι αναίσθητη. *eene anestheetee*
He can't breathe/move.	Δεν μπορεί να αναπνεύσει/κινηθεί. *THen boree na anapnefsee/keeneethee*
Don't move him.	Μην τον μετακινήσετε. *meen ton metakeeneesete*

INJURIES ➤ 162; DIRECTIONS ➤ 94

Legal matters Νομικά θέματα

What's your insurance company?	Ποιά είναι η ασφαλιστική εταιρία σας; *pia eene ee asfaleesteekee etereea sas*
What's your name and address?	Ποιό είναι το όνομα και η διεύθυνσή σας; *peeo eene to onoma ke ee THee-eftheensee sas*
He ran into me.	Με χτύπησε. *me khteepeese*
She was driving too fast/close.	Οδηγούσε πολύ γρήγορα/πολύ κοντά. *oTHeeghoose polee ghreeghora/konda*
I had the right of way.	Είχα προτεραιότητα. *eekha protereoteeta*
I was (only) driving at … km/h.	Έτρεχα μόνο … χιλιόμετρα την ώρα. *etrekha mono me … kheeleeometra teen ora*
I'd like an interpreter.	Θα ήθελα έναν/μια διερμηνέα. *tha eethela enan/mia THee ermeenea*
I didn't see the sign.	Δεν είδα την πινακίδα. *THen eeTHa teen peenakeeTHa*
He/She saw it happen.	Αυτός/αυτή είδε τι συνέβη. *aftos/aftee eeTHe tee seenevee*
The registration number was …	Ο αριθμός κυκλοφορίας ήταν … *o areethmos keekloforeeas eetan*

Μπορώ να δω …, παρακαλώ;	Can I see your …, please?
την άδεια οδήγησης	driver's license
το πιστοποιητικό της ασφάλισης	insurance card
την άδεια κυκλοφορίας	vehicle registration
Τι ώρα συνέβηκε;	What time did it happen?
Πού συνέβηκε;	Where did it happen?
Ήταν κανείς άλλος αναμεμειγμένος;	Was anyone else involved?
Υπάρχουν μάρτυρες;	Are there any witnesses?
Τρέχατε.	You were speeding.
Δεν δουλεύουν τα φώτα σας.	Your lights aren't working.
Πρέπει να πληρώσετε πρόστιμο.	You'll have to pay a fine (on the spot).
Πρέπει να κάνετε δήλωση στο τμήμα.	We need you to make a statement at the station.

TIME ➤ 220

Asking directions
Ρωτώντας το δρόμο

Excuse me, please!	Παρακαλώ! *parakalo*
How do I get to …?	Πώς πάνε στο/στη …; *pos pane sto/stee*
Where is …?	Πού είναι …; *poo eene*
Can you show me on the map where I am?	Μπορείτε να μου δείξετε στο χάρτη πού είμαι; *boreete na moo THeeksete sto khartee poo eeme*
I've lost my way.	Έχασα το δρόμο μου. *ekhasa to THromo moo*
Can you repeat that please?	Μπορείτε να το επαναλάβετε; *boreete na to epanalavete*
More slowly, please.	Πιο αργά, παρακαλώ. *peeo argha, parakalo*
Thanks for your help.	Ευχαριστώ για τη βοήθεια σας. *efkhareesto ya tee voeetheea sas*

Traveling by car Ταξιδεύοντας με το αυτοκίνητο

Is this the right road for …?	Αυτός είναι ο σωστός δρόμος για …; *aftos eene o sostos THromos ya*
How far is it to … from here?	Πόσο απέχει ο/η/το … από εδώ; *poso apekhee o/ee/to … apo eTHo*
Where does this road lead?	Πού πάει αυτός ο δρόμος; *poo paee aftos o THromos*
How do I get onto the highway [motorway]?	Πώς πάω στην Εθνικη οδό; *pos pao steen ethneekee oTHo*
What's the next town called?	Πώς λέγεται η επόμενη πόλη; *pos leyete ee epomenee polee*
How long does it take by car?	Πόση ώρα είναι με το αυτοκίνητο; *posee ora eene me to aftokeeneeto*

– seeghnomee, parakalo. pos pane sto seeTHeeroTHromeeko stathmo?
– parte to treeto steno sta areestera ke eene eftheea.
– treeto sta areestera. eene makreea?
– eene pende lepta me ta poTHya.
– efkhareesto ya teen voeetheea sas.
– parakalo.

COMMUNICATION DIFFICULTIES ➤ 11

Location Θέση

Είναι ...	It's ...
ευθεία	straight ahead
στα αριστερά	on the left
στα δεξιά	on the right
από την άλλη μεριά του δρόμου	on the other side of the street
στη γωνία	on the corner
στη γωνία λίγο πιο κάτω	around the corner
στην κατεύθυνση προς ...	in the direction of ...
απέναντι .../πίσω ...	opposite .../behind ...
δίπλα στο/στη .../μετά ...	next to .../after ...
Πάρτε ...	Go down the .../Take the ...
τον παράδρομο/τον κεντρικό δρόμο	side street/main street
το τρίτο στενό στα δεξιά	third right
Περάστε ...	Cross the ...
την πλατεία/την γέφυρα	square/bridge
Στρίψτε αριστερά ...	Turn left ...
μετά τα πρώτα φώτα	after the first traffic lights
στο δεύτερο σταυροδρόμι	at the second intersection [crossroad]

By car Με το αυτοκίνητο

Είναι ... από δω.	It's ... of here.
βόρεια/νότια	north/south
ανατολικά/δυτικά	east/west
Πάρτε το δρόμο για ...	Take the road for ...
Είστε σε λάθος δρόμο.	You're on the wrong road.
Πρέπει να πάτε πίσω στο ...	You'll have to go back to ...
Ακολουθήστε τα σήματα για ...	Follow the signs for ...

How far? Πόσο απέχει;

Είναι ...	It's ...
κοντά/όχι πολύ μακριά/μακριά	close/not far/a long way
πέντε λεπτά με τα πόδια	5 minutes on foot
δέκα λεπτά με το αυτοκίνητο	10 minutes by car
περίπου εκατό μέτρα πιο κάτω	about 100 meters down the road

TIME ➤ 220; NUMBERS ➤ 216

Road signs Σήματα

ΜΟΝΟ ΓΙΑ ΠΡΟΣΒΑΣΗ	access only
ΠΑΡΑΚΑΜΨΗ	detour [diversion]
ΔΩΣΤΕ ΠΡΟΤΕΡΑΙΟΤΗΤΑ	yield [give way]
ΧΑΜΗΛΗ ΓΕΦΥΡΑ	low bridge
ΜΟΝΟΔΡΟΜΟΣ	one-way street
ΟΔΟΣ ... ΚΛΕΙΣΤΗ	road closed
ΣΧΟΛΕΙΟ	school
ΑΝΑΨΤΕ ΤΑ ΦΩΤΑ ΠΟΡΕΙΑΣ	use headlights

Town plan Χάρτης της πόλης

αεροδρόμιο	*aeroTHromeeo*	airport
αθλητικό στάδιο	*athleeteeko staTHeeo*	playing field [sports ground]
αστυνομικό τμήμα	*asteenomeeko tmeema*	police station
βρισκόσαστε εδώ	*vreeskosaste eTHo*	you are here
γραφείο πληροφοριών	*ghrafeeo pleeroforeeon*	information office
δημόσιο κτίριο	*THeemoseeo kteereeo*	public building
διάβαση πεζών	*THeeavasee pezon*	pedestrian crossing
διαδρομή λεωφορείων	*THeeaTHromee leoforeeon*	bus route
εκκλησία	*ekleeseea*	church
θέατρο	*theatro*	theater
κινηματογράφος	*keeneematoghrafos*	movie theater [cinema]
παλιά πόλη	*paleÂa polee*	old town
πάρκο	*parko*	park
πεζόδρομος	*pezoTHromos*	pedestrian precinct
πιάτσα ταξί	*peeatsa taksee*	taxi stand [rank]
προκυμαία	*prokeemea*	harborfront
στάδιο	*staTHeeo*	stadium
σταθμός	*stathmos*	station
σταθμός μετρό	*stathmos metro*	subway [metro] station
στάση λεωφορείων	*stasee leoforeeon*	bus stop
ταχυδρομείο	*takheeTHromeeo*	post office
τουαλέττες	*tooaletes*	toilets
υπόγεια διάβαση	*eepoyeea THeeavasee*	underpass
χώρος στάθμευσης	*khoros stathmefsees*	parking lot [car park]

DICTIONARY ➤ 169; SIGHTSEEING ➤ 97–107

Sightseeing

Tourist information office EOT/KOT

Tourist information offices.are known as EOT (**eleeneekos orghaneesmos tooreesmoo** or **eot**) in Greece, and KOT (**keepreeakos orghaneesmos tooreesmoo** or **kot**) in Cyprus. They can be found in most tourist resorts and major towns. The principal tourist attractions are the ancient sites.

Where's the tourist office?	Πού είναι το γραφείο τουρισμού; *poo eene to ghrafeeo tooreezmoo*
What are the main points of interest?	Ποιά είναι τα κυριότερα αξιοθέατα; *pia eene ta keereeotera akseeotheata*
We're here for …	Είμαστε εδώ για … *eemaste eTHO ya*
only a few hours	λίγες ώρες μόνο *leeyes ores mono*
a day	μια ημέρα *mia eemera*
a week	μια εβδομάδα *mia evTHomaTHa*
Can you recommend …?	Μπορείτε να συστήσετε …; *boreete na seesteesete*
a sightseeing tour	μια ξενάγηση στα αξιοθέατα *mia ksenayeesee sta akseeotheata*
an excursion	μια εκδρομή *mia ekTHromee*
a boat trip	μια εκδρομή με βάρκα *mia ekTHromee me varka*
Are these leaflets free?	Αυτά τα φυλλάδια είναι δωρεάν; *afta ta feelaTHeea eene THorean*
Do you have any information on …?	Έχετε πληροφορίες για …; *ekhete pleeroforee-es ya*
Are there any trips to …?	Υπάρχουν ταξίδια για …; *eeparkhoon takseeTHya ya*

DAYS OF THE WEEK ➤ 218; DIRECTIONS ➤ 94

Excursions Εκδρομές

How much does the tour cost?	Πόσο κοστίζει η περιήγηση; *poso kosteezee ee peree-eeyeesee*
Is lunch included?	Συμπεριλαμβάνεται το μεσημεριανό; *seembereelamvanete to meseemeryano*
Where do we leave from?	Από πού φεύγουμε; *apo poo fevghoome*
What time does the tour start?	Τι ώρα αρχίζει η εκδρομή; *tee ora arkheezee ee ekTHromee*
What time do we get back?	Τι ώρα θα επιστρέψουμε; *tee ora tha epeestrepsoome*
Do we have free time in …?	Έχουμε ελεύθερο χρόνο στο …; *ekhoome eleftihero khrono sto*
Is there an English-speaking guide?	Υπάρχει Αγγλόφωνος ξεναγός; *eeparkhee anglofonos ksenaghos*

On tour Στην ξενάγηση

Are we going to see …?	Θα δούμε …; *tha THoome*
We'd like to have a look at the …	Θα θέλαμε να ρίξουμε μια ματιά … *tha thelame na reeksoome mia mateea*
Can we stop here …?	Μπορούμε να σταματήσουμε εδώ …; *boroome na stamateesoome eTHo*
to take photographs	για να πάρουμε φωτογραφίες *ya na paroome fotoghrafee-es*
to buy souvenirs	για να αγοράσουμε σουβενίρ *ya na aghorasoome sooveneer*
to use the bathroom [toilet]	για την τουαλέττα *ya teen tooaleta*
Would you take a photo of us, please?	Μπορείτε να μας πάρετε μια φωτογραφία, παρακαλώ; *boreete na mas parete mia fotoghrafeea parakalo*
How long do we have here/ in …?	Πόση ώρα έχουμε εδώ/στο …; *posee ora ekhoome eTHo/sto*
Wait! … isn't back yet.	Περιμένετε! … δεν έχει γυρίσει ακόμη. *pereemenete! … THen ekhee yeereesee akomee*
Stop the bus! My child is feeling sick.	Σταματήστε το λεωφορείο! το παιδί μου δεν αισθάνεται καλά. *stamateeste to leoforeeo! to peTHee moo THen esthanete kala*

Sights Τα αξιοθέατα

Where is the …	Πού είναι …;	*poo eene*
art gallery	η γκαλερί τέχνης	*ee galeree tekhnees*
botanical garden	ο βοτανικός κήπος	*o votaneekos keepos*
castle	το κάστρο	*to kastro*
cathedral	ο καθεδρικός ναός	*o katheTHreekos naos*
chapel	το παρεκκλήσι	*to parekleesee*
church	η εκκλησία	*ee ekleeseea*
city wall	το τείχος	*to teekhos*
downtown area	το κέντρο της πόλης	*to kendro tees polees*
fountain	το συντριβάνι	*to seendreevanee*
harbor	το λιμάνι	*to leemanee*
market	η αγορά	*ee aghora*
memorial/monument	το μνημείο	*to mneemeeo*
monastery	το μοναστήρι/η μονή (on road signs)	*to monasteeree/ee monee*
museum	το μουσείο	*to mooseeo*
old town	η παλιά πόλη	*ee paleea polee*
opera house	η όπερα	*ee opera*
palace	τα ανάκτορα	*ta anaktora*
park	το πάρκο	*to parko*
parliament building	η Βουλή	*ee voolee*
shopping area	η εμπορική περιοχή	*ee emboreekee pereeokhee*
statue	το άγαλμα	*to aghalma*
temple	ναός	*naos*
(ancient) theater	το (αρχαίο) θέατρο	*to arkheo theatro*
tower	ο πύργος	*o peerghos*
town hall	το Δημαρχείο	*to THeemarkheeo*
viewpoint	το πανόραμα	*to panorama*
Can you show me on the map?	Μπορείτε να μου δείξετε στο χάρτη;	*boreete na moo THeeksete sto khartee*

DIRECTIONS ➤ 94

Admission Είσοδος

Most sites and museums are closed at least once a week – usually Monday. Admission is often free on Sunday.

If you want to visit a monastery it is best to avoid religious service times (early morning, sunset) and lunchtime. The tourist office or tourist police will have more detailed local opening hours.

Is the … open to the public?	Είναι το … ανοιχτό στο κοινό; *eene to … aneekhto sto keeno*
What are the opening hours?	Ποιές είναι οι ώρες λειτουργίας; *pee-es eene ee ores leetooryeeas*
When does it close?	Τί ώρα κλείνει; *tee ora kleenee*
Is … open on Sundays?	Είναι το … ανοιχτό τις Κυριακές; *eene to … aneekhto tees keereeakes*
When's the next guided tour?	Πότε είναι η επόμενη ξενάγηση; *pote eene ee epomenee ksenayeesee*
Do you have a guidebook (in English)?	Έχετε ένα ταξιδιωτικό οδηγό (στα Αγγλικά); *ekhete ena takseeTHeeoteeko oTHeegho (sta angleeka)*
Can I take photos?	Μπορώ να πάρω φωτογραφίες; *boro na paro fotoghrafee-es*
Is there access for the disabled?	Υπάρχει πρόσβαση για άτομα με ειδικές ανάγκες; *eeparkhee prozvasee ya atoma me eeTHeekes ananges*
Is there an audioguide in English?	Υπάρχει ξενάγηση με κασέτα στα Αγγλικά; *eeparkhee ksenayeesee me kaseta sta angleeka*

Paying/Tickets Πληρωμή/Εισιτήρια

How much is the entrance fee?	Πόσο κάνει η είσοδος; *poso kanee ee eesoTHos*
Are there discounts for …?	Υπάρχει μειωμένο εισιτήριο για …; *eeparkhee meeomeno eeseeteereeo ya*
children/students	παιδιά/φοιτητές *peTHya/feeteetes*
senior citizens	συνταξιούχους *seendakseeookhoos*
1 adult and 2 children, please.	Ένας ενήλικας και δύο παιδιά, παρακαλώ. *enas eneeleekas ke THeeo peTHya parakalo*

TIME ➤ 220

– pende eeseeteereea, parakalo.
eeparkhee meeomeno eeseeteereeo?

– ne. ya peTHya ke seendakseeookhoos eene THeeo evro.

– THeeo eneeleekes ke treea peTHya, parakalo.

– kanee teserees kheeleeaTHes okhtakosee-es, parakalo.

ΕΛΕΥΘΕΡΗ ΕΙΣΟΔΟΣ	free admission
ΑΝΟΙΧΤΟ	open
ΚΛΕΙΣΤΟ	closed
ΣΟΥΒΕΝΙΡ	gift shop
ΤΕΛΕΥΤΑΙΑ ΕΙΣΟΔΟΣ ΣΤΙΣ 5 μμ	last entry at 5 p.m.
Η ΕΠΟΜΕΝΗ ΞΕΝΑΓΗΣΗ ΣΤΙΣ …	next tour at …
ΑΠΑΓΟΡΕΥΕΤΑΙ Η ΕΙΣΟΔΟΣ	no entry
ΑΠΑΓΟΡΕΥΕΤΑΙ Η ΦΩΤΟΓΡΑΦΗΣΗ ΜΕ ΦΛΑΣ	no flash photography
ΩΡΕΣ ΛΕΙΤΟΥΡΓΙΑΣ	visiting hours

Impressions Εντυπώσεις

It's …	Είναι … *eene*
amazing	καταπληκτικό *katapleekteeko*
beautiful	όμορφο *omorfo*
boring	βαρετό *vareto*
breathtaking	φαντασμαγορικό *fandazmaghoreeko*
impressive	εντυπωσιακό *endeeposeeako*
incredible	απίστευτο *apeestefto*
interesting	ενδιαφέρον *enTHeeaferon*
magnificent	μεγαλοπρεπές *meghaloprepes*
romantic	ρομαντικό *romandeeko*
strange	παράξενο *parakseno*
superb	έξοχο *eksokho*
terrible	φοβερό *fovero*
ugly	άσχημο *askheemo*
It's good value	Είναι καλή τιμή. *eene kalee teemee*
It's a rip-off.	Είναι κλεψιά. *eene klepseea*
I like it.	Μου αρέσει. *moo aresee*
I don't like it.	Δεν μου αρέσει. *THen moo aresee*

Tourist glossary
Οδηγός εκθεμάτων

λουτρά	*lootra*	baths
αμφιθέατρο(ν)	*amfeetheatro(n)*	amphitheater
εκκλησία	*ekleeseea*	church
μονή	*monee*	monastery
τάφος	*tafos*	grave, tomb
το μουσείο	*to mooseeo*	museum
εικόνα	*eekona*	icon
ακρόπολις	*akropolees*	fortified city
ανάκτορα	*anaktora*	palace
κίονας	*keeonas*	column
ναός	*naos*	temple
άγαλμα	*aghalma*	statue

αρχαιολογία	*arkheoloyeea*	archaeology
αρχαία	*arkhea*	antiquities
αρχιτεκτονική	*arkheetektoneekee*	architecture
(βυζαντινή)	*(veezandeenee)*	(Byzantine)
τέχνη	*tekhnee*	art
αγγειοπλαστική	*angeeoplasteekee*	ceramics / pottery
διάζωμα	*THeeazoma*	frieze
κοσμήματα	*kozmeemata*	jewelry
ψηφιδωτό	*pseefeeTHoto*	mosaic
πίνακας	*peenakas*	painting
γλυπτό	*ghleepto*	sculpture
ταπετσαρία	*tapetsareea*	tapestry

Who/What/When? Ποιός/Τί/Πότε;

What's that building?	Τί είναι αυτό το κτίριο; *tee eene afto to kteereeo*
Who was the …?	Ποιός ήταν ο/η …; *peeos eetan o/ee*
architect	αρχιτέκτονας *arkheetektonas*
artist	καλλιτέχνης *kaleetekhnees*
painter	ζωγράφος *zoghrafos*
When was it built/painted?	Πότε κτίστηκε/ζωγραφίστηκε; *pote kteesteeke/zoghrafeesteeke*

Temple architectural styles

Δωρικός ρυθμός *THoreekos reethmos*

Doric style – famous for its simplicity and perfect symmetry. The best example is the Parthenon, on the Acropolis of Athens.

Ιωνικός ρυθμός *eeoneekos reethmos*

Ionic style – The column capital is in the form of a spiral, sometimes with intricate decorations. Example: the Temple of Athena Nike on the Acropolis.

Κορινθιακός ρυθμός *koreentheeakos reethmos*

Corinthian style – Columns are similar to Ionic, but the capital is decorated with thistle leaves. The Temple of Olympian Zeus in Athens is of this style.

Αττικός ρυθμός *ateekos reethmos*

Attic style – generally refers to the style of art in Athens (Attica).

Church styles

Βασιλική *vaseeleekee*

Basilica – early form of Christian church. Rectangular in shape, later ones have a single dome.

Βυζαντινός ρυθμός *veezandeenos reethmos*

Byzantine style – churches built in the shape of a cross, with a main central dome and four smaller ones at each point of the cross. More elaborate churches are made in the shape of a double cross (8 points) with a dome at each point. The Hagia Sophia built in A.D. 537 (in Istanbul, Turkey) became the prototype.

History

What period is that?	Ποιάς περιόδου είναι αυτό; *pias pereeoTHoo eene afto*

Κυκλαδικός πολιτισμός *keeklaTHeekos poleeteezmos* 3200–1100 B.C.

Cycladic civilization; ruins can be found on the island of Thira or Santorini.

Μινωικός πολιτισμός *meenoeekos poleeteezmos* c.2500–c.1500 B.C.

Minoan civilization; ruins at Knossos and Phaestos on Crete.

Μυκηναϊκός πολιτισμός
meekeenaeekos poleeteezmos 1600–1100 B.C.
Mycenaean civilization, centered on Mycenae.

Ελληνοπερσικοί πόλεμοι
eleenoperseekee polemee c. 500 B.C.
Greco-Persian wars; battles of Marathon and Salamis.

Κλασσική εποχή *klaseekee epokhee* 500–400 B.C.
Classical period. Flourishing of all art. Building of the Acropolis and the temples of Olympian Zeus in Athens and Artemis at Ephesus.

Ελληνιστικοί χρόνοι *eleeneesteekee khronee*
late 4th–1st century B.C.
Hellenistic period. Rise of Macedonia under Philip and later his son Alexander the Great. Expansion of "Hellas" to Afghanistan.

Ρωμαϊκοί χρόνοι *romaeekee khronee* 27 B.C.–A.D. 330
Roman period. Greece becomes a Roman province.

Βυζαντινή Αυτοκρατορία
veezandeenee aftokratoreea 330–1453
Foundation of Eastern Roman Empire in 330 A.D., also known as the Byzantine Empire. Capital moves from Rome to Constantinople.

Τουρκοκρατία *toorkokrateea* 1453–1821
Turkish occupation ended by the Greek War of Independence (1821–1829).

Νεοελληνική εποχή *neoeleeneekee epokhee* 1829–present
Modern Greek period

Religious services Θρησκευτικές λειτουργίες

The prevalent religion in Greece is Greek Orthodox. As a tourist, you will find the religious service fascinating, the ritual having barely changed since the early Byzantine years (see above). The head of the Eastern Orthodox Church is the patriarch, who is based in Istanbul. The main churches stay open all day. You will not be allowed into a church or a monastery if you are wearing shorts, a mini skirt, or a sleeveless top/dress.

(Greek) Orthodox Church	(Ελληνική) Ορθόδοξος εκκλησία *eleeneekee orthoTHoksos ekleeseea*
Catholic/Protestant Church	Καθολική/Διαμαρτυρόμενη εκκλησία *katholeekee/THeeamarteeromenee ekleesseea*
mosque	τζαμί *tzamee*
synagogue	συναγωγή *seenaghoyee*
What time is …?	Τι ώρα είναι …; *tee ora eene*
mass/the service	η λειτουργία *ee leetooryeea*

In the countryside Στην εξοχή

I'd like a map of …	Θα ήθελα ένα χάρτη … *tha eethela ena khartee*
this region	αυτής της περιοχής *aftees tees pereeokhees*
walking routes	διαδρομών περιήγησης *THeeaTHromon peree-eeyeesees*
cycle routes	ποδηλατόδρομων *poTHeelatoTHromon*
How far is it to …?	Πόσο μακριά είναι για …; *poso makreea eene ya*
Is there a right of way?	Υπάρχει προτεραιότητα; *eeparkhee protereoteeta*
Is there a scenic route to …?	Υπάρχει μονοπάτι/γραφικός δρόμος για …; *eeparkhee monopatee/ghrafeekos THromos ya*
Can you show me on the map?	Μπορείτε να μου δείξετε στο χάρτη; *boreete na moo THeeksete sto khartee*
I'm lost.	Έχω χαθεί. *eho khathee*

Organized walks Οργανωμένοι περίπατοι

When does the guided walk/hike set out?	Πότε ξεκινάει ο περίπατος/η πεζοπορία με τον ξεναγό; *pote ksekeenaee o pereepatos/ee pezoporeea me ton ksenagho*
When will we return?	Πότε θα επιστρέψουμε; *pote tha epeestrepsoome*
What is the walk/hike like?	Πώς είναι ο περίπατος/η πεζοπορία; *pos eene o pereepatos/ee pezoporeea*
gentle/medium/tough	ομαλός/μέτριος/δύσκολος *omalos/metreeos/THeeskolos*
Where do we meet?	Πού θα συναντηθούμε; *poo tha seenandeethoome*
I'm exhausted.	Είμαι ξεθεωμένος/-η. *eeme ksetheomenos/-ee*
What kind of … is that?	Τι είδους … είναι αυτό; *tee eeTHoos … eene afto*
animal/bird	ζώο/πουλί *zoo/poolee*
flower/tree	λουλούδι/δέντρο *loolooTHee/THendro*

HIKING GEAR ➤ 145

Geographic features
Γεωγραφικά χαρακτηριστικά

bridge	η γέφυρα *ee yefeera*
cave	το σπήλαιο *to speeleo*
cliff	ο γκρεμός *o gremos*
farm	η φάρμα *ee farma*
field	το χωράφι *to khorafee*
forest	το δάσος *to THasos*
hill	ο λόφος *o lofos*
lake	η λίμνη *ee leemnee*
mountain	το βουνό, το όρος (on maps) *to voono, to oros*
mountain pass	το ορεινό πέρασμα *to oreeno perazma*
nature reserve	ο εθνικός δρυμός *o ethneekos THreemos*
panorama	το πανόραμα *to panorama*
park	ο κήπος/το πάρκο *o keepos/to parko*
path	το μονοπάτι *to monopatee*
peak	η κορυφή *ee koreefee*
picnic area	η περιοχή για πικ-νικ *ee pereeokhee ya "picnic"*
pond	η λιμνούλα *ee leemnoola*
rapids	το ρεύμα ποταμού *to revma potamoo*
ravine	η ρεματιά *ee remateea*
river	ο ποταμός *o potamos*
sea	η θάλασσα *ee thalasa*
spa	τα ιαματικά λουτρά *ta eeamateeka lootra*
stream	το ρυάκι *to reeakee*
valley	η κοιλάδα *ee keelaTHa*
viewing point	η πανοραμική θέση *ee panorameekee thesee*
village	το χωριό *to khoryo*
vineyard/winery	ο αμπελώνας/η οινοποιεία *o ambelonas/ee eenopee-eea*
waterfall	ο καταρράχτης *o katarakhtees*
wood	το δάσος *to THasos*

Leisure

Events Εκδηλώσεις

The tourist police and EOT can provide a list of cultural events in the area. For Athens the EOT publication *Athina* and the English newspaper *Athens News* give a comprehensive guide of what's on, where to eat, current exhibits etc. A separate magazine *Music Hall*, giving a diary of events, is published by **megharo mooseekees**.

Do you have a program of events?	Έχετε έναν οδηγό θεαμάτων; *ekhete enan oTHeegho theamaton*
Can you recommend a …?	Μπορείτε να συστήσετε ένα … *boreete na seesteesete ena*
ballet/concert	μπαλέτο/συναυλία *baleto/seenavleea*
movie [film]	ταινία *teneea*
opera	όπερα *opera*
ancient tragedy/comedy	αρχαία τραγωδία/κωμωδία *arkhea traghoTHeea/ komoTHeea*
When does it start/end?	Τι ώρα αρχίζει/τελειώνει; *tee ora arkheezee/teleeonee*

Availability Διαθεσιμότητα

During the Athens festival (**festeeval atheenon**) in the summer (June-September), information and tickets for performances at the Theater of Herodeion Attikon and Epidauros can be obtained from the ticket office at Stadiou 4 St. Tickets for other performances can be bought directly from the theater box office.

Where can I get tickets?	Πού μπορώ να βρω εισιτήρια; *poo boro na vro eeseeteereea*
Are there any seats for tonight?	Υπάρχουν θέσεις για απόψε; *eeparkhoon thesees ya apopse*
There are … of us.	Είμαστε … *eemaste*

Tickets Εισιτήρια

How much are the seats?	Πόσο κοστίζουν οι θέσεις; *poso kosteezoon ee thesees*
Do you have anything cheaper?	Έχετε τίποτα φτηνότερο; *ekhete teepota fteenotero*
I'd like to reserve …	Θα ήθελα να κλείσω … *tha eethela na kleeso*
3 for Sunday matinée/evening	τρία για την απογευματινή/βραδινή της Κυριακή *treea ya tee apoyevmateenee/vraTHeenee tees keereeakees*

Ποιός/-ά/-ό είναι … της πιστωτικής σας κάρτας;	What's your credit card …?
ο αριθμός/το είδος	number/type
η ημερομηνία λήξεως	expiration [expiry] date
Παρακαλώ, να παραλάβετε τα εισιτήρια …	Please pick up the tickets …
μέχρι τις … μ.μ.	by … p.m.
στο γραφείο κρατήσεων	at the reservations desk

(May I have) a program, please?	(Μπορώ να έχω) ένα πρόγραμμα, παρακαλώ; *(boro na ekho) ena proghrama parakalo*
Where's the coatcheck [cloakroom]?	Πού είναι η γκαρνταρόμπα; *poo eene ee gardaromba*

ΚΡΑΤΗΣΕΙΣ ΘΕΣΕΩΝ	advance reservations
ΕΙΣΙΤΗΡΙΑ ΓΙΑ ΑΠΟΨΕ	tickets for today

– *boro na sas voeetheeso?*
– tha eethela treea eeseeteereea ya teen apopseenee seenavleea.
– *veveos.*
– boro na pleeroso me peestoteekee karta?
– *maleesta, keeree-e.*
– tote tha khreeseemopee-eeso VISA.
– *efkhareesto … eepoghrapste eTHo, parakalo..*

NUMBERS ➤ 216

Movies [Cinema] Κινηματογράφος

After a sharp decline in the 1980s, movie theaters are experiencing a revival in Greece. There is at least one movie theater in most resorts. And if you are there in the summer, it is worth going to an open air theater – watching a film on a warm summer evening with the rising moon and a star-studded sky as a backdrop is a unique experience.

Foreign films are always subtitled, so you should have no problem finding English-language films.

What's playing at the movies [cinema] tonight?	Τι παίζει ο κινηματογράφος απόψε; *tee pezee o keeneematoghrafos ·apopse*
Is the film dubbed/subtitled?	Η ταινία είναι μεταγλωττισμένη/με υπότιτλους; *ee teneea eene metaghloteezmenee/me eepoteetloos*
Is the film in the original English?	Η ταινία είναι στα Αγγλικά; *ee teneea eene sta angleeka*
Who's the main actor/actress?	Ποιός είναι ο πρωταγωνιστής; *peeos eene o protaghoneestees*
A …, please.	… , παρακαλώ. *… parakalo*
box of popcorn	ένα πακέτο ποπ-κορν *ena paketo "popcorn"*
chocolate ice cream	ένα παγωτό σοκολάτα *ena paghoto sokolata*
hot dog	ένα χοτ-ντογκ *ena "hot dog"*
soft drink/soda	ένα αναψυκτικό *ena anapseekteeko*
small/regular/large	μικρό/μέτριο/μεγάλο *meekro/metreeo/meghalo*

Theater Θέατρο

What's playing at the … Theater?	Τι παίζεται στο Θέατρο …; *tee pezete sto theatro*
Who's the playwright?	Ποιός είναι ο δραματουργός; *peeos eene o THramatoorghos*
Do you think I'd enjoy it? I don't know much Greek.	Νομίζετε ότι θα το ευχαριστηθώ; Δεν μιλώ πολλά Ελληνικά. *nomeezete otee tha to efkhareesteetho? THen meelo pola eleeneeka*

Opera / Ballet / Dance
Όπερα/Μπαλέτο/Χορός

Who's the composer / soloist?	Ποιός είναι ο συνθέτης/ο σολίστας; *peeos eene o seenthetees/o soleestas*
Is formal evening dress required?	Χρειάζεται βραδυνό ένδυμα; *khreeazete vraTHeeno enTHeema*
Where's the opera house?	Πού είναι η Όπερα; *poo eene ee opera*
Who's dancing?	Ποιός χορεύει; *peeos khorevee*
I'm interested in contemporary / folk dance.	Με ενδιαφέρει ο μοντέρνος χορός/οι παραδοσιακοί χοροί. *me enTHeeaferee o mondernos khoros/ee paraTHoseakee khoree*

Music / Concerts Μουσική/Συναυλίες

Where's the concert hall?	Πού είναι η αίθουσα συναυλιών; *poo eene ee ethoosa seenavleeon*
Which orchestra / band is playing?	Ποιά ορχήστρα/ποιό συγκρότημα παίζει; *peea orkheestra/peeo seegroteema pezee*
What are they playing?	Τί παίζουν; *tee pezoon*
Who's the conductor?	Ποιός είναι ο διευθυντής ορχήστρας; *peeos eene o THeeeftheendees orkheestras*
Who's the support band?	Ποιό είναι το βοηθητικό συγκρότημα; *peeo eene to voeetheeteeko seengroteema*
I really like …	Με ενδιαφέρει … *me enTHeeaferee*
folk music	η δημοτική μουσική *ee THeemoteekee mooseekee*
jazz	η τζαζ *ee "jazz"*
pop	η ποπ *ee "pop"*
rock music	η μουσική ροκ *ee mooseekee "rock"*
soul music	η σόουλ *ee so-ool*
rembetika (traditional Greek music)	τα ρεμπέτικα *ta rembeteeka*
Have you ever heard of her / him?	Τον/Την έχετε ακουστά; *ton/teen ekhete akoosta*

Nightlife Νυχτερινή ζωή

What is there to do in the evenings?	Τι μπορώ να κάνω τα βράδυα; *tee boro na kano ta vraTHya*
Can you recommend a good …?	Μπορείτε να συστήσετε ένα καλό …; *boreete na seesteesete ena kalo*
Is there a … in town?	Υπάρχει … στην πόλη; *eeparkhee … steen polee*
(music) bar	μπαρ (με μουσική) *"bar" (me mooseekee)*
casino	καζίνο *"casino"*
discotheque	ντισκοτέκ *deeskotek*
gay club	κλαμπ για ομοφυλόφιλους *"club" ya omofeelofeeloos*
nightclub	νυχτερινό κέντρο *neekhtereeno kendro*
restaurant (with live Greek music)	εστιατόριο (με ζωντανή ελληνική μουσική) *esteeatoreeo (me zondanee eleeneekee mooseekee)*
Is there a floor show / cabaret?	Υπάρχει ζωντανό σώου/καμπαρέ; *eeparkhee zondano "show"/"cabaret"*
How do I get there?	Πώς πάω εκεί; *pos pao ekee*

Admission Είσοδος

What time does the show start?	Τι ώρα αρχίζει το σώου; *tee ora arkheezee to "show"*
Is evening dress required?	Χρειάζεται βραδυνό ένδυμα; *khreeazete vraTHeeno enTHeema*
Is a reservation necessary?	Είναι απαραίτητη η κράτηση; *eene apareteetee ee krateesee*
Do we need to be members?	Χρειάζεται να είμαστε μέλη; *khreeazete na eemaste melee*
How long will we have to stand in line [queue]?	Πόση ώρα πρέπει να περιμένουμε στην ουρά; *posee ora prepee na pereemenoome steen oora*
I'd like a good table.	Θα ήθελα ένα καλό τραπέζι. *tha eethela ena kalo trapezee*

TIME ➤ *220; TAXI* ➤ *84*

Children Παιδιά

Can you recommend something for the children?	Μπορείτε να μας συστήσετε κάτι για τα παιδιά; *boreete na mas seesteesete katee ya ta peTHeea*
Where can I change the baby's diaper [nappy]?	Που μπορώ να αλλάξω την πάνα του μωρού; *poo boro na alakso teen pana too moroo*
Where are the bathrooms [toilets]?	Πού είναι οι τουαλέττες; *poo eene ee tooaletes*
amusement arcade	αίθουσα ψυχαγωγίας *ethoosa pseekhaghoyeeas*
fairground	λούνα-παρκ *loona-park*
kiddie [paddling] pool	ρηχή πισίνα *reekhee peeseena*
playground	παιδική χαρά *peTHeekee khara*
play group	παιδικός σταθμός *peTHeekos stathmos*
zoo	ζωολογικός κήπος *zooloyeekos keepos*

Baby-sitting Φύλαξη παιδιών

Can you recommend a reliable baby-sitter?	Μπορείτε να συστήσετε μια υπεύθυνη μπέιμπυ-σίτερ; *boreete na seesteesete mia eepeftheenee "babysitter/dada*
Is there constant supervision?	Υπάρχει συνεχής επίβλεψη; *eeparkhee seenekhees epeevlepsee*
Is the staff properly trained?	Οι βοηθοί είναι καλά εκπαιδευμένοι; *ee voeethee eene kala ekpeTHevmenee*
When can I drop them off?	Πότε μπορώ να τα αφήσω; *pote boro na ta afeeso*
I'll pick them up at …	Θα τα πάρω στις … *tha ta paro stees*
We'll be back by …	Θα είμαστε πίσω στις … *tha eemaste peeso stees*
What age is he/she?	Τι ηλικίας είναι; *tee eeleekeeas eene*
She's 3 and he's 18 months.	Αυτή είναι τριών χρονών και αυτός δεκαοχτώ μηνών. *aftee eene treeon khronon ke aftos THekaokhto meenon*

Sports Αθλητισμός

The most popular sports in Greece are basketball (**kalathosfereesee**) – even the smallest towns have their own basketball team – followed closely by soccer (**poTHosfero**). Soccer matches are usually played on Sunday. The main stadiums are **panatheenaeeko staTHeeo** in Athens and **staTHeeo kara-eeskakee** in Piraeus.

Water sports are very popular on the islands and in coastal areas. However, you need a special permit to dive with oxygen tanks.

Winter skiing has gained popularity in the last few years – and there are 16 ski resorts on the mainland. Ask EOT for details on locations and snow conditions.

Spectating Ως θεατής

Is there a soccer [football] game [match] this Sunday?	Υπάρχει αγώνας ποδοσφαίρου αυτή τη Κυριακή; *eeparkhee aghonas poTHosferoo aftee teen keereeakee*
Which teams are playing?	Ποιές ομάδες παίζουν; *pee-es omaTHes pezoon*
Can you get me a ticket?	Μπορείτε να μου βρείτε ένα εισιτήριο; *boreete na moo vreete ena eeseeteereeo*
What's the admission charge?	Πόσο κάνει η είσοδος; *poso kanee ee eesoTHos*
Where's the racetrack [racecourse]?	Πού είναι το ιπποδρόμιο; *poo eene to eepoTHromeeo*
Where can I place a bet?	Πού μπορώ να βάλω στοίχημα; *poo boro na valo steekheema*
athletics	τα αθλήματα στίβου *ta athleemata steevoo*
basketball	η καλαθοσφαίρηση, το μπάσκετ *ee kalathosfereesee, to "basket"*
cycling	η ποδηλασία *ee poTHeelaseea*
golf	το γκόλφ *to "golf"*
horse racing	οι ιπποδρομίες *ee eepoTHromee-es*
sailing	η ιστιοπλοΐα *ee eesteeoploeea*
soccer [football]	το ποδόσφαιρο *to poTHosfero*
swimming	η κολύμβηση *ee koleemveesee*
tennis	το τέννις *to "tennis"*
volleyball	το βόλεϋ *to "volley"*
water-skiing	το θαλάσσιο σκι *to thalaseeo "ski"*

Playing Το παιχνίδι

Where's the nearest ...?	Πού είναι ο/το κοντινότερος/-ο ...; *poo eene o/to kondeenoteros/-o*
golf course	γήπεδο γκόλφ *yeepeTHo "golf"*
sports club	αθλητικός όμιλος *athleeteekos omeelos*
Where are the tennis courts?	Πού είναι τα γήπεδα τέννις; *poo eene ta yeepeTHa "tennis"*
What's the charge per ...?	Ποιό είναι το κόστος για ... *peeo eene to kostos ya*
day/round/hour	την ημέρα/το παιχνίδι/την ώρα *teen eemera/to pekhneeTHee/teen ora*
Do I need to be a member?	Πρέπει να είμαι μέλος; *prepee na eeme melos*
Where can I rent ...?	Πού μπορώ να νοικιάσω ...; *poo boro na neekeeaso*
boots	μπότες *botes*
clubs	μπαστούνια *bastooneea*
equipment	εξοπλισμό *eksopleezmo*
a racket	μια ρακέτα *mia raketa*
Can I get lessons?	Μπορώ να πάρω μαθήματα; *boro na paro matheemata*
Do you have a fitness room?	Έχετε δωμάτιο γυμναστικής; *ekhete THomateeo yeemnasteekees*
Can I join in?	Μπορώ να συμμετάσχω; *boro na seemetaskho*

Λυπάμαι. Είναι όλα κλεισμένα.	I'm sorry, we're booked up.
Υπάρχει μια προκαταβολή των ...	There is a deposit of ...
Τι μέγεθος είστε;	What size are you?
Χρειαζόσαστε μια φωτογραφία διαβατηρίου.	You need a passport size photo.

ΑΠΑΓΟΡΕΥΕΤΑΙ ΤΟ ΨΑΡΕΜΑ	no fishing
ΑΠΟΔΥΤΗΡΙΑ	changing

At the beach Στην παραλία

Greek beaches are mostly free and often offer a range of water sports. The beaches run by EOT require an entrance fee, but they tend to have more facilities. The use of jet-skis is restricted to a few beaches only, at a certain distance from the land, and at specific hours (ask at your resort). In most island and mainland resorts, it is acceptable to lie on the beach topless, but ask for information on nudist beaches. If in doubt, don't go topless unless you see others first. Greeks rarely go topless, and you may cause offense if you sunbathe topless on a beach frequented by locals.

Is the beach …?	Είναι η παραλία …; *eene ee paraleea*
pebbly / sandy	με χαλίκια/με άμμο *me khaleekeea/me amo*
Is there a … here?	Υπάρχει … εδώ *eeparkhee … eTHo*
children's pool	παιδική πισίνα *peTHeekee peeseena*
swimming pool	πισίνα *peeseena*
indoor / open-air	κλειστή/ανοιχτή *kleestee/aneekhtee*
Is it safe to swim / dive here?	Είναι ασφαλές εδώ για κολύμπι/κατάδυση; *eene asfales eTHo ya koleembee/ kataTHeesee*
Is it safe for children?	Είναι ασφαλές για παιδιά; *eene asfales ya ta peTHya*
Is there a lifeguard?	Υπάρχει ναυαγοσώστης; *eeparkhee navaghosostees*
Is this a nudist beach?	Αυτή είναι παραλία για γυμνιστές; *aftee eene paraleea ya yeemneestes*
I want to rent a / some …	Θέλω να νοικιάσω … *thelo na neekeeaso*
deck chair	μια σεζ-λονγκ *mia sez-long*
diving equipment	εξοπλισμό για υποβρύχιο κολύμπι *eksopleezmo ya eepovreekheeo koleembee*
jet-ski	ένα τζετ-σκι *ena "jet-ski"*
motorboat	μια εξωλέμβιο *mia eksolemveeo*
sailing boat	ένα ιστιοπλοϊκό *ena eesteeoploeeko*
umbrella [sunshade]	μια ομπρέλλα *mia ombrela*
water skis	θαλάσσια σκί *thalaseea "ski"*
windsurfer	ένα γουίντσερφ *ena "windsurfer"*

Skiing Χειμερινό σκί

Skiing has become very popular in the last few years – with 16 ski resorts on all the main summits on the mainland. Ask EOT for details on locations and snow conditions.

I'd like to rent …	Θα ήθελα να νοικιάσω … *tha eethela na neekeeaso*
poles	μπαστούνια του σκι *bastooneea too "ski"*
skates	παγοπέδιλα *paghopeтнeela*
ski boots/skis	μπότες του σκι/σκι *botes too "ski"/"ski"*
These are too …	Αυτά είναι πολυ … *afta eene polee*
big/small	μεγάλα/μικρά *meghala/meekra*
loose/tight	φαρδιά/στενά *farтнeea/stena*
A lift pass for a day/ 5 days.	Μια άδεια για μια ημέρα/πέντε ημέρες. *mia aтнeea ya mia eemera/pende eemeres*
I'd like to join the ski school.	Θα ήθελα να γραφτώ στη σχολή σκι. *tha eethela na ghrafto stee skholee "ski".*
I'm a beginner.	Είμαι αρχάριος/αρχάρια. *eeme arkhareeos/arkhareea*
I'm experienced.	Είμαι έμπειρος/έμπειρη. *eeme embeeros/embeeree*

ΤΕΛΕΣΕΖ	cable car/gondola
ΤΕΛΕΦΕΡΙΚ	chair lift

On the slopes Στην πίστα σκι

Is this slope suitable for …?	Αυτή η πλαγιά είναι κατάλληλη για …; *aftee ee playa eene kataleelee ya*
beginners	αρχάριους *arkhareeoos*
average skiers	μέτριους σκιερ *metreeoos skee-er*
good skiers	καλούς σκιέρ *kaloos skee-er*
Where does the ski school meet?	Πού συγκεντρώνεται η σχολή σκι; *poo seegendronete ee skholee "ski"*
Are the chair lifts in operation?	Λειτουργούν οι τελεσέζ; *leetoorghoon ee telesez*

Making Friends

Introductions Συστάσεις

Greeks always shake hands when they meet for the first time, and also on subsequent meetings. With close friends, it is customary to exchange kisses on both cheeks when meeting and parting.

When you meet people for the first time, it is more polite to address them by their surname until prompted to use their first name.

GRAMMAR

Greek has a formal and an informal form of "you": **ya sas/ya sou**. The informal is used only between friends or when addressing children. Use the formal **ya sas** unless prompted to do otherwise.

Hello, we haven't met.	Χαίρετε, δεν γνωριζόμαστε. *kherete THen ghnoreezomaste*
My name is …	Λέγομαι … *leghome*
May I introduce …?	Να σας συστήσω … *na sas seesteeso*
John, this is …	Γιάννη, από εδώ ο/η … *yeeanee apo eTHo o/ee*
Pleased to meet you.	Χαίρω πολύ. *khero polee*
What's your name?	Πώς λέγεστε; *pos leyeste*
How are you?	Πώς είσαι (Πώς είστε); *pos eese (pos eeste)*
Fine, thanks. And you?	Καλά, ευχαριστώ. Εσύ; (Εσείς;) *kala, efkhareesto. esee (esees)*

– ya sou, tee kanees?
– kala, efkhareesto. esee?
– kala, efkhareesto.

Where are you from?
Από πού είσαι (είστε);

Where do you come from?	Από πού είσαι (είστε); *apo poo eese (eeste)*
I'm from …	Είμαι από … *eeme apo*
Australia	την Αυστραλία *teen afstraleea*
Britain	την Βρεταννία *teen vretaneea*
Canada	τον Καναδά *ton kanaTHa*
England	την Αγγλία *teen angleea*
Ireland	την Ιρλανδία *teen eerlanTHeea*
Scotland	τη Σκωτία *tee skoteea*
the U.S.	τις Ηνωμένες Πολιτείες *tees eenomenes poleetee-es*
Wales	την Ουαλλία *teen ooaleea*
Where do you live?	Πού μένεις (μένετε); *poo menees (menete)*
What part of … are you from?	Από ποιό μέρος …. είσαι (είστε); *apo peeo meros …. eese (eeste)*
Greece	της Ελλάδας *tees elaTHas*
Cyprus	της Κύπρου *tees keeproo*
We come here every year.	Ερχόμαστε εδώ κάθε χρόνο. *erkhomaste eTHo kathe khrono*
It's my/our first visit	Είναι η πρώτη μου/μας επίσκεψη. *eene ee protee moo/mas epeeskepsee*
Have you ever been to Britain/the U.S.?	Έχεις (έχετε) πάει ποτέ στη Βρετανννία/ στις Ηνωμένες Πολιτείες; *ekhees (ekhete) pae pote stee vretaneea/ stees eenomenes poleetee-es*
Do you like it here?	Σου (σας) αρέσει εδώ; *soo (sas) aresee eTHo*
I love (the) … here.	Μου αρέσει … εδώ. *moo aresee … eTHo*
I don't care for (the) … here.	Δεν με ενδιαφέρει … εδώ. *THen me enTHeeaferee … eTHo*
architecture	η αρχιτεκτονική *ee arkheetektoneekee*
countryside	η εξοχή *ee eksokhee*
cuisine	η κουζίνα *ee koozeena*

Who are you with?

Με ποιόν/ποιάν είσαι (είστε);

Who are you with?	Με ποιόν/ποιάν είσαι (είστε); *me peeon/pian eese (eeste)*
I'm on my own.	Είμαι μόνος/-η μου. *eeme monos/-ee moo*
I'm with a friend.	Είμαι με ένα φίλο/μια φίλη μου. *eeme me ena feelo/mia feelee moo*
I'm with my …	Είμαι με … μου. *eeme me … moo*
wife	τη γυναίκα *tee yeeneka*
husband	τον άνδρα *ton anTHra*
family	την οικογένειά *teen eekoyeneea*
children	τα παιδιά *ta peTHya*
parents	τους γονείς *toos ghonees*
boyfriend / girlfriend	το φίλο/τη φίλη *to feelo/tee feelee*
father / mother	τον πατέρα/τη μητέρα *ton patera/tee meetera*
son / daughter	το γιό/την κόρη *to yo/teen koree*
brother / sister	τον αδελφό/την αδελφή *ton aTHelfo/ teen aTHelfee*
uncle / aunt	το θείο/τη θεία *to theeo/tee theea*
Are you married?	Είσαι (είστε) παντρεμένος/-η; *eese (eeste) pandremenos/-ee*
I'm …	Είμαι … *eeme*
married / single	παντρεμένος(-η)/ελεύθερος(-η) *pandremenos(-ee)/eleftheros(-ee)*
divorced / separated	διαζευγμένος(-η) *deeazevghmenos(-ee)*
We live together.	Συζούμε. *seezoome*
Do you have any children?	Έχετε παιδιά; *ekhete peTHya*
2 boys and a girl.	Δύο αγόρια και ένα κορίτσι. *THeeo aghoreea ke ena koreetsee*
How old are they?	Πόσων χρονών είναι; *poson khronon eene*
They're 10 and 12.	Είναι δέκα και δώδεκα. *eene THeka ke THoTHeka*

What do you do? Τι δουλειά κάνετε;

What do you do?	Τι δουλειά κάνεις (κάνετε); *tee THooleea kanees (kanete)*
What are you studying?	Τι σπουδάζεις (σπουδάζετε); *tee spooTHazees (spooTHazete)*
I'm studying …	Σπουδάζω … *spooTHazo*
I'm in …	Είμαι … *eeme*
business	στο εμπόριο *sto emboreeo*
engineering	στη μηχανική *stee meekhaneekee*
retail	στις λιανικές πωλήσεις *stees leeaneekes poleesees*
sales	στις πωλήσεις *stees poleesees*
Who do you work for …?	Για ποιόν δουλεύετε; *ya peeon THoolevete*
I work for …	Δουλεύω για … *THoolevo ya*
I'm a/an …	Είμαι … *eeme*
accountant	λογιστής/λογίστρια *loyeestees/loyeestreea*
housewife	(ν)οικοκυρά *(n)eekokeera*
student	φοιτητής/φοιτήτρια *feeteetees/feeteetreea*
I'm …	Είμαι … *eeme*
retired	συνταξιούχος *seendakseeookhos*
self-employed	ελεύθερος επαγγελματίας *eleftheros epangelmateeas*
between jobs	μεταξύ εργασιών *metaksee erghaseeon*
What are your hobbies/interests?	Ποιά είναι τα χόμπυ/ενδιαφέροντά σου (σας); *pia eene ta khombee/enTHeeaferonda soo (sas)*
I like …	Μου αρέσει … *moo aresee*
music	η μουσική *ee mooseekee*
reading	το διάβασμα *to THeeavasma*
sports	ο αθλητισμός *o athleeteezmos*
Would you like to play …	Θέλεις (θέλετε) να παίξουμε … *thelees (thelete) na peksoome*
cards/chess	χαρτιά/σκάκι *kharteea/skakee*
backgammon	τάβλι *tavlee*

PROFESSIONS, JOBS, INTERESTS ➤ DICTIONARY

What weather! Τί καιρός!

What a lovely day!	Τί όμορφη ημέρα! *tee omorfee eemera*
What awful weather!	Τί απαίσιος καιρός! *tee apeseeos keros*
It's so cold/hot today!	Κάνει τόσο κρύο/τόση ζέστη σήμερα! *kanee toso kreeo/tosee zestee seemera*
Is it usually this hot?	Κάνει συνήθως τόση ζέστη; *kanee seeneethos tosee zestee*
Do you think it's going to … tomorrow?	Νομίζεις (νομίζετε) ότι θα …. αύριο; *nomeezees (nomeezete) otee tha … avreeo*
be a nice day	είναι ωραία ημέρα *eene orea eemera*
rain	βρέξει *vreksee*
snow	χιονίσει *kheeoneesee*
What is the weather forecast?	Τί λέει η πρόβλεψη του καιρού; *tee lee-e ee provlepsee too keroo*
It's …	Έχει … *ekhee*
sunny	ήλιο *eeleeo*
cloudy	συννεφιά *seenefeea*
foggy	ομίχλη *omeekhlee*
wintry [frosty]	παγετό *payeto*
icy	πάγο *pagho*
rainy	βροχερό καιρό *vrokhero kero*
snowy	χιόνι *kheeonee*
stormy	καταιγίδες *kateyeeTHes*
windy	αέρα *aera*
Has the weather been like this for long?	Ο καιρός είναι έτσι εδώ και πολύ καιρό; *o keros eene etsee eTHo ke polee kero*
There will be a heat-wave tomorrow.	Αύριο θα έχουμε καύσωνα. *avreeo tha ekhoome kafsona*

ΠΡΟΒΛΕΨΗ ΚΑΙΡΟΥ	weather forecast

Enjoying your trip?
Περνάς (περνάτε) καλά στο ταξίδι σου (σας);

Κάνεις (κάνετε) διακοπές;	Are you on vacation?
Πώς ήρθες (ήρθατε) εδώ;	How did you get here?
Πώς ήταν το ταξίδι σου (σας);	How was your trip?
Πού μένεις (μένετε);	Where are you staying?
Πόσο καιρό είσαι (είστε) εδώ;	How long have you been here?
Πόσο καιρό θα μείνεις (μείνετε);	How long are you staying?
Τί έχεις (έχετε) κάνει μέχρι τώρα;	What have you done so far?
Πού θα πας (πάτε) μετά;	Where are you going next?
Περνάς (περνάτε) καλά τις διακοπές σου (σας);	Are you enjoying your vacation?

I'm here on …	Είμαι εδώ … *eeme eTHo*
business	για δουλειά *ya THooleea*
vacation [holiday]	για διακοπές *ya THeeakopes*
We came by …	Ήρθαμε με … *eerthame me*
train/bus/plane	το τραίνο/το λεωφορείο/το αεροπλάνο *to treno/to leoforeeo/to aeroplano*
car/ferry	το αυτοκίνητο/το φέρρυ-μπωτ *to aftokeeneeto/to feree-bot*
I have a rental [hire] car.	Έχω νοικιάσει αυτοκίνητο. *ekho neekeeasee aftokeeneeto*
We're staying in …	Μένουμε σε … *menoome se*
an apartment	διαμέρισμα *THeeamereezma*
a hotel/campsite	σε ξενοδοχείο/σε κάμπιγκ *se ksenoTHokheeo/se kambeeng*
with friends	με φίλους *me feeloos*
Can you suggest …?	Μπορείς (μπορείτε) να προτείνεις (προτείνετε) …; *borees (boreete) na proteenees (proteenete)*
things to do	κάτι να κάνουμε *katee na kanoome*
places to eat	μέρη για φαγητό *meree ya fayeeto*
We're having a great/horrible time.	Περνάμε ωραία/απαίσια. *pername orea/apeseea*

Invitations Προσκλήσεις

Would you like to have dinner with us on …?	Θέλεις (θέλετε) να έρθεις (έρθετε) για βραδυνὸ στις …; *thelees (thelete) na erthees (erthete) ya vraTHeeno stees*
May I invite you to lunch?	Θα ήθελα να σε (σας) καλέσω για μεσημεριανὸ. *tha eethela na se (sas) kaleso ya meseemereeano*
Can you come for a drink this evening?	Μπορεὶς να έρθεις (μπορεὶτε να έρθετε) για ένα ποτὸ απὸψε το βράδυ; *borees na erthees (boreete na erthete) ya ena poto apopse to vraTHee*
We are having a party. Can you come?	Κάνουμε ένα πάρτυ. Μπορεὶς να έρθεις; *kanoome ena "party". borees na erthees*
May we join you?	Να έρθουμε μαζὶ σας; *na erthoome mazee sas*
Would you like to join us?	Θέλεις να έρθεις (θέλετε να έρθετε) μαζὶ μας; *thelees na erthees (thelete na erthete) mazee mas*

Going out Έξοδος

What are your plans for …?	Ποιὰ εὶναι τα σχὲδιὰ σου (σας) για …; *pia eene ta skheTHeea soo (sas) ya*
today / tonight	σὴμερα/απὸψε *seemera/apopse*
tomorrow	αὺριο *avreeo*
Are you free this evening?	Είστε ελεὺθερη απὸψε; *eeste eleftheree apopse*
Would you like to …?	Θα ήθελες (θα θέλατε) να …; *tha eetheles (tha thelate) na*
go dancing	πάμε για χορὸ *pame ya khoro*
go for a drink / meal	πάμε για ένα ποτὸ/για φαγητὸ *pame ya ena poto/ya fayeeto*
go for a walk	πάμε ένα περὶπατο *pame ena pereepato*
go shopping	πάμε για ψώνια *pame ya psoneea*
Where would you like to go?	Πού θα ήθελες (θα θέλατε) να πάμε; *poo tha eetheles (tha thelate) na pame*
I'd like to go to …	Θα ήθελα να πάω … *tha eethela na pao*
I'd like to see …	Θα ήθελα να δω … *tha eethela na THo*
Do you like …?	Σου αρέσει …; *soo aresee*

Accepting/Declining
Δέχομαι/Απορρίπτω την πρόταση

Thank you. I'd love to.	Θαύμα. Θα το ήθελα πολύ. *thavma. tha to eethela polee*
Thank you, but I'm busy.	Σας ευχαριστώ, αλλά είμαι πολύ απασχολημένος/-η. *sas efkhareesto ala eeme polee apaskholeemenos/-ee*
May I bring a friend?	Μπορώ να φέρω ένα φίλο/μια φίλη; *boro na fero ena feelo/mia feelee*
Where shall we meet?	Πού θα συναντηθούμε; *poo tha seenandeethoome*
I'll meet you …	Θα σε συναντήσω … *tha se seenandeeso*
in the bar	στο μπαρ *sto bar*
in front of your hotel	μπροστά στο ξενοδοχείο *brosta sto ksenoTHokheeo*
I'll call for you at 8.	Θα περάσω να σε πάρω στις οχτώ. *tha peraso na se paro stees okhto*
Could we make it a bit later/earlier?	Μπορούμε να πούμε λίγο αργότερα/νωρίτερα; *boroome na poome leegho arghotera/noreetera*
How about another day?	Τί θα έλεγες για άλλη μέρα; *tee tha eleyes ya alee mera*
That will be fine.	Εντάξει. *endaksee*

Dining out/in Τρώγοντας έξω/στο σπίτι

If you are invited to a Greek's home for a meal, always take a gift – flowers, something for the home, chocolates, etc. – as you can be sure a lot of effort will be put into feeding you well!

Let me buy you a drink.	Να σε κεράσω ένα ποτό. *na se keraso ena poto*
Do you like …?	Σου αρέσει …; *soo aresee*
What are you going to have?	Τί θα πάρεις; *tee tha parees*
Thank you for the meal.	Σε (σας) ευχαριστώ για το γεύμα. *se (sas) efkhareesto ya to yevma*
That was a lovely meal.	Ήταν ένα θαυμάσιο γεύμα. *eetan ena thavmaseeo yevma*

TIME ➤ 220

Encounters Συναντήσεις

Are you waiting for someone?	Περιμένετε κάποιον; *pereemenete kapeeon*
Do you mind if I …?	Σας πειράζει να …; *sas peerazee na*
sit here/smoke	καθήσω εδώ/καπνίσω *katheeso eTHo/kapneeso*
Can I buy you a drink?	Μπορώ να σε (σου) κεράσω ένα ποτό; *boro na se (sas) keraso ena poto*
I'd love to have some company.	Θα μου άρεσε πολύ η παρέα. *tha moo arese polee ee parea*
Why are you laughing?	Γιατί γελάς (γελάτε); *yatee yelas (yelate)*
Is my Greek that bad?	Τόσο άσχημα είναι τα Ελληνικά μου; *toso askheema eene ta eleeneeka moo*
Shall we go somewhere quieter?	Πάμε κάπου πιο ήσυχα; *pame kapoo peeo eeseekha*
Leave me alone, please!	Σας παρακαλώ, αφήστε με ήσυχη! *sas parakalo afeeste me eeseekhee*
You look great!	Είσαι πολύ όμορφος/όμορφη! *eese polee omorfos/omorfee*
May I kiss you?	Μπορώ να σε φιλήσω; *boro na se feeleeso*
I'm not ready for that.	Δεν είμαι ακόμη έτοιμος/-η για αυτό. *THen eeme akomee eteemos/-ee ya afto*
I'm afraid we've got to leave now.	Λυπάμαι, πρέπει να φύγουμε τώρα. *leepame prepee na feeghoome tora*
Thanks for the evening.	Σε ευχαριστώ για τη βραδυά. *se efkhareesto ya tee vraTHya*
Can I see you again tomorrow?	Μπορώ να σε ξαναδώ αύριο; *boro na se ksanaTHo avreeo*
See you soon.	Θα σε δω σύντομα. *tha se THo seendoma*
Can I have your address?	Μπορώ να έχω τη διεύθυνσή σου (σας); *boro na ekho tee THee-eftheensee soo (sas)*
This is our address in the U.S./Britain.	Αυτή είναι η διεύθυνσή μας στις Ηνωμένες Πολιτείες/στη Βρετανία. *aftee eene ee THee-eftheensee mas stees eenomenes poleetee-es/stee vretaneea*

SAFETY ➤ *65*

Telephoning Στο τηλέφωνο

OTE (**orghaneezmos teelepeekeenoneeon elaTHos**) is the company responsible for Greek telecommunications.

You will have no problems making a phone call in Greece. There are plenty of phone booths, even in remote areas, both coin and card operated (you can purchase cards from most kiosks).

In addition kiosks often have metered phones. You don't need any change; simply make the phone call and pay after you've finished.

May I have your telephone number?	Μπορώ να έχω τον αριθμό τηλεφώνου σου (σας); *boro na ekho ton areethmo teelefonoo soo (sas)*
Here's my number.	Ορίστε ο αριθμός τηλεφώνου μου. *oreeste o areethmos teelefonoo moo*
Please call me.	Παρακαλώ, πάρε (πάρτε) με τηλέφωνο. *parakalo pare (parte) me teelefono*
I'll give you a call.	Θα σε (σας) πάρω τηλέφωνο. *tha se (sas) paro teelefono*
Where's the nearest telephone booth?	Πού είναι ο κοντινότερος τηλεφωνικός θάλαμος; *poo eene o kondeenoteros teelefoneekos thalamos*
May I use your phone?	Μπορώ να χρησιμοποιήσω το τηλέφωνό σας; *boro na khreeseemopee-eeso to teelefono sas*
It's an emergency.	Είναι επείγον. *eene epeeghon*
Do you have a telephone directory for …?	Έχετε τηλεφωνικό κατάλογο για …; *ekhete teelefoneeko katalogho ya*
How much is it to phone the U.S./Britain?	Πόσο κάνει το τηλεφώνημα για τις Ηνωμένες Πολιτείες/Βρεταννία; *poso kanee to telefoneema ya tees eenomenes poleetee-es/vretaneea*
What's the number/ area [dialling] code for …?	Ποιός είναι ο αριθμός/κωδικός για …; *peeos eene o areethmos/koTHeekos ya*
I'd like a phone card, please.	Θα ήθελα μια τηλεκάρτα, παρακαλώ; *tha eethela mia teelekarta parakalo*
I'd like to call collect [reverse the charges].	Θα ήθελα να καλέσω με χρέωση στον παραλήπτη. *tha eethela na kaleso me khreosee ston paraleeptee*

Speaking Μιλώντας

Hello. This is …	Εμπρός. Είμαι ο/η … *embros. eeme o/ee*
I'd like to speak to …	Θα ήθελα να μιλήσω με τον/την … *tha eethela na meeleeso me ton/teen*
Extension …	Εσωτερική γραμμή … *esotereekee ghramee*
Speak louder/more slowly, please.	Μιλάτε πιο δυνατά/πιο αργά, παρακαλώ. *meelate peeo THeenata/peeo argha parakalo*
Could you repeat that, please?	Μπορείτε να το επαναλάβετε; *boreete na to epanalavete*
I'm afraid he's/she's not in.	Λυπάμαι, αλλά δεν είναι εδώ. *leepame ala THen eene eTHo*
You've got the wrong number.	Έχετε λάθος νούμερο. *ekhete lathos noomero*
Just a moment.	Μισό λεπτό. *meeso lepto*
Hold on, please.	Περιμένετε, παρακαλώ. *pereemenete parakalo*
When will he/she be back?	Πότε θα επιστρέψει; *pote tha epeestrepsee*
Will you tell him/her that I called?	Μπορείτε να του/της πείτε ότι πήρα τηλέφωνο; *boreete na too/tees peete otee peera teelefono*
My name is …	Λέγομαι … *leghome*
Would you ask him/her to call me?	Μπορείτε να του/της ζητήσετε να με πάρει τηλέφωνο; *boreete na too/tees zeeteesete na me paree teelefono*
May I leave a message, please?	Μπορώ να αφήσω ένα μήνυμα, παρακαλώ; *boro na afeeso ena meeneema parakalo*
I must go now.	Πρέπει να πηγαίνω τώρα. *prepee na peeyeno tora*
Nice to speak to you.	Χάρηκα πού μιλήσαμε. *khareeka poo meeleesame*
I'll be in touch.	Θα έρθω σε επαφή. *tha ertho se epafee*
Bye.	Αντίο. *andeeo*

Stores & Services

Shopping can be a great pleasure in Greece. Apart from the standard department stores, you can wander through flea markets and seek out the small handicraft stores that line the narrow alleys of most islands and old towns. Haggling is expected in souvenir stores (don't be put off by the price tag), handicraft stores, and outdoor markets, but in other stores the prices are fixed.

ESSENTIAL

I'd like …	Θα ήθελα … *tha eethela*
Do you have …?	Έχετε …; *ekhete*
How much is that?	Πόσο κάνει αυτό; *poso kanee afto*
Thank you.	Ευχαριστώ. *efkhareesto*

ΑΝΟΙΧΤΟ	open
ΚΛΕΙΣΤΟ	closed

Stores and services
Καταστήματα και υπηρεσίες

Where is ...? Πού είναι ...;

Where's the nearest ...?	Πού είναι το κοντινότερο ...; *poo eene to kondeenoteroo*
Where's there a good ...?	Πού υπάρχει ένα καλό ...; *poo eeparkhee ena kalo*
Where's the shopping mall [centre]?	Πού είναι η εμπορική περιοχή; *poo eene ee emboreekee pereeokhee*
Is it far from here?	Είναι μακριά από δώ; *eene makreea apo eTHo*
How do I get there?	Πώς πάνε εκεί; *pos pane ekee*

Stores Καταστήματα

antique store	το κατάστημα με αντίκες *to katasteema me anteekes*
bakery	το αρτοποιείο *to artopee-eeo*
bank	η τράπεζα *ee trapeza*
barber	το κουρείο *to kooreeo*
bookstore	το βιβλιοπωλείο *to veevleeopoleeo*
butcher	το κρεοπωλείο *to kreopoleeo*
camera store	το φωτογραφείο *to fotoghrafeeo*
clothing store [clothes shop]	το κατάστημα ρούχων *to katasteema rookhon*
delicatessen	τυριά-αλλαντικά *teerya alandeeka*
department store	το πολυκατάστημα *to poleekatasteema*
drugstore	το φαρμακείο *to farmakeeo*
fish store [fishmonger]	το ιχθυοπωλείο *to eekhtheeopoleeo*
florist	το ανθοπωλείο *to anthopoleeo*
gift store	το κατάστημα με είδη δώρων *to katasteema me eeTHee THoron*
greengrocer	το οπωροπωλείο *to oporopoleeo*
grocery store	παντοπωλείο *pandopoleeo*
health food store	το κατάστημα με υγιεινές τροφές *to katasteema me eeyee-eenes trofes*

jeweler	το κοσμηματοπωλείο *to kozmeematopoleeo*
kiosk	το περίπτερο *to pereeptero*
liquor store [off-licence]	το κατάστημα ποτών *to katasteema poton*
market	η αγορά *ee aghora*
pastry store	το ζαχαροπλαστείο *to zakharoplasteeo*
pharmacy [chemist]	το φαρμακείο *to farmakeeo*
record / music store	το δισκάδικο *to THeeskaTHeeko*
second-hand store	το κατάστημα μεταχειρισμένων ειδών *to katasteema metakheereezmenon eeTHon*
shoe store	το κατάστημα υποδημάτων *to katasteema eepoTHeematon*
shopping mall [centre]	η εμπορική περιοχή *ee emboreekee pereeokhee*
souvenir store	το κατάστημα σουβενίρ *to katasteema "souvenir"*
sporting goods store	το κατάστημα αθλητικών *to katasteema athleeteekon*
supermarket	το σουπερμάρκετ *to "supermarket"*
tobacconist	το καπνοπωλείο *to kapnopoleeo*
toy store	το κατάστημα παιχνιδιών *to katasteema pekhneeTHyon*

Services Υπηρεσίες

clinic	η κλινική *ee kleeneekee*
dentist	ο οδοντίατρος *o oTHondeeatros*
doctor	ο γιατρός *o yatros*
dry cleaner	το καθαριστήριο *to kathareesteereeo*
hairdresser (ladies / men)	το κομμωτήριο *to komoteereeo*
hospital	το νοσοκομείο *to nosokomeeo*
library	η βιβλιοθήκη *ee veevleeotheekee*
optician	ο οπτικός *o opteekos*
police station	το αστυνομικό τμήμα *to asteenomeeko tmeema*
post office	το ταχυδρομείο *to takheeTHromeeo*
travel agency	το ταξιδιωτικό γραφείο *to takseeTHeeoteeko ghrafeeo*

Opening hours Ώρες λειτουργίας

Most stores are open daily from 8:30 a.m. to 3:00 p.m. in the winter and 8:00 a.m. to 2:30 p.m. in the summer. On Tuesdays, Thursdays and Fridays they reopen at 5:00 p.m. and stay open until 8:30 p.m. (5:30 pm until 9:00 p.m. in the summer). Most stores are open on Saturdays from 8:30 a.m. until 3:00 p.m. Supermarkets and department stores are open from 9:00 a.m. to 9:00 p.m. Monday through Saturday and some are open for a half day on Sunday.

When does the … open/shut?	Πότε ανοίγει/κλείνει ο/η/το …; *pote aneeyee/kleenee o/ee/to*
Are you open in the evening?	Είστε ανοιχτά το απόγευμα; *eeste aneekhta to apoyevma*
Do you close for lunch?	Κλείνετε το μεσημέρι; *kleenete to meseemeree*
Where is the …?	Πού είναι …; *poo eene*
cashier [cash desk]	το ταμείο *to tameeo*
elevator [lift]	το ασανσέρ *to asanser*
escalator	οι κυλιόμενες σκάλες *ee keeleeomenes skales*
store guide	ο οδηγός καταστήματος *o oTHeeghos katasteematos*
It's in the basement.	Είναι στο υπόγειο. *eene sto eepoyeeo*
It's on the … floor.	Είναι στο … *eene sto*
first [ground *(Brit.)*]	ισόγειο *eesoyeeo*
second [first *(Brit.)*]	πρώτο όροφο *proto orofo*
Where's the … department?	Πού είναι το τμήμα …; *poo eene to tmeema*

ΑΝΟΙΧΤΟ ΟΛΗΜΕΡΙΣ	open all day
ΚΛΕΙΣΤΟ ΤΟ ΜΕΣΗΜΕΡΙ	closed for lunch
ΩΡΕΣ ΕΜΠΟΡΙΟΥ	business hours
ΕΙΣΟΔΟΣ	entrance
ΣΚΑΛΑ	stairs
ΕΞΟΔΟΣ	exit
ΕΞΟΔΟΣ ΚΙΝΔΥΝΟΥ	(emergency) exit
ΕΞΟΔΟΣ ΣΕ ΠΕΡΙΠΤΩΣΗ ΠΥΡΚΑΙΑΣ	fire exit

Service Εξυπηρέτηση

Can you help me?	Μπορείτε να με βοηθήσετε; *boreete na me voeetheesete*
I'm looking for …	Ψάχνω για … *psakhno ya*
I'm just browsing.	Απλώς κοιτάω. *aplos keetao*
It's my turn.	Είναι η σειρά μου. *eene ee seera moo*
Do you have any …?	Έχετε καθόλου …; *ekhete katholoo*
I'd like to buy …	Θα ήθελα να αγοράσω … *tha eethela na aghoraso*
Could you show me …?	Μπορείτε να μου δείξετε …; *boreete na moo THeeksete*
How much is this / that?	Πόσο κάνει αυτό/εκείνο; *poso kanee afto/ekeeno*
That's all, thanks.	Τίποτε άλλο. Ευχαριστώ. *teepote alo. efkhareesto*

Καλημέρα/καλησπέρα σας.	Good morning / afternoon.
Σας εξυπηρετεί κανείς;	Are you being served?
Τί θα θέλατε;	What would you like?
Μισό λεπτό να το ελέγξω.	One moment, I'll just check that for you.
Τίποτε άλλο;	Is that everything? / Anything else?

– boro na sas voeetheeso!

– okhee, efkhareesto. aplos keetao.

– endaksee …

– parakalo.

– ne. boro na sas voeetheeso?

– poso kanee afto?

– Mmm… meeso lepto na to elenkso … kanee 6 evro.

ΕΞΥΠΗΡΕΤΗΣΗ ΠΕΛΑΤΩΝ	customer service
ΑΥΤΟΕΞΥΠΗΡΕΤΗΣΗ	self-service
ΕΙΔΙΚΗ ΠΡΟΣΦΟΡΑ	clearance
ΕΚΠΤΩΣΕΙΣ	sale

Preference Προτίμηση

I want something …	Θέλω κάτι … *thelo katee*
It must be …	Πρέπει να είναι … *prepee na eene*
big / small	μεγάλο/μικρό *meghalo/meekro*
cheap / expensive	φτηνό/ακριβό *fteeno/akreevo*
dark / light	σκούρο/ανοιχτό *skooro/aneekhto*
light / heavy	ελαφρύ/βαρύ *elafree/varee*
oval / round / square	οβάλ/στρογγυλό/τετράγωνο *oval/strongeelo/tetraghono*
genuine / imitation	αυθεντικό/απομίμηση *afthendeeko/apomeemeesee*
I don't want anything too expensive.	Δεν θέλω κάτι πολύ ακριβό. *THen thelo katee polee akreevo*
In the region of … euros.	Γύρω στις … ευρώ. *yeero stees … evro*

Τί … θα θέλατε;	What … would you like?
χρώμα/σχήμα	color / shape
ποιότητα/ποσότητα	quality / quantity
Τί είδος θα θέλατε;	What sort would you like?
Περίπου σε τι τιμή σκεφτόσαστε;	What price range are you thinking of?

Do you have anything …?	Έχετε κάτι …; *ekhete katee*
larger	μεγαλύτερο *meghaleetero*
better quality	καλύτερης ποιότητας *kaleeterees peeoteetas*
cheaper	φτηνότερο *fteenotero*
smaller	μικρότερο *meekrotero*
Can you show me …?	Μπορείτε να μου δείξετε …; *boreete na moo THeeksete*
that / this one	εκείνο/αυτό *ekeeno/afto*
these / those ones	αυτά/εκείνα *afta/ekeena*
the one in the window / display case	αυτό στη βιτρίνα *afto stee veetreena*
some others	μερικά άλλα *mereeka ala*

COLORS ➤ 143

Conditions of purchase Όροι αγοράς

Is there a guarantee?	Υπάρχει εγγύηση; *eeparkhee engee-eesee*
Are there any instructions with it?	Υπάρχουν οδηγίες; *eeparkhoon oTHeeyee-es*

Out of stock Εξαντλημένα

Λυπάμαι, δεν έχουμε άλλα.	I'm sorry, we don't have any.
Έχουν τελειώσει.	We're out of stock.
Μπορώ να σας δείξω κάτι άλλο/ένα άλλο είδος;	Can I show you something else/ a different sort?
Να σας το παραγγείλουμε;	Shall we order it for you?

Can you order it for me?	Μπορείτε να μου το παραγγείλετε; *boreete na moo to parangeelete?*
How long will it take?	Πόσο καιρό θα πάρει; *poso kero tha paree?*
Where else might I get ...?	Πού αλλού μπορώ να βρω ...; *poo aloo boro na vro?*

Decision Απόφαση

That's not quite what I want.	Δεν είναι ακριβώς αυτό που θέλω. *THen eene akreevos afto poo thelo*
No, I don't like it.	Όχι, δεν μου αρέσει. *okhee, THen moo aresee*
That's too expensive	Είναι πολύ ακριβό. *eene polee akreevo*
I'd like to think about it.	Θα ήθελα να το σκεφτώ. *tha eethela na to skefto*
I'll take it.	Θα το πάρω. *tha to paro*

– *boreete na moo THeeksete ekeeno to ... ekee, parakalo?*
– veveos. na sas to katevasso.
– *efkhareesto. ... mmm, THen eene akreevos afto poo thelo.*
– ekhoome ala steel ke THeeaforeteeka khromata.
– *okhee. sas efkhareesto.*

Paying Πληρωμή

Most credit cards are accepted in large stores and hotels, and you can also use them in ATMs [cash machines] at major banks. Smaller businesses usually accept only cash.

Where do I pay?	Πού πληρώνω; *poo pleerono*
How much is that?	Πόσο κάνει; *poso kanee*
Could you write it down, please?	Μπορείτε να το γράψετε, παρακαλώ; *boreete na to ghrapsete parakalo*
Do you accept …?	Δέχεστε …; *THekheste*
traveler's checks [cheques]	ταξιδιωτικές επιταγές *takseeTHeeoteekes epeetayes*
I'll pay …	Θα πληρώσω … *tha pleeroso*
by cash	τοις μετρητοίς *tees metreetees*
by credit card	με πιστωτική κάρτα *me peestoteekee karta*
I don't have any smaller change.	Δεν έχω τίποτε μικρότερο. *THen ekho teepote meekrotero*
Sorry, I don't have enough money.	Συγγνώμη, δεν έχω αρκετά χρήματα. *seeghnomee THen ekho arketa khreemata*

Πώς θα πληρώσετε;	How will you pay?
Η συναλλαγή δεν εγκρίθηκε/ δεν έγινε δεκτή.	This transaction has not been approved / accepted.
Αυτή η κάρτα δεν ισχύει.	This card is not valid.
Μπορώ να έχω κάποια ταυτότητα;	May I have some identification?
Εχετε ψιλά/τίποτε μικρότερο;	Do you have any smaller change?

Could I have a receipt, please?	Μπορώ να έχω απόδειξη παρακαλώ; *boro na ekho apoTHeeksee parakalo*
I think you've given me the wrong change.	Νομίζω ότι μου δώσατε λάθος ρέστα. *nomeezo otee moo THosate lathos resta*

ΤΑΜΕΙΟ	cash desk
Η ΚΛΟΠΗ ΤΙΜΩΡΕΙΤΑΙ ΜΕ ΠΡΟΣΤΙΜΟ	shoplifters will be fined

Complaints Παράπονα

This doesn't work.	Αυτό είναι ελαττωματικό. *afto eene elatomateeko*
Where can I make a complaint?	Πού μπορώ να παραπονεθώ; *poo boro na paraponetho*
Can I exchange this, please?	Μπορείτε να μου το αλλάξετε; *boreete na moo to alaksete*
I'd like a refund.	Θα ήθελα την επιστροφή των χρημάτων μου. *tha eethela teen epeestrofee ton khreematon moo*
Here's the receipt.	Ορίστε η απόδειξη. *oreeste ee apoTHeeksee*
I don't have the receipt.	Δεν έχω την απόδειξη. *THen ekho teen apoTHeksee*
I'd like to see the manager.	Θα ήθελα να δω το διευθυντή. *tha eethela na THo to THee-eftheendee*

Repairs/Cleaning Επισκευές/Καθαριστήριο

This is broken. Can you repair it?	Αυτό είναι σπασμένο. Μπορείτε να μου το διορθώσετε; *afto eene spazmeno. boreete na moo to THeeorthosete*
Do you have … for this?	Έχετε … γι' αυτό; *ekhete … yafto*
a battery	μπαταρία *batareea*
replacement parts	ανταλλακτικά *andalakteeka*
There's a problem with the …	Υπάρχει πρόβλημα με τον/την/το … *eeparkhee provleema me ton/teen/to*
I'd like this …	Θα ήθελα να μου … αυτό. *tha eethela na moo … afto*
cleaned	καθαρίσετε *kathareesete*
pressed	σιδερώσετε *seeTHerosete*
When will it/they be ready?	Πότε θα είναι έτοιμο; *pote tha eene eteemo*
This isn't mine.	Αυτό δεν είναι δικό μου. *afto THen eene THeeko moo*
There's … missing.	Λείπει ένας/μια/ένα … *leepee enas/mia/ena*

TIME ➤ 220; DATE ➤ 218

Bank / Currency exchange
Τράπεζα/Ανταλλαγή συναλλάγματος

Changing money in Greece is not a problem. All major foreign currencies, travelers checks [cheques] and Eurocheques are widely accepted at all banks and currency exchanges. In addition, automatic cash dispensers (look for theATM sign) can be found ouside most main banks and accept VISA, MasterCard, EC, American Express, Eurocard, etc.

Banks open at 7:30 a.m. or 8:00 a.m. and close at 2:30 p.m. (1:30 p.m. on Fridays). Centrally located banks are also open on Saturdays. Currency exchanges stay open until late at night.

Where's the nearest …?	Πού είναι η κοντινότερη …; *poo eene ee kondeenoteree*
bank	η τράπεζα *ee trapeza*
currency exchange [bureau de change]	ανταλλαγή συναλλάγματος *andalaghee seenalaghmatos*

ΩΘΗΣΑΤΕ/ΕΛΞΑΤΕ/ΠΙΕΣΑΤΕ	push / pull / press
ΑΝΟΙΧΤΟ/ΚΛΕΙΣΤΟ	open / closed
ΤΑΜΕΙΟ	cashiers

Changing money Αλλαγή χρημάτων

Can I exchange foreign currency here?	Μπορώ να αλλάξω ξένο συνάλλαγμα εδώ; *boro na alakso kseno seenalaghma eTHo*
I'd like to change some dollars / pounds into euros.	Θα ήθελα να αλλάξω μερικά δολλάρια/λίρες σε ευρώ. *tha eethela na alakso mereeka THolareea/leeres se evro*
I want to cash some traveler's checks [cheques].	Θα ήθελα να εξαργυρώσω μερικές ταξιδιωτικές επιταγές. *tha eethela na eksaryeeroso mereekes takseeTHyoteekes epeetayes*
What's the exchange rate?	Ποιά είναι η τιμή συναλλάγματος; *pia eene ee teemee seenalaghmatos*
How much commission do you charge?	Πόση προμήθεια χρεώνετε; *posee promeetheea khreonete*
I've lost my traveler's checks [cheques]. These are the numbers.	Έχασα τις ταξιδιωτικές επιταγές μου. Ορίστε οι αριθμοί. *ekhasa tees takseeTHyoteekes epeetayes moo. oreeste ee areethmee*

Security Ασφάλεια

Μπορώ να δω …;	Could I see …?
το διαβατήριο σας	your passport
την ταυτότητά σας	some identification
την τραπεζική κάρτα σας	your bank card
Ποιά είναι η διεύθυνσή σας;	What's your address?
Πού μένετε;	Where are you staying?
Συμπληρώστε αυτό το έντυπο, παρακαλώ.	Fill in this form, please.
Παρακαλώ υπογράψτε εδώ.	Please sign here.

ATMs [Cash machines] Αυτόματες Ταμειολογιστικές Μηχανές (A.T.M.)

Can I withdraw money on my credit card here?	Μπορώ να κάνω ανάληψη με την πιστωτική κάρτα μου εδώ; *boro na kano analeepsee me teen peestoteekee karta moo eTHo*
Where are the ATMs [cash machines]?	Πού είναι οι αυτόματες μηχανες; *poo eene ee aftomates meekhanes*
Can I use my … card in the cash machine?	Μπορώ να χρησιμοποιήσω την κάρτα … σε αυτόματη μηχανή; *boro na khreeseemopee-eeso teen karta … se aftomatee meekhanee*
The cash machine has eaten my card.	Η αυτόματη μηχανή πήρε την κάρτα μου. *ee aftomatee meekhanee peere teen karta moo*

ΞΕΝΟ ΣΥΝΑΛΛΑΓΜΑ	foreign currency
ΠΡΟΜΗΘΕΙΑ	bank charges

In 2002 the oldest currency in Europe, the Greek drachma, was replaced with the common European currency, the euro (ευρώ, pronounced *evro*), divided into 100 cents (λεπτό, *lepto*).

Coins: 1, 2, 5, 10, 20, 50 c.; €1, 2

Notes: €5, 10, 20, 50, 100, 200, 500

Pharmacy Φαρμακείο

All phamacists in Greece must hold a pharmacology degree and are generally extremely helpful at treating minor ailments. Many medications that are prescription only in other countries can be bought over the counter. Additionally, insulin is free at all pharmacies. Pharmacies work on a rota system and there will always be one open 24 hours a day. Read the list on display in all pharmacy windows to find the nearest.

Where's the nearest (all-night) pharmacy?	Πού είναι το κοντινότερο (εφημερεύον) φαρμακείο; *poo eene to kondeenotero (efeemerevon) farmakeeo*
What time does the pharmacy open/close?	Τί ώρα ανοίγει/κλείνει το φαρμακείο; *tee ora aneeyee/kleenee to farmakeeo*
Can you make up this prescription for me?	Μπορείτε να μου φτιάξετε αυτή τη συνταγή; *boreete na moo fteeaksete aftee tee seendayee*
Shall I wait?	Να περιμένω; *na pereemeno*
I'll come back for it.	Θα επιστρέψω. *tha epeestrepso*

Dosage instructions Δοσολογία

How much should I take?	Πόσο πρέπει να πάρω; *poso prepee na paro*
How often should I take it?	Πόσο συχνά πρέπει να το παίρνω; *poso seekhna prepee na to perno*
Is it suitable for children?	Είναι κατάλληλο για παιδιά; *eene kataleelo ya peтнya*

Πάρτε … χάπια/… κουταλιές …	Take … tablets/… teaspoons …
πριν/μετά το γεύμα	before/after meals
με νερό	with water
ολόκληρα	whole
το πρωί/το βράδυ	in the morning/at night
για … ημέρες	for … days

ΔΗΛΗΤΗΡΙΟ	poison
ΜΟΝΟ ΓΙΑ ΕΞΩΤΕΡΙΚΗ ΧΡΗΣΗ	for external use only
ΔΕΝ ΠΑΙΡΝΕΤΑΙ ΑΠΟ ΤΟ ΣΤΟΜΑ	not to be taken internally

DOCTOR ➤ 161

Asking advice Ζητώντας συμβουλή

What would you recommend for ...?	Τι συνιστάτε για ... *tee seeneestate ya*
a cold	το κρυολόγημα *to kreeoloyeema*
a cough	το βήχα *to veekha*
diarrhea	τη διάρροια *tee THeeareea*
hay fever	την αλλεργία σε γύρη *teen aleryeea se yeeree*
insect bites	το τσίμπημα από έντομο *to tseembeema apo endomo*
motion [travel] sickness	ναυτία *nafteea*
a sore throat	πονόλαιμο *ponolemo*
sunburn	τα εγκαύματα ήλιου *ta egavmata eeleeoo*
an upset stomach	το στομαχόπονο *to stomakhopono*
Can I get it without a prescription?	Μπορώ να το πάρω χωρίς συνταγή γιατρού; *boro na to paro khorees seendayee yatroo*

Over-the-counter treatment
Εξυπηρέτηση στο φαρμακείο

Can I have a(n)/some ...?	Μπορώ να έχω ...; *boro na ekho*
antiseptic cream	μια αντισηπτική κρέμα *mia andeeseeptеekee krema*
aspirin	μια ασπιρίνη *mia aspeereenee*
adhesive bandage [plaster]	αυτοκόλλητους επιδέσμους *aftokoleetoos epeeTHezmoos*
condoms	προφυλακτικά *profeelakteeka*
cotton [wool]	βαμβάκι *vamvakee*
cough syrup	σιρόπι για το βήχα *seeropee ya to veekha*
gauze [bandage]	γάζα *ghaza*
insect repellent/spray	εντομοαπωθητικό/εντομοκτόνο *endomoapotheeteeko/endomoktono*
pain killers	παυσίπονα *pafseepona*
vitamin tablets	βιταμίνες *veetameenes*

Toiletries Καλλυντικά

I'd like a/an/ some …	Θα ήθελα … *tha eethela*
after shave	ένα άφτερ σέιβ *ena "after-shave"*
after-sun lotion	το γαλάκτωμα για μετά την ηλιοθεραπεία *to ghalaktoma ya meta teen eeleeotherapeea*
deodorant	ένα αποσμητικό *ena apozmeeteeko*
razor blades	ξυραφάκια *kseerafakeea*
sanitary napkins [towels]	σερβιέττες *servee-etes*
soap	ένα σαπούνι *ena sapoonee*
suntan lotion	κρέμα/λάδι ήλιου *krema/laTHee eeleeoo*
tampons	ταμπόν *tambon*
tissues	χαρτομάντηλα *khartomandeela*
toilet paper	χαρτί υγείας *khartee eeyeeas*
toothbrush	μια οδοντόβουρτσα *mia oTHondovoortsa*
toothpaste	μια οδοντόκρεμα *mia oTHondokrema*

Haircare Φροντίδα για τα μαλλιά

comb	η χτένα *ee khtena*
conditioner	το γαλάκτωμα για τα μαλλιά *to ghalaktoma ya ta maleea*
hair brush	η βούρτσα *ee voortsa*
hair mousse	ο αφρός χτενίσματος, η μους *o afros khteneezmatos, ee moos*
hair spray	η λακ *ee lak*
shampoo	το σαμπουάν *to sampooan*

For the baby Για το μωρό

baby food	το φαγητό για μωρά *to fayeeto ya mora*
baby wipes	υγρά μαντηλάκια *eeghra mandeelakeea*
diapers [nappies]	οι πάνες μωρού *ee panes moroo*
sterilizing solution	το αποστειρωτικό διάλυμα *to aposteeroteeko THeealeema*

Clothing Ρουχισμός

General Γενικά

I'd like …	Θα ήθελα … *tha eethela*
Do you have any …?	Έχετε καθόλου …; *ekhete katholoo*

ΓΥΝΑΙΚΕΙΑ	ladieswear
ΑΝΔΡΙΚΑ	menswear
ΠΑΙΔΙΚΑ ΡΟΥΧΑ	childrenswear

Color Χρώμα

I'm looking for something in …	Ψάχνω κάτι σε … *psakhno katee se*
beige	μπεζ *bez*
black	μαύρο *mavro*
blue	μπλε *ble*
brown	καφέ *kafe*
green	πράσινο *praseeno*
gray	γκρίζο *greezo*
orange	πορτοκαλί *portokalee*
pink	ροζ *roz*
purple	μωβ *mov*
red	κόκκινο *kokeeno*
white	άσπρο *aspro*
yellow	κίτρινο *keetreeno*
light …	ανοιχτό … *aneekhto*
dark …	σκούρο … *skooro*
I want a darker/lighter shade.	Θέλω μια σκουρότερη/ανοιχτότερη απόχρωση. *thelo mia skooroteree/aneekhtoteree apokhrosee*
Do you have the same in …?	Έχετε το ίδιο σε …; *ekhete to eeTHyo se*

Clothes and accessories
Ρούχα και αξεσουάρ

belt	η ζώνη *ee zonee*
bikini	το μπικίνι *to beekeenee*
blouse	η μπλούζα *ee blooza*
bra	το σουτιέν *to sootee-en*
briefs	το κυλοτάκι/σλιπ *to keelotakee/sleep*
coat	το παλτό *to palto*
dress	το φόρεμα *to forema*
handbag	η τσάντα *ee tsanda*
hat	το καπέλλο *to kapelo*
jacket	το σακάκι *to sakakee*
jeans	το μπλου-τζην *to blootzeen*
leggings	το κολλάν *to kolan*
pants (U.S.)	το παντελόνι *to pandelonee*
pantyhose [tights]	το καλτσόν *to kaltson*
scarf	το κασκώλ *to kaskol*
shirt	το πουκάμισο *to pookameeso*
shorts	το σόρτς *to sorts*
skirt	η φούστα *ee foosta*
socks	οι κάλτσες *ee kaltses*
suit (men's)	το κουστούμι *to koostoomee*
suit (women's)	το ταγιέρ *to tayer*
sunglasses	τα γυαλιά ήλιου *ta yaleea eeleeoo*
sweater	το πουλόβερ *to poolover*
sweatshirt	η αθλητική μπλούζα *ee athleeteekee blooza*
swimming trunks	το μαγιώ *to mayo*
swimsuit	το ολόσωμο μαγιώ *to olosomo mayo*
T-shirt	το μπλουζάκι *to bloozakee*
tie	η γραβάτα *ee ghravata*
trousers	το παντελόνι *to pandelonee*
with long/short sleeves	με μακριά/κοντά μανίκια *me makreea/konda maneekeea*
with a V-/round neck	με βε/με στρογγυλή λαιμόκοψη *me ve/me strongeelee lemokopsee*

Shoes Παπούτσια

boots	οι μπότες *ee botes*
flip-flops	οι σαγιονάρες *ee sayonares*
running [training] shoes	τα αθλητικά παπούτσια *ta athleeteeka papootseea*
sandals	τα πέδιλα *ta peTHeela*
shoes	τα παπούτσια *ta papootseea*
slippers	οι παντόφλες *ee pandofles*

Walking/Hiking gear Εξοπλισμός για πεζοπορία

knapsack	το σακκίδιο *to sakeeTHeeo*
hiking boots	οι μπότες πεζοπορίας *ee botes pezoporeeas*
waterproof jacket	το αδιάβροχο *to aTHeeavrokho*
windbreaker [cagoule]	το αδιάβροχο μπουφάν *to aTHeeavrokho boofan*

Fabric Ύφασμα

I want something in …	Θέλω κάτι σε … *thelo katee se*
cotton	βαμβακερό *vamvakero*
denim	ντένιμ *"denim"*
lace	δαντέλλα *THandela*
leather	δερμάτινο *THermateeno*
linen	λινό *leeno*
wool	μάλλινο *maleeno*
Is this …?	Αυτό είναι …; *afto eene*
pure cotton	αγνό βαμβάκι *aghno vamvakee*
synthetic	συνθετικό *seentheteeko*
Is it hand/machine washable?	Πλένεται στο χέρι/στο πλυντήριο; *plenete sto kheree/sto pleendeereeo*

ΠΛΕΝΕΤΑΙ ΜΟΝΟ ΣΤΟ ΚΑΘΑΡΙΣΤΗΡΙΟ	dry clean only
ΠΛΕΝΕΤΑΙ ΣΤΟ ΧΕΡΙ	handwash only
ΜΗΝ ΤΟ ΣΙΔΕΡΩΣΕΤΕ	do not iron

Does it fit? Μου κάνει;

Can I try this on?	Μπορώ να το δοκιμάσω; *boro na to THokeemaso*
It fits well. I'll take it.	Μου κάνει. Θα το πάρω. *moo kanee. tha to paro*
It doesn't fit.	Δεν μου κάνει. *THen moo kanee*
It's too…	Είναι πολύ … *eene polee*
short/long	κοντό/μακρύ *kondo/makree*
tight/loose	στενό/φαρδύ *steno/farTHee*
Do you have this in size …?	Το έχετε στο μέγεθος …; *to ekhete sto meyethos*
What size is this?	Τι μέγεθος είναι αυτό; *tee meyethos eene afto*
Could you measure me, please?	Μπορείτε να με μετρήσετε, παρακαλώ; *boreete na me metreesete parakalo*
I don't know Greek sizes.	Δεν ξέρω τα ελληνικά μεγέθη. *THen ksero ta eleeneeka meyethee*

Size Μέγεθος

Continental sizes are used in Greece. Use the tables below to convert, but remember that they are only a rough guide as sizes vary considerably.

	Dresses/Suits						**Women's shoes**			
American	8	10	12	14	16	18	6	7	8	9
British	10	12	14	16	18	20	$4^{1/2}$	$5^{1/2}$	$6^{1/2}$	$7^{1/2}$
Continental	36	38	40	42	44	46	37	38	40	41

	Shirts				**Men's shoes**								
American / **British**	15	16	17	18	5	6	7	8	$8^{1/2}$	9	$9^{1/2}$	10	11
Continental	38	41	43	45	38	39	41	42	43	43	44	44	45

εξαιρετικά μεγάλος	extra large (XL)
μεγάλος	large (L)
μέτριος	medium (M)
μικρός	small (S)

1 centimeter (cm.) = 0.39 in.	1 inch = 2.54 cm.
1 meter (m.) = 39.37 in.	1 foot = 30.5 cm.
10 meters = 32.81 ft.	1 yard = 0.91 m.

Health and beauty
Υγεία και ομορφιά

I'd like a …	Θα ήθελα … *tha eethela*
facial	έναν καθαρισμό προσώπου *enan kathareezmo prosopoo*
manicure	ένα μανικιούρ *ena maneekeeoor*
massage	ένα μασάζ *ena masaz*
waxing	μια χαλάουα *mia khalaooa*

Hairdresser/Hairstylist Στο κομμωτήριο

I'd like to make an appointment for …	Θα ήθελα να κλείσω ένα ραντεβού για … *tha eethela na kleeso ena randevoo ya*
Can you make it a bit earlier/later?	Μπορείτε λίγο νωρίτερα/αργότερα; *boreete leegho noreetera/arghotera*
I'd like a …	Θα ήθελα … *tha eethela*
cut and blow-dry	κούρεμα και πιστολάκι *koorema ke peestolakee*
shampoo and set	σαμπουάν και χτένισμα *sampooan ke khteneezma*
trim	διόρθωμα *THeeorthoma*
I'd like my hair …	Θα ήθελα … *tha eethela*
colored/tinted	να μου βάψετε τα μαλλιά *na moo vapsete ta malee*
highlighted	ανταύγειες *andavyee-es*
permed	μια περμανάντ *mia permanand*
Don't cut it too short.	Μη τα κόψετε πολύ κοντά. *mee ta kopsete polee konda*
A little more off the …	Κόψτε λίγο ακόμα από … *kopste leegho akoma apo*
back/front	πίσω/μπρος *peeso/bros*
neck/sides	το λαιμό/τα πλάγια *to lemo/ta playa*
top	πάνω *pano*
That's fine, thanks.	Εντάξει, ευχαριστώ. *endaksee, efkhareesto*

Household articles
Είδη οικιακής χρήσεως

I'd like a(n)/some … Θα ήθελα ένα/λίγο … *tha eethela ena/leegho*

alumin(i)um foil	αλουμινόχαρτο *aloomeenokharto*
bottle opener/corkscrew	ένα τιρμπουσόν *ena teermbooson*
can opener	ένα ανοιχτήρι *ena aneekhteeree*
candles	κεριά *kerya*
clothes pins [pegs]	μανταλάκια *mandalakeea*
light bulb	μια λάμπα *mia lamba*
matches	σπίρτα *speerta*
paper napkins	χαρτοπετσέτες *khartopetsetes*
plastic wrap [cling film]	διαφανή μεμβράνη *THeeafanee memvranee*
plug	μια πρίζα *mia preeza*
scissors	ένα ψαλίδι *ena psaleeTHee*
screwdriver	ένα κατσαβίδι *ena katsaveeTHee*

Cleaning items Είδη καθαρισμού

bleach	χλωρίνη *khloreenee*
dish cloth	πανί για τα πιάτα *panee ya ta piata*
dishwashing detergent [washing-up liquid]	υγρό πιάτων *eeghro piaton*
garbage [refuse] bags	σακκούλες σκουπιδιών *sakooles skoopeeTHeeon*
kitchen cloth	απορροφητική πετσέτα κουζίνας *aporofeeteekee petseta koozeenas*
detergent [washing powder]	απορρυπαντικό *aporeepandeeko*

Crockery/Cutlery Πιατικά/Μαχαιροπήρουνα

cups	τα φλυτζάνια *ta fleetzaneea*
forks	τα πηρούνια *ta peerooneea*
glasses	τα ποτήρια *ta poteerya*
knives	τα μαχαίρια *ta makherya*
plates	τα πιάτα *ta piata*
spoons	τα κουτάλια *ta kootaleea*
teaspoons	τα κουταλάκια *ta kootalakeea*

Jeweler Στο κοσμηματοπωλείο

Could I see …?	Μπορώ να δω …; *boro na THo*
this/that	αυτό/εκείνο *afto/ekeeno*
It's in the window/ display cabinet.	Είναι στη βιτρίνα. *eene stee veetreena*
I'd like a(n)/some …	Θα ήθελα … *tha eethela*
alarm clock	ένα ξυπνητήρι *ena kseepneeteeree*
battery	μια μπαταρία *mia batareea*
bracelet	ένα βραχιόλι *ena vrakheeolee*
brooch	μια καρφίτσα *mia karfeetsa*
chain	μια αλυσίδα *mia aleeseeTHa*
clock	ένα ρολόι *ena roloee*
earrings	σκουλαρίκια *skoolareekeea*
necklace	ένα κολλιέ *ena kolee-e*
ring	ένα δαχτυλίδι *ena THakhteeleeTHee*
watch	ένα ρολόι *ena roloee*

Materials Υλικά

Is this real silver/gold?	Αυτό είναι αληθινό ασήμι/χρυσό; *afto eene aleetheeno aseemee/khreeso*
Is there any certification for it?	Υπάρχει σφραγίδα επάνω; *eeparkhee sfrayeeTHa epano*
Do you have anything in …?	Έχετε τίποτα σε … ; *ekhete teepota se*
copper	χαλκό *khalko*
crystal	κρύσταλλο *kreestalo*
cut glass	σκαλιστό γυαλί *skaleesto yaloo*
diamond	διαμάντι *THyamandee*
gold	χρυσό *khreeso*
gold-plate	επίχρυσο *epeekhreeso*
pearl	μαργαριτάρι *marghareetaree*
pewter	κασσίτερο *kaseetero*
platinum	πλατίνα *plateena*
silver	ασήμι *aseemee*
silver-plate	επάργυρο *eparyeero*

Newsstand [Newsagent] / Bookstore
Περίπτερο/Βιβλιοπωλείο

Yellow-colored kiosks (**pereeptera**) can be found on most street corners and at key locations in towns and cities and are a ubiquitous part of everyday life. Greek and foreign newspapers and magazines are sold there as well as tobacco, candy, beer, bus tickets, and more. The more sophisticated kiosks also sell books, maps, guides, and souvenirs.

Do you sell English-language books / newspapers?	Πουλάτε αγγλικά βιβλία/αγγλικές εφημερίδες; *poolate angleeka veevleea/angleekes efeemereeTHes*
I'd like a(n) / some ...	Θα ήθελα ... *tha eethela*
book	ένα βιβλίο *ena vevleeo*
candy [sweets]	καραμέλες *karameles*
chewing gum	μια τσίχλα *mia tseekhla*
chocolate bar	μια σοκολάτα *mia sokolata*
(pack of) cigarettes	ένα πακέτο τσιγάρα *ena paketo tseeghara*
cigars	πούρα *poora*
dictionary	ένα λεξικό *ena lekseeko*
Greek-English	Ελληνο-Αγγλικό *eleeno-angleeko*
guidebook of ...	έναν τουριστικό οδηγό του/της ... *enan tooreesteeko oTHeegho too/tees*
lighter	έναν αναπτήρα *enan anapteera*
magazine	ένα περιοδικό *ena pereeoTHeeko*
map of ...	ένα χάρτη της ... *ena khartee tees*
matches	σπίρτα *speerta*
newspaper	μια εφημερίδα *mia efeemereeTHa*
American / English	αμερικάνικη/αγγλική *amereekaneekee/angleekee*
paper	χαρτί *khartee*
pen	ένα στυλό *ena steelo*
postcard	μια κάρτα *mia karta*
stamps	γραμματόσημα *ghramatoseema*
tobacco	καπνό *kapno*
writing pad	ένα μπλοκ *ena blok*

Photography Φωτογραφικά

I'm looking for a … camera.	Ψάχνω για μια … φωτογραφική μηχανή. *psakhno ya mia fotoghrafeekee meekhanee*
automatic	αυτόματη *aftomatee*
compact	συμπαγής *seembayees*
disposable	μιας χρήσεως *mias khreeseos*
SLR	μονοοπτική ρεφλέξ *monoopteekee refleks*
battery	μπαταρία *batareea*
camera case	θήκη της μηχανής *theekee tees meekhanees*
(electronic) flash	(ηλεκτρονικό) φλας *(eelektroneeko) flas*
filter	φίλτρο *feeltro*
lens	φακός *fakos*
lens cap	κάλυμμα του φακού *kaleema too fakoo*

Film/Processing Φιλμ/Εμφάνιση

I'd like a … film for this camera.	Θα ήθελα ένα … φιλμ για αυτή τη φωτογραφική μηχανή. *tha eethela ena … "film" ya aftee tee fotoghrafeekee meekhanee*
black and white	ασπρόμαυρο *aspromavro*
color	έγχρωμο *enkhromo*
I'd like this film developed, please.	Θα ήθελα να μου εμφανίσετε αυτό το φίλμ, παρακαλώ. *tha eethela na moo emfaneesete afto to "film" parakalo*
Would you enlarge this, please?	Μπορείτε να μου μεγενθύνετε αυτό, παρακαλώ; *boreete na moo meyentheenete afto parakalo*
How much do … exposures cost?	Πόσο κοστίζουν οι … στάσεις; *poso kosteezoon ee … stasees*
When will the photos be ready?	Πότε θα είναι έτοιμες οι φωτογραφίες; *pote tha eene eteemes ee fotoghrafee-es*
I'd like to collect my photos. Here's the receipt.	Θα ήθελα να πάρω τις φωτογραφίες μου. Ορίστε η απόδειξη. *tha eethela na paro tees fotoghrafee-es moo. oreeste ee apoTHeeksee*

Police Αστυνομία

If you have witnessed or been the victim of a crime, report it to the tourist police or directly to the police. The tourist police always have an English-speaking interpreter on duty. If arrested for any reason you should ask for an interpreter. Note: possession of drugs is punishable by five years imprisonment and a large fine. Traffic offences are dealt with by a separate body known as the **trokhea**.

The emergency police number is 100.

Where's the nearest police station?	Πού είναι το κοντινότερο αστυνομικό τμήμα; *poo eene to kondeenotero asteenomeeko tmeema*
Does anyone here speak English?	Μιλάει κανείς εδώ Αγγλικά; *meelaee kanees eTHo angleeka*
I want to report an ...	Θέλω να αναφέρω .... *thelo na anafero*
accident/attack	ένα ατύχημα/μια επίθεση *ena ateekheema/mia epeethesee*
My child is missing.	Λείπει το παιδί μου. *leepee to peTHee moo*
Here's a photo of him/her.	Να μια φωτογραφία του/της. *na mia fotoghrafeea too/tees*
I need an English-speaking lawyer.	Χρειάζομαι έναν αγγλόφωνο δικηγόρο. *khreeazome enan anglofono THeekeeghoro*
I need to make a phone call.	Χρειάζεται να κάνω ένα τηλεφώνημα. *khreeazete na kano ena teelefoneema*
I need to contact the American/British consulate.	Χρειάζεται να έρθω σε επαφή με το ... αμερικάνικο/βρεταννικό Προξενείο. *khreeazete na ertho se epafee me to amereekaneeko/vretaneeko prokseneeo*

Μπορείτε να τον/την περιγράψετε;	Can you describe him/her?
άνδρας/γυναίκα	male/female
ξανθός(-η)/μελαχρινός(-η)	blond/brunette
με κόκκινα/με γκρίζα μαλλιά	red-headed/gray-haired
με μακριά/κοντά μαλλιά/φαλακρός	long hair/short hair/balding
με ύψος περίπου ...	approximate height ...
ηλικίας (περίπου) ...	aged (approximately) ...
φορούσε ...	he/she was wearing ...

CLOTHES ➤ 144; COLORS ➤ 143

Lost property/Theft Απώλεια/Κλοπή

I want to report a theft/ break-in.	Θέλω να καταγγείλω μια κλοπή/μια διάρρηξη. *thelo na katangeelo mia klopee/mia THeeareeksee*
My car's been broken into.	Μού διέρρηξαν το αυτοκίνητο. *moo THee-ereeksan to aftokeeneeto*
I've lost my …	Έχασα … *ekhasa*
My … has been stolen.	Μου έκλεψαν … μου. *moo eklepsan … moo*
camera	τη φωτογραφική μηχανή *tee fotoghrafeekee meekhanee*
(rental) car	το (νοικιασμένο) αυτοκίνητο *to (neekeeazmeno) aftokeeneeto*
credit cards	τις πιστωτικές κάρτες *tees peestoteekes kartes*
handbag	την τσάντα *teen tsanda*
money	τα χρήματα *ta khreemata*
passport	το διαβατήριο *to THeeavateereeo*
purse/wallet	το πορτοφόλι *to portofolee*
watch	το ρολόι *to roloee*
What shall I do?	Τί να κάνω; *tee na kano*
I need a police report for my insurance claim.	Χρειάζομαι ένα πιστοποιητικό της αστυνομίας για την ασφάλειά μου. *khreeazome ena peestopee-eeteeko tees asteenomeeas ya teen asfaleea moo*

Τί λείπει;	What's missing?
Πότε συνέβηκε;	When did it happen?
Πού μένετε;	Where are you staying?
Από πού το πήραν;	Where was it taken from?
Πού ήσασταν εκείνη την ώρα;	Where were you at the time?
Θα σας βρούμε ένα/ μια διερμηνέα.	We're getting an interpreter for you.
Θα κοιτάξουμε το ζήτημα.	We'll look into the matter.
Παρακαλώ, συμπληρώστε αυτό το έντυπο.	Please fill in this form.

Post office Ταχυδρομείο

Mailboxes are yellow and bear the initials ELTA. The post office is open from 8 a.m. to 8 p.m., except Wednesdays and Saturdays when it shuts at around 1 p.m. Main post offices are open Sunday mornings.

Stamps can also be bought at some kiosks and stores that sell postcards.

General queries Γενικές ερωτήσεις

Where is the nearest/ main post office?	Πού είναι το κοντινότερο/κεντρικό ταχυδρομείο; *poo eene to kondeenotero/ kendreeko takheeTHromeeo*
What time does the post office open/close?	Τι ώρα ανοίγει/κλείνει το ταχυδρομείο; *tee ora aneeyee/kleenee to takheeTHromeeo*
Does it close for lunch?	Κλείνει το μεσημέρι; *kleenee to meseemeree*
Where's the mailbox [postbox]?	Πού είναι το ταχυδρομικό κουτί; *poo eene to takheeTHromeeko kootee*

Buying stamps Αγοράζοντας γραμματόσημα

A stamp for this postcard/ letter, please.	Ένα γραμματόσημο γι' αυτή τη κάρτα/ γράμμα, παρακαλώ. *ena ghramatoseemo yaftee teen karta/ghrama, parakalo*
A ...-cent stamp, please.	Ένα γραμματόσημο των ... λεπτών, παρακαλώ. *ena ghramatoseemo ton ... lepton parakalo*
What's the postage for a postcard/letter to ...?	Πόσο κάνει αυτή η κάρτα/αυτό το γράμμα για ...; *poso kanee aftee ee karta/afto to ghrama ya*
Is there a stamp machine here?	Υπάρχει μηχανή για γραμματόσημα εδώ; *eeparkhee meekhanee ya ghramatoseema eTHo*

– kherete. tha eethela na steelo aftes tees kartes stees eenomenes poleetee-es.

– poses?

– enea, parakalo.

– kanoon 50 x 9 (peneenda) lepta (epee enea): 4.5 (teserameesee) evro, parakalo.

Sending parcels Στέλνοντας πακέτα

I want to send this package by …	Θέλω να στείλω αυτό το πακέτο … *thelo na steelo afto to paketo*
airmail	αεροπορικώς *aeroporeekos*
special delivery	επείγον *epeeghon*
registered mail	συστημένο *seesteemeno*
It contains …	Περιέχει … *peree-ekhee*

Παρακαλώ συμπληρώστε αυτήν την τελωνειακή δήλωση.	Please fill in the customs declaration.
Ποιά είναι η αξία;	What is the value?
Τι είναι μέσα;	What's inside?

Other services Άλλες υπηρεσίες

I'd like a phonecard, please.	Θα ήθελα μια τηλεκάρτα, παρακαλώ. *tha eethela mia teelekarta parakalo*
20/50/100 units	Είκοσι/πενήντα/εκατό μονάδες *eekosee/peneenda/ekato monaTHes*
Do you have a photocopier/ fax machine here?	Έχετε φωτοτυπικό/φαξ εδώ; *ekhete fototeepeeko/"fax" eTHo*
I'd like to send a message by fax/e-mail.	Θα ήθελα να στείλω ένα φαξ/"e-mail". *tha eethela na steelo ena "fax"/ "e-mail"*
Can I access the Internet here?	Μπορώ να έχω πρόσβαση στο Ιντερνέτ από εδώ; *boro na ekho prosvasee sto "internet" apo eTHo*
What are the charges per hour?	Πόσο χρεώνεται η ώρα; *poso khreonete ee ora*
How do I log on?	Πώς συνδέομαι; *pos seenTHeome*

ΓΡΑΜΜΑΤΟΣΗΜΑ	stamps
ΤΗΛΕΓΡΑΦΗΜΑΤΑ	telegrams
ΟΛΕΣ ΟΙ ΥΠΗΡΕΣΙΕΣ	all transactions
ΠΟΣΤ ΡΕΣΤΑΝΤ	general delivery [poste restante]
ΕΠΟΜΕΝΗ ΣΥΛΛΟΓΗ	next collection …
ΠΑΚΕΤΑ	parcels

Gifts Δώρα

Typical local souvenirs
Παραδοσιακά σουβενίρ

You can buy some imaginative and unusual souvenirs for a reasonable price. Shop around at souvenir stalls, and don't be afraid to haggle. Many of the handicrafts, especially jewelry and pottery, are handmade, so quality, design, and price will vary from store to store. Greek jewelry is intricate and beautifully made, some of the designs being copies of Byzantine jewelry bearing the dolphin, lion, ram, snake, and owl – the five animal symbols of ancient Greece.

You will also find a range of leather goods: belts, sandals, wallets, and bags. Hand-woven rugs and carpets of all sizes, embroidered tablecloths, decorative lace, icons and as a more unusual souvenir, a wooden backgammon board, all make good presents.

Some food products also make excellent gifts. Here are a few exportable products:

olives	ελιές *elee-es*
olive oil	λάδι *laTHee*
thyme honey	Θυμαρίσιο μέλι *theemareeseeo melee*
Turkish delight	λουκούμι *lookoomee*
ground Greek coffee	ελληνικός καφές *eleeneekos kafes*
dried Corinthian currants	κορινθιακή σταφίδα *koreentheeakee stafeeTHa*
pistachio nuts	φυστίκια *feesteekeea*
halva	χαλβάς *khalvas*

Note that there is a ban on the export of all wild bulbs and orchids and endangered wildlife, including bird's eggs, tortoise shell, feathers, and stuffed animals.

Gifts Δώρα

bottle of wine	ένα μπουκάλι κρασί *ena bookalee krasee*
box of pastries	ένα κουτί γλυκά *ena kootee ghleeka*
calendar	ένα ημερολόγιο *ena eemeroloyeeo*
key ring	ένα μπρελόκ *ena brelok*
postcard	μια κάρτα *mia karta*
T-shirt	ένα μπλουζάκι *ena bloozakee*

Music Μουσική

I'd like a …	Θα ήθελα … *tha eethela*
cassette	μια κασέτα *mia kaseta*
compact disc	ένα κόμπακτ ντισκ *ena "CD"*
record	ένα δίσκο *ena THeesko*
videocassette	μια βιντεοκασέτα *mia veendeokaseta*
Which singers are popular? And which bands?	Ποιοί τραγουδιστές είναι δημοφιλείς; Και ποιά συγκροτήματα; *pee-ee traghooTHeestes eene THeemofeelees? ke pia seengroteemata*

Toys and games Παιχνίδια

I'd like a toy/game …	Θα ήθελα ένα παιχνίδι … *tha eethela ena pekhneeTHee*
for a boy	για ένα αγόρι *ya ena aghoree*
for a 5-year-old girl	για ένα πεντάχρονο κορίτσι *ya ena pendakhrono koreetsee*
pail and shovel [bucket and spade]	ο κουβάς και το φτυαράκι *o koovas ke to fteearakee*
chess/backgammon set	ένα σκάκι/τάβλι *ena skakee/tavlee*
doll	μια κούκλα *mia kookla*
electronic game	ένα ηλεκτρονικό παιχνίδι *ena eelektroneeko pekhneeTHee*
teddy bear	ένα αρκουδάκι *ena arkooTHakee*

Antiques Αντίκες

There are restrictions on exporting certain antiques and antiquities, so it is best to check in advance with the customs authorities before purchasing.

How old is this?	Πόσο παλιό είναι αυτό; *poso paleeo eene afto*
Can you send it to me?	Μπορείτε να μου το στείλετε; *boreete na moo to steelete*
Will I have problems with customs?	Θα έχω προβλήματα με το τελωνείο; *tha ekho provleemata me to teloneeo*
Is there a certificate of authenticity?	Υπάρχει πιστοποιητικό αυθεντικότητας; *eeparkhee peestopee-eeteeko afthendeekoteetas*

HISTORICAL PERIODS ➤ 104

Supermarket / Minimart
Σουπερμάρκετ/Παντοπωλείο

Large-scale self-service hypermarkets and supermarkets can be found on the outskirts of most towns and smaller ones nearer city centers. There are several large chains, including: **alfaveeta**, **vaseelopoolos**, **veropoolos**, **mareenopoolos**, and **hellas spar**. They are all good value. Note: there will usually be someone to serve you in smaller local stores, so it's better not to pick things up yourself.

At the supermarket Στο σουπερμάρκετ

Excuse me. Where can I find ...?	Συγγνώμη. Πού μπορώ να βρω ...; *seeghnomee. poo boro na vro*
Do I pay for this here or at the checkout?	Να πληρώσω για αυτό εδώ ή στο ταμείο; *na pleeroso ya afto eTHo ee sto tameeo*
Where are the shopping carts [trolleys] / baskets?	Πού είναι τα καροτσάκια/καλάθια; *poo eene ta karotsakeea/kalatheea*
Is there a ... here?	Υπάρχει τμήμα με ... εδώ; *eeparkhee tmeema me ... eTHo*
delicatessen	τυριά-αλλαντικά *teerya alandeeka*
pasta section	ζυμαρικά *zeemareeka*

ΨΩΜΙ ΚΑΙ ΓΛΥΚΑ	bread and cakes
ΕΙΔΗ ΚΑΘΑΡΙΣΜΟΥ	cleaning products
ΓΑΛΑΚΤΟΚΟΜΙΚΑ	dairy products
ΦΡΕΣΚΑ ΨΑΡΙΑ	fresh fish
ΦΡΕΣΚΟ ΚΡΕΑΣ	fresh meat
ΦΡΕΣΚΑ ΠΡΟΙΟΝΤΑ	fresh produce
ΚΑΤΕΨΥΓΜΕΝΑ	frozen foods
ΕΙΔΗ ΟΙΚΙΑΚΗΣ ΧΡΗΣΕΩΣ	household goods
ΠΟΥΛΕΡΙΚΑ	poultry
ΕΙΔΙΚΗ ΠΡΟΣΦΟΡΑ	special promotion
ΚΟΝΣΕΡΒΕΣ ΦΡΟΥΤΩΝ/ ΛΑΧΑΝΙΚΩΝ	canned fruit / vegetables
ΠΟΤΑ	wines and spirits

Weights and measures

- **1 kilogram** or **kilo** (**kg.**) = **1000 grams** (**g.**); **100 g.** = 3.5 oz.; **1 kg.** = 2.2 lb; 1 oz. = 28.35 g.; 1 lb. = 453.60 g.
- 1 liter (l.) = 0.88 imp. quart or 1.06 U.S. quart; 1 imp. quart = 1.14 l.; 1 U.S. quart = 0.951 l.; 1 imp. gallon = 4.55 l.; 1 U.S. gallon = 3.8 l.

Food hygiene Διατροφή

ΚΑΤΑΝΑΛΩΣΗ ... ΗΜΕΡΕΣ ΜΕΤΑ ΤΟ ΑΝΟΙΓΜΑ	eat within ... days of opening
ΔΙΑΤΗΡΕΙΤΑΙ ΣΤΟ ΨΥΓΕΙΟ	keep refrigerated
ΚΑΤΑΛΛΗΛΟ ΓΙΑ ΦΟΥΡΝΟΥΣ ΜΙΚΡΟΚΥΜΑΤΩΝ	microwaveable
ΞΑΝΑΘΕΡΜΑΝΕΤΕ ΠΡΙΝ ΤΗΝ ΚΑΤΑΝΑΛΩΣΗ	reheat before eating
ΑΝΑΛΩΣΗ ΜΕΧΡΙ ...	sell by ...
ΚΑΤΑΛΛΗΛΟ ΓΙΑ ΧΟΡΤΟΦΑΓΟΥΣ	suitable for vegetarians

At the minimart Στο παντοπωλείο

I'd like some of that/those.	Θα ήθελα μερικά από αυτά/εκείνα. *tha eethela mereeka apo afta/ekeena*
That's all, thanks.	Τίποτε άλλο. Ευχαριστώ. *teepote alo. efkhareesto*
I'd like a(n)/some ...	Θα ήθελα ... *tha eethela*
kilo of apples	ένα κιλό μήλα *ena keelo meela*
half-kilo of tomatoes	μισό κιλό ντομάτες *meeso keelo domates*
100 grams of cheese	εκατό γραμμάρια τυρί *ekato ghramareea teeree*
liter of milk	ένα λίτρο γάλα *ena leetro ghala*
six eggs	εξι αυγά *eksee avgha*
... slices of ham	... μερικές φέτες ζαμπόν *... mereekes fetes zambon*
bottle of wine	ένα μπουκάλι κρασί *ena bookalee krasee*
carton of milk	ένα κουτί γάλα *ena kootee ghala*
jar of jam	ένα βάζο μαρμελάδα *ena vazo marmelatha*
bag of potato chips [crisps]	ένα πακέτο τσιπς *ena paketo "chips"*

– tha eethela meeso keelo apo afto to teeree, parakalo.
– *afto?*
– ne, teen feta, parakalo.
– *veveos. teepote alo?*
– ke tesera komateea spanakopeeta, parakalo.
– *oreeste.*

Provisions / Picnic Τρόφιμα/Πικνίκ

apples	τα μήλα *ta meela*
bananas	οι μπανάνες *ee bananes*
beer	η μπύρα *ee beera*
bottle of wine	το μπουκάλι κρασί *to bookalee krasee*
butter	το βούτυρο *to vooteero*
cheese	το τυρί *to teeree*
chocolate	η σοκολάτα *ee sokolata*
cookies [biscuits]	τα μπισκότα *ta beeskota*
grapes	τα σταφύλια *ta stafeeleea*
ice cream	το παγωτό *to paghoto*
instant coffee	ο νεσκαφές *o neskafes*
milk	το γάλα *to ghala*
oranges	τα πορτοκάλια *ta portokaleea*
potato chips [crisps]	τα τσιπς *ta "chips"*
salt	το αλάτι *to alatee*
soft drink / soda	το αναψυκτικο *to anapseekteeko*
sugar	η ζάχαρη *ee zakharee*
tea bags	τα φακελλάκια τσαγιού *ta fakelakeea tsayoo*
yogurt	το γιαούρτι *to yaoortee*

Some of the most common types of bread are:

χωριάτικο *khoryateeko:* Brown bread

ολικής αλέσεως *oleekees aleseos:* Wholegrain bread

άσπρο/πολυτελείας *aspro/poleeteleeas*: Both are types of white bread. **poleeteleeas** is made from more refined flour than **aspro** and is more expensive

σιμιγδαλένιο *seemeeghthaleneeo* Semolina bread

MEAT ➤ 46; VEGETABLES ➤ 47

Health

Doctors in Greece are well trained but sometimes poor facilities affect the quality of healthcare. However, for simple ailments you should be in good hands. The E111 form will cover all EU citizens on the Greek national health service for any emergency treatment (including dental treatment). Non-EU citizens should take out a health insurance policy before traveling.

No immunization is necessary before coming to Greece, but it is best to make sure you are up-to-date on your tetanus shots.

Doctor (General) Γιατρός (Γενικά)

Where can I find a doctor/dentist?	Πού μπορώ να βρω ένα γιατρό/οδοντίατρο; *poo boro na vro ena yatro/oTHondeeatro*
Where's there a doctor who speaks English?	Πού υπάρχει γιατρός που να μιλά Αγγλικά; *poo eeparkhee yatros poo na meela angleeka*
What are the office [surgery] hours?	Ποιές είναι οι ώρες ιατρίου; *pee-es eene ee ores eeatreeoo*
Could the doctor come to see me here?	Μπορεί να έρθει να με δει εδώ ο γιατρός; *boree na erthee na me THee eTHo o yatros*
Can I make an appointment for … ?	Μπορώ να κλείσω ένα ραντεβού για … ; *boro na kleeso ena randevoo ya*
tomorrow	αύριο *avreeo*
as soon as possible	όσο το δυνατόν πιο σύντομα *oso to THeenaton peeo seendoma*
It's urgent.	Είναι επείγον. *eene epeeghon*
I've got an appointment with Doctor …	Έχω ραντεβού με τον κύριο/κυρία … *ekho randevoo me ton keereeo/keereea*

TIME ➤ 220; DATE ➤ 218

– boro na kleeso ena randevoo oso to THeenaton peeo seendoma?
– *eemaste yematee seemera. eene epeeghon?*
– ne.
– *boroome-na sas valoome stees THeka ke tetarto me ton keereeo …*
– THeka ke tetarto. efkhareesto polee

Accident and injury Ατύχημα και τραυματισμός

My … is hurt/injured.	… μου χτύπησε/τραυματίστηκε. *… moo khteepeese/travmateesteeke*
husband/wife	Ο άνδρας/η γυναίκα *o anTHras/ee yeeneka*
son/daughter	ο γιος/η κόρη *o yos/ee koree*
friend	Ο φίλος/η φίλη *o feelos/ee feelee*
baby	Το μωρό *to moro*
He/She is …	Είναι … *eene*
unconscious	αναίσθητος/-η *anestheetos/-ee*
(seriously) injured	σοβαρά τραυματισμένος/-η *sovara travmateezmenos/-ee*
He/she is bleeding (heavily)	Αιμορραγεί σοβαρά. *emorayee sovara*
I have a(n) …	Έχω … *ekho*
blister	μια φουσκάλα *mia fooskala*
boil	ένα σπυρί *ena speeree*
bruise	μια μελανιά *mia melaneea*
burn	ένα έγκαυμα *ena egavma*
cut	ένα κόψιμο *ena kopseemo*
graze	μια γρατζουνιά *mia ghratzooneea*
insect bite	ένα τσίμπημα από έντομο *ena tseembeema apo endomo*
lump	ένα σβώλο *ena zvolo*
rash	ένα εξάνθημα *ena eksantheema*
sting	ένα τσίμπημα *ena tseembeema*
swelling	ένα πρήξιμο *ena preekseemo*
wound	μια πληγή *mia pleeyee*
My … hurts.	Με πονάει … *me ponaee*

PARTS OF THE BODY ➤ *166*

Symptoms Συμπτώματα

I've been feeling ill for … days.	Αισθάνομαι άρρωστος εδώ και … ημέρες *esthanome arostos eTHo ke … eemeres*
I feel …	Αισθάνομαι … *esthanome*
feverish	σαν να έχω πυρετό *san na ekho peereto*
sick	άρρωστος *arostos*
I feel …	Έχω … *ekho*
dizzy	ζαλάδες *zalaTHes*
faint	λιποθυμίες *leepotheemee-es*
I've been vomiting.	Έκανα εμετό. *ekana emeto*
I've got diarrhea.	Έχω διάρροια. *ekho THeeareea*
It hurts here.	Με πονάει εδώ. *me ponaee eTHo*
I have (a/an) …	Έχω … *ekho*
backache	πόνο στη πλάτη *pono steen platee*
cold	κρυολόγημα *kreeoloyeema*
earache	πόνο στο αυτί *pono sto aftee*
headache	πονοκέφαλο *ponokefalo*
sore throat	πονόλαιμο *ponolemo*
stomachache	στομαχόπονο *stomakhopono*
sunstroke	ηλίαση *eeleeasee*

Health conditions Κατάσταση υγείας

I am …	Έχω … *ekho*
asthmatic	άσθμα *asthma*
handicapped	αναπηρία *anapeereea*
I am …	Είμαι … *eeme*
deaf	κουφός/-ή *koofos/-ee*
diabetic	διαβητικός/-ή *THeeaveeteekos/-ee*
epileptic	επιληπτικός/-ιά *epeeleepteekos/-eea*
(… months) pregnant	(… μηνών) έγκυος *(meenon) engeeos*
I have a heart condition/ high blood pressure.	Έχω πρόβλημα καρδιάς/υψηλή πίεση *ekho provleema karTHyas/ eepseelee pee-esee*

Doctor's inquiries Ερωτήσεις γιατρού

Πόσο καιρό αισθάνεστε έτσι;	How long have you been feeling like this?
Είναι η πρώτη φορά που το παθαίνετε;	Is this the first time you've had this?
Παίρνετε άλλα φάρμακα;	Are you taking any other medication?
Είστε αλλεργικός σε τίποτα;	Are you allergic to anything?
Έχετε κάνει εμβόλιο τετάνου;	Have you been vaccinated against tetanus?
Έχει κοπεί η όρεξή σας;	Have you lost your appetite?

Examination Εξέταση

Θα πάρω τη θερμοκρασία/την πίεσή σας.	I'll take your temperature/blood pressure.
Σηκώστε το μανίκι σας παρακαλώ.	Roll up your sleeve, please.
Παρακαλώ γδυθείτε ως τη μέση.	Please undress to the waist.
Παρακαλώ ξαπλώστε.	Please lie down.
Ανοίξτε το στόμα σας.	Open your mouth.
Πάρτε μια βαθιά αναπνοή.	Breathe deeply.
Παρακαλώ βήξτε.	Cough, please.
Πού πονάει;	Where does it hurt?
Πονάει εδώ;	Does it hurt here?

Diagnosis Διάγνωση

Θέλω να βγάλετε μια ακτινογραφία.	I want you to have an X-ray.
Θέλω ένα δείγμα αίματος/κοπράνων/ούρων.	I want a specimen of your blood/stools/urine.
Θέλω να δείτε έναν ειδικό.	I want you to see a specialist.
Θέλω να πάτε στο νοσοκομείο.	I want you to go to a hospital.
Είναι ...	It's ...
σπασμένο/στραμπουληγμένο	broken/sprained
εξαρθρωμένο/σχισμένο	dislocated/torn

Έχετε	You have (a/an) …
σκωληκοειδίτιδα	appendicitis
κυστίτιδα	cystitis
γρίππη	flu
τροφική δηλητηρίαση	food poisoning
κάταγμα	fracture
γαστρίτιδα	gastritis
κοίλη	hernia
φλεγμονή του/της	inflammation of …
ιλαρά	measles
πνευμονία	pneumonia
ισχυαλγία	sciatica
αμυγδαλίτιδα	tonsilitis
όγκο	tumor
αφροδισιακό νόσημα	venereal disease
Είναι μολυσμένο.	It's infected.
Είναι μεταδοτικό.	It's contagious.

Treatment Θεραπεία

Θα σας δώσω …	I'll give you …
ένα αντισηπτικό	an antiseptic
ένα παυσίπονο	a painkiller
Θα σας γράψω συνταγή για …	I'm going to prescribe …
μια δόση αντιβιοτικά	a course of antibiotics
υπόθετα	(some) suppositories
Είσαστε αλλεργικός/-ή σε κανένα φάρμακο;	Are you allergic to any medication?
Παίρνετε … κάθε … ώρες/ πριν τα γεύματα.	Take … every … hours/ before meals.
Θέλω να επιστρέψετε σε … ημέρες.	I'd like you to come back in … days.
Συμβουλευτείτε ένα γιατρό όταν επιστρέψετε στην πατρίδα σας.	Consult a doctor when you get home.

Parts of the body
Μέρη του σώματος

arm	χέρι *kheree*
back	πλάτη *platee*
bone	οστό *osto*
breast/chest	στήθος *steethos*
ear	αυτί *aftee*
eye	μάτι *matee*
face	πρόσωπο *prosopo*
finger	δάχτυλο *THakhteelo*
foot	πόδι *poTHee*
hand	χέρι *kheree*
head	κεφάλι *kefalee*
heart	καρδιά *karTHya*
jaw	σαγόνι *saghonee*
kidney	νεφρό *nefro*
knee	γόνατο *ghonato*
leg	πόδι *poTHee*
liver	ήπαρ (medical), συκώτι *eepar, seekotee*
mouth	στόμα *stoma*
muscle	μυς *mees*
neck	αυχένας *afkhenas*
nose	μύτη *meetee*
rib	πλευρό *plevro*
shoulder	ώμος *omos*
skin	δέρμα *THerma*
spine	σπονδυλική στήλη *sponTHeeleekee steelee*
stomach	στομάχι *stomakhee*
throat	λαιμός *lemos*
thumb	αντίχειρας *andeekheeras*
toe	δάχτυλο ποδιού *THakhteelo poTHyoo*
tongue	γλώσσα *ghlosa*
vein	φλέβα *fleva*

Gynecologist Στο γυναικολόγο

I have ...	Έχω ... *ekho*
abdominal pains	πόνους στη κοιλιά *ponoos steen keeleea*
period pains	πόνους περιόδου *ponoos pereeoTHoo*
a vaginal infection	κολπική μόλυνση *kolpeekee moleensee*
I haven't had my period for ... months.	Δεν έχω περίοδο εδώ και ... μήνες. *THen ekho pereeoTHo eTHo ke ... meenes*
I'm on the Pill.	Παίρνω το αντισυλληπτικό χάπι. *perno to andeeseeleepteeko khapee*

Hospital Νοσοκομείο

Please notify my family.	Παρακαλώ ειδοποιήστε την οικογένειά μου. *parakalo eeTHopee-eeste teen eekoyeneea moo*
What are the visiting hours?	Ποιές είναι οι ώρες επισκεπτηρίου; *pee-es eene ee ores epeeskepteereeoo*
I'm in pain.	Πονάω. *ponao*
I can't eat/sleep.	Δεν μπορώ να φάω/κοιμηθώ. *THen boro na fao/keemeetho*
When will the doctor come?	Πότε θα έρθει ο γιατρός; *pote tha erthee o yatros*
Which ward is ... in?	Σε ποιά πτέρυγα είναι ο/η ... ; *se pia ptereegha eene o/ee*

Optician Στον οφθαλμίατρο

I'm near- [short-] sighted/ far- [long-] sighted.	Είμαι μύωπας/πρεσβύωπας. *eeme meeopas/prezveeopas*
I've lost ...	Έχασα ... *ekhasa*
one of my contact lenses	έναν από τους φακούς επαφής μου. *enan apo toos fakoos epafees moo*
my glasses	τα γυαλιά μου *ta yaleea moo*
a lens	ένα φακό *ena fako*
Could you give me a replacement?	Μπορείτε να μου το αντικαταστήσετε; *boreete na moo to andeekatasteesete*

Dentist Οδοντίατρος

I have a toothache.	Έχω πονόδοντο. *ekho ponoTHonto*
This tooth hurts.	Αυτό το δόντι με πονάει. *afto to THondee me ponaee*
I've lost/broken a tooth/crown/cap.	Έχασα/έσπασα ένα δόντι/μια κορώνα/ένα σφράγισμα. *ekhasa/espasa ena THondee/mia korona/ena sfrayeezma*
I've lost a filling.	Έχασα ένα σφράγισμα. *ekhasa ena sfrayeezma*
Can you repair this denture?	Μπορείτε να φτιάξετε αυτή την τεχνητή οδοντοστοιχία; *boreete na fteeaksete aftee teen tekhneetee oTHondosteekheea*
I don't want it extracted.	Δεν θέλω να μου το βγάλετε. *THen thelo na moo to vghalete*

Θα σας κάνω μια ένεση/ένα τοπικό αναισθητικό.	I'm going to give you an injection/a local anesthetic.
Χρειάζεστε ένα σφράγισμα/μια κορώνα.	You need a filling/cap/crown.
Πρέπει να το βγάλω.	I'll have to take it out.
Μπορώ να το διορθώσω μόνο προσωρινά.	I can only fix it temporarily.
Ελάτε σε … ημέρες.	Come back in … days.
Μη φάτε τίποτα για … ώρες.	Don't eat anything for … hours.

Payment and insurance Πληρωμή και ασφάλεια

How much do I owe you?	Τι σας οφείλω; *tee sas ofeelo*
I have insurance.	Έχω ασφάλεια. *ekho asfaleea*
Can I have a receipt for my health insurance?	Μπορώ να έχω μια απόδειξη για την ασφάλεια υγείας μου; *boro na ekho mia apoTHeeksee ya teen asfaleea eeyeeas moo*
Do you have… ?	Έχετε … ; *ekhete*
Form E111/health insurance	το έντυπο E111/ασφάλεια υγείας *to endeepo epseelon ekaton endeka/asfaleea eeyeeas*

MAKING APPOINTMENTS ➤ 161

Dictionary
English – Greek

A-Z

Most terms in this dictionary are either followed by an example or cross-referenced to pages where the word appears in a phrase. The notes below provide some basic grammar guidelines.

Nouns

The gender of a noun is indicated by the article preceding it: **o** for masculine (m), **ee** for feminine (f), and **to** for neuter (n).

masculine	ο καφές	**o kafes**	the coffee
feminine	η μπύρα	**ee beera**	the beer
neuter	το τρένο	**to treno**	the train

There is no easy way to form the plural but if you clearly state a number along with the noun (➤ 216), then you will be easily understood.

Greek nouns have cases – that is a noun's ending is dependent on the position of the word in the sentence, for example whether it is the subject or the object. For this reason you will see the same noun with slightly different endings in different phrases. Don't worry too much about this. Use the form given in the dictionary if in doubt.

Adjectives

Adjectives agree with the noun they are describing in gender, case, and number. In this dictionary the (nominative) masculine form is given. The most common ending for a feminine adjective is **-ee** and for the neuter **-o**.

Verbs

Verbs are shown in the first person singular (I eat, I go, etc.). Below are three of the main categories of regular verbs in the present tense. Using the endings indicated after -, you can use a large number of verbs competently. Greeks generally use the polite "you" form of verbs (**esees**). The informal form (**esee**) is used amongst friends and with children, but don't worry too much – you will not be considered rude, just friendly!

Verb ends in:	-ω **-o** *(I have)*	-ώ **-o** *(I am thirsty)*	-όμαι **-ome** *(I think)*
egho *(I)*	**ekh-o**	**THeeps-o**	**skeft-ome**
esee *(you, informal)*	**ekh-ees**	**THeeps-as**	**skeft-ese**
aftos/aftee/afto *(he/she/it)*	**ekh-ee**	**THeeps-a (-aee)**	**skeft-ete**
emees *(we)*	**ekh-oume**	**THeeps-oume**	**skeft-omaste**
esees *(you, formal & pl.)*	**ekh-ete**	**THeeps-ate**	**skeft-este**
aftee/aftes/afta *(they m/f/n)*	**ekh-oon**	**THeeps-oon**	**skeft-onde**

A-Z

A

a few λίγα leegha 15
a little λίγο leegho 15
a lot πολύ polee 15
a.m. π.μ. pro meseemvreeas
about *(approximately)* περίπου, γύρω pereepoo 15
abscess απόστημα n aposteema
abseiling αναρρίχηση f anareekheesee
access πρόσβαση f prozvasee 100
accessories αξεσουάρ n aksesooar 144
accident ατύχημα n ateekheema 92, 152; **accidentally** κατά λάθος kata lathos 28
accompaniments συνοδεία φαγητού f seenoTHeea fagheetoo 38
accompany, to συνοδεύω seenoTHevo 65
accountant λογιστής m loyeestees
ace *(cards)* άσσος m asos
acne ακμή f akmee
adaptor προσαρμοστής m prosarmostees 26
address διεύθυνση f THe-eeftheensee 84, 93, 94, 126
adhesive bandages αυτοκόλλητοι επίδεσμοι mpl, λευκοπλάστ aftokoleetee epeeTHezmee, lefkoplast 141
adjoining room διπλανό δωμάτιο n THeeplano THomateeo 22
admission: what's the admission charge? πόσο κάνει η είσοδος; poso kanee ee eesoTHos 114
adult ενήλικας eneeleekas 81, 100
aerial *(car/tv)* κεραία f kerea
after *(place)* μετά meta 95; *(time)* μετά meta 13
after-sun lotion γαλάκτωμα για μετά την ηλιοθεραπεία n ghalaktoma ya meta teen eeleeotherapeea 142
afternoon, in the το απόγευμα to apoyevma 221
age ηλικία f eeleekeea 152
ago πριν από, εδώ και preen apo, eTHo ke 13
agree: I agree συμφωνώ seemfono
air conditioning κλιματισμός m kleemateezmos 22, 24
air pump αντλία αέρος f andleea aeros 87
air-freshener αποσμητικό χώρου n apozmeeteeko khoroo
airline αεροπορία f aeroporeea
airmail αεροπορικώς aeroporeekos 155
airport αεροδρόμιο n aeroTHromeeo 96
airsteward/hostess αεροσυνοδός aeroseenoTHos
aisle seat διάδρομος m THeeaTHromos 69
Albania Αλβανία f alvaneea
alcoholic (drink) οινοπνευματώδες (ποτό) eenopnevmatoTHes (poto)
all όλοι olee
allergic, to be είμαι αλλεργικός/-ή eeme alergheekos/-ee 164, 165
allergy αλλεργία f aleryeea
allowed: is it allowed? επιτρέπεται; epeetrepete
alone μόνος monos 120
alphabet αλφάβητο n alfaveeto
already ήδη eeTHee 28
also επίσης epeesees 19
aluminium foil αλουμινόχαρτο n aloomeenokharto 148
always πάντα panda 13
am: I am είμαι eeme
amazing καταπληκτικό katapleekteeko 101
ambassador πρεσβευτής m prezveftees
amber κεχριμπάρι n kekhreembaree
ambulance ασθενοφόρο n asthenoforo 92
American *(adj)* αμερικάνικος amereekaneekos 150, 152; *(n)* Αμερικαν-ός, -ίδα amereekan-os, -eeTHa
amount ποσό n poso 42

amusement arcade αίθουσα ψυχαγωγίας f ethoosa pseekhaghoyeeas 113
and και ke 19
angling ψάρεμα n psarema
animal ζώο n zo-o 106
another άλλο alo 21; **~ time** άλλη φορά alee fora 125
antibiotics αντιβιοτικά n andeeveeoteeka 165
anticeptic αντισηπτικό n andeeseepteeko 165
antique αντίκα f anteeka 157; **~ store** κατάστημα με αντίκες n katasteema me anteekes 130
antiquities αρχαιολογικός χώρος m arkheoloyeekos khoros
antiseptic cream αντισηπτική κρέμα f andeeseepteekee krema 141
anyone else κανείς άλλος kanees alos 93
anything cheaper κάτι φτηνότερο katee fteenotero 21
apartment διαμέρισμα n THeeamereezma 28
apologize: I apologize ζητώ συγγνώμη zeeto seeghnomee
appendicitis σκωληκοειδίτιδα f skoleekoeeTHeeteeTHa 165
appendix σκωληκοειδίτιδα f skoleekoeeTHeeteeTHa
appetizer ορεκτικό n oreekteeko 43
apple μήλο n meelo 106
appointment ραντεβού n randevoo 161; **to make an ~** κλείνω ένα ραντεβού kleeno ena randevoo 147
approximately περίπου pereepoo 152
April Απρίλιος m apreeleeos 218
archery τοξοβολία f toksovoleea
architect αρχιτέκτονας arkheetektonas 104; **architecture** αρχιτεκτονική f arkheetektoneekee 119
are you ... είστε ...; eeste
area code κωδικός m koTHeekos 127
arm χέρι n kheree 166
around *(time)* περίπου pereepoo
arrange: can you arrange it? μπορείτε να το κανονίσετε; boreete na to kanoneesete
arrest, to be under είσαστε υπό σύλληψη eesaste eepo seeleepsee
arrive, to φτάνω ftano 68, 71, 76
art τέχνη f tekhnee; **~ gallery** γκαλερί τέχνης f galeree tekhnees 99
artificial sweetener ζακχαρίνη f zakkhareenee 38
artist καλλιτέχνης kaleetekhnees 104
as soon as possible όσο το δυνατόν πιο σύντομα oso to THeenaton peeo seendoma
ashore, to go πάω στην ξηρά pao steen kseera
ashtray σταχτοδοχείο n stakhtoTHokheeo 39
ask: I asked for ... ζήτησα ... zeeteesa 41
asleep, to be κοιμάμαι keemame
aspirin (soluble) ασπιρίνη (διαλυόμενη) f aspeereenee (THeealeeomenee) 141
asthmatic, to be έχω άσθμα ekho asthma 163
astringent στυπτικό n steepteeko
at *(time)* στις stees 13; **at least** τουλάχιστον toolakheeston 23
athletics αθλήματα στίβου npl athleemata steevoo 114
attack *(criminal)* επίθεση f epeethesee 152; *(medical)* κρούσμα kroozma
attendant βοηθός voeethos
attractive ελκυστικός elkeesteekos
August Αύγουστος m avghoostos 218
aunt θεία f theea 120
Australia Αυστραλία f afstraleea 119
Australian *(n)* Αυστραλός afstralos
authenticity αυθεντικότητα f afthendeekoteeta 157

A–Z

automatic (car) αυτόματο (αυτοκίνητο) aftomato (aftokeeneeto) 86
automatic camera αυτόματη φωτογραφική μηχανή f aftomatee fotoghrafeekee meekhanee 151
autumn φθινόπωρο n ftheenoporo 219

B

baby μωρό n moro 39, 113, 162; **~ seat** καρέκλα μωρού f karekla moroo; **~ food** φαγητό για μωρά n fayeeto ya mora 142
back πλάτη f platee 166; **~ache** πόνος στη πλάτη ponos steen platee 163
backgammon τάβλι n tavlee 121
bad κακό kako 14
baggage πράγματα npl, αποσκευές fpl pragmata, aposkeves 32, 67, 69, 71; **~ reclaim** παραλαβή αποσκευών f paralavee aposkevon 71; **~ check** φύλαξη αποσκευών f feelaksee aposkevon 73
baked στο φούρνο sto foorno
bakery αρτοποιείο n / φούρνος m artopee-eeo / fournos 130
balcony μπαλκόνι n balkonee 29
ballet μπαλλέτο n baleto 108, 111
banana μπανάνα f banana 160
band *(musical group)* συγκρότημα n seengroteema 111, 157
bandage γάζα f ghaza 141
bank τράπεζα f trapeza 130, 138; **~ account** λογαριασμός τραπέζης m logharyazmos trapezees; **~ loan** τραπεζικό δάνειο n trapezeeko THaneeo
bar μπαρ n "bar" 26, 112
barber κουρείο n kooreeo 130
basement υπόγειο n eepoyeeo 132
basket καλάθι n kalathee 158
basketball μπάσκετ μπολ m, καλαθοσφαίρηση f basket bol, kalathosfereesee 114
bath: to take a ~ κάνω μπάνιο kano baneeo
bathroom μπάνιο n baneeo 26, 29
battery μπαταρία f batareea 137, 151
battle site πεδίο μάχης n peTHeeo makhees
be able, to μπορώ boro 18
be, to *(see also* **am, are***)* είμαι eeme
beach παραλία f paraleea 116
beans όσπρια npl ospreea 47
beard γένια npl yeneea
beautiful όμορφος omorfos 101
because επειδή epeeTHee 15; **because of** λόγω logho 15
bed κρεββάτι krevatee 21; **~ and breakfast** διαμονή με πρωινό THeeamonee me proeeno 24
bedding σεντόνια npl sendoneea 29
bedroom υπνοδωμάτιο n eepnoTHomateeo 29
bee μέλισσα f meleesa
beer μπύρα f beera 40, 160
before *(time)* πριν (από) preen (apo) 13, 221
beginner αρχάριος arkhareeos 117
beginning αρχή f arkhee
beige μπεζ bez 143
belong: this belongs to me αυτό μου ανήκει afto moo aneekee
belt ζώνη f zonee 144
berth κουκέτα f kooketa 74, 77
better καλύτερο kaleetero 14
bib ποδιά μωρού f poTHya moroo
bicycle ποδήλατο n poTHeelato 83; **bicycle parts** 82
bidet μπιντέ n beede
big μεγάλος meghalos 14, 134, 117; **bigger** μεγαλύτερο meghaleetero 24
bikini μπικίνι n "bikini" 144
bill λογαριασμός m logharyazmos 32
binoculars κυάλια n keealeea
bird πουλί n poolee 106
biscuits μπισκότα npl beeskota 160

bite *(insect)* τσίμπημα n tseembeema
bitten: I've been bitten by a dog με δάγκωσε ένας σκύλος me THangose enas skeelos
bitter πικρός peekros 41
black μαύρος mavros 143; *(coffee)* σκέτος m sketos 40; **~ and white film** *(camera)* ασπρόμαυρο φιλμ aspromavro "film" 151
bladder ουροδόχος κύστη f ooroTHokhos keestee
blanket κουβέρτα f kooverta 27
bleach χλωρίνη f khloreenee 148
bleeding, to be αιμορραγώ emoragho 92, 162
blinds n περσίδες fpl perseeTHes 25
blister φουσκάλα f fooskala 162
blocked, to be έχει βουλώσει ekhee voolosee 25
blood αίμα n ema 164; **~ group** ομάδα αίματος f omaTHa ematos ; **~ pressure** πίεση f pee-esee 163
blouse μπλούζα f blooza 144
blue μπλε ble 143
boarding card κάρτα επιβιβάσεως f karta epeeveevaseos 70
boat πλοίο n pleeo 81; **~ trip** ταξίδι με πλοίο n takseeTHee me pleeo 81
body: parts of the ~ μέρη του σώματος meree too somatos 166
boil σπυρί n speeree 162
boiled βραστό vrasto
boiler θερμοσίφωνας m thermoseefonas 29
bone οστό n osto 166
book βιβλίο n veevleeo 11, 150
book, to *(reserve)* κλείνω kleeno; **booked up, to be** όλα κλεισμένα ola kleezmena 115; **booking** *(restaurant)* κράτηση f krateesee
booklet of tickets δεσμίδα εισιτηρίων f THezmeeTHa eeseeteereeon 79
bookstore βιβλιοπωλείο n veevleeopoleeo 130, 150
boots μπότες fpl botes 115, 145
border *(country)* σύνορα npl seenora
boring βαρετό vareto 101
born: I was born ... Γεννήθηκα ... yeneetheeka
borrow: may I borrow the ...? Μπορώ να δανειστώ το/τη ...; boro na THaneesto to/tee
botanical garden βοτανικός κήπος m votaneekos keepos 99
bottle μπουκάλι n bookalee 37, 159; **~ of wine** μπουκάλι κρασί n bookalee krasee 156, 160; **~-opener** τιρμπουσόν n teerbooson 148
bow *(ship)* πλώρη f ploree
bowel έντερο n endero
box office γραφείο κρατήσεων n ghrafeeo krateeseon
boxing μποξ n boks
boy αγόρι n aghoree 120, 157
boyfriend φίλος m feelos 120
bra σουτιέν n sootee-en 144
bread ψωμί n psomee 38
break, to σπάζω spazo 28
break-in διάρρηξη f THeeareeksee 153
breakdown *(car)* βλάβη f vlavee 88
breakfast πρωινό n proeeno 26, 27
breast στήθος n steethos 166
breathe, to αναπνέω anapneo 92
breathtaking φαντασμαγορικό fandazmaghoreeko 101
bridge γέφυρα f ghefeera 96, 107
bridge *(cards)* μπριτζ m "bridge"
briefcase τσάντα γραφείου f, χαρτοφύλακας m tsanda ghrafeeoo,
briefs κυλοτάκι, σλιπ n keelotakee, sleep 144
bring, to φέρνω ferno
Britain Βρετανία f vretaneea 119
British *(adj)* βρετανικός vretaneekos 152; *(n)* Βρετανός vretanos
brochure φυλλάδιο n feelaTHeeo

A-Z

A-Z

broken σπασμένος spazmenos 137, 164

bronchitis βρογχίτιδα f vronkheeteeTHa

broom σκούπα f skoopa

brother αδελφός m aTHelfos 120

brown καφέ kafe 143

browse, to κοιτάω keetao 133

bruise μελανιά f melaneea 162

brush βούρτσα f voortsa

buffet car τραπεζαρία τραίνου f trapezareea trenoo

build, to κτίζω kteezo 104

building κτίριο n kteereeo

Bulgaria Βουλγαρία f voolghareea

bureau de change γραφείο συναλλάγματος n ghrafeeo seenalaghmatos 138

burger χάμπουργκερ n khamboorger 40

burglary *(see also* **theft***)* κλοπή f klopee

burn έγκαυμα n engavma 162

burst pipe σπασμένος σωλήνας m spazmenos soleenas

bus λεωφορείο n leoforeeo 70, 78, 79, 98; **~ route** διαδρομή λεωφορείων f THeeaTHromee leoforeeon 96; **~ station** σταθμός λεωφορείων m stathmos leoforeeon 78; **~ stop** στάση λεωφορείου f stasee leoforeeoo 65, 96

business: on ~ για δουλειά ya THooleea 66; **~ class** μπίζνες "business" 68; **~ trip** ταξίδι για δουλειά takseeTHee ya THooleea 123

busy *(occupied)* απασχολημένος apaskholeemenos 125

but αλλά ala 19

butane gas υγραέριο n eeghraereeo 30, 31

butcher shop κρεοπωλείο n kreopoleeo 130

butter βούτυρο n vooteero 38, 43, 160

button κουμπί n koombee

buy, to αγοράζω aghorazo 67, 80

by *(time)* μέχρι mekhree 13; **by car** με το αυτοκίνητο me to aftokeeneeto 17, 94; **by cash** τοις μετρητοίς tees metreetees 136; **by credit card** με πιστωτική κάρτα me peestoteekee karta 17

bye! αντίο! andeeo

C

cabaret καμπαρέ n "cabaret" 112

cabin καμπίνα f kambeena 81

café καφετέρια f kafetereea 35, 40

cagoule αδιάβροχο μπουφάν n aTHeeavrokho boofan 145

cake κέηκ n "cake" 40

calendar ημερολόγιο n eemeroloyeeo 156

call, to καλώ kalo 92; *(telephone)* παίρνω τηλέφωνο perno teelefono 127, 128; **call the police!** καλέστε την αστυνομία! kaleste teen asteenomeea 92; **~ collect** με χρέωση του παραλήπτη me khreosee too paraleeptee 127

camcorder φορητή βιντεοκάμερα f foreetee videokamera

camera φωτογραφική μηχανή f fotoghrafeekee meekhanee 151; **~ case** θήκη μηχανής f theekee meekhanees 151; **~ store** φωτογραφικά npl, κατάστημα με φωτογραφικά είδη n fotoghrafeeka, katasteema me fotoghrafeeka eeTHee 151

campbed κρεββάτι εκστρατείας n krevatee ekstrateeas 31

camping κατασκήνωση f, κάμπιγκ n kataskeenosee, "camping" 30, 31; **~ equipment** εξοπλισμός κάμπιγκ eksopleezmos "camping" 31

campsite χώρος κάμπινγκ/για κατασκήνωση m khoros "camping"/ya kataskeenosee 30

can: can I? μπορώ; boro 18; **can I have?** μπορώ να έχω; boro na ekho 18; **can you help me?** μπορείτε να με βοηθήσετε; boreete na me voeetheesete 18; **can you recommend?** μπορείτε να συστήσετε; boreete na seesteesete 112

can opener ανοιχτήρι n aneekhteeree 148

Canada Καναδάς m kanaTHas 119

Canadian *(n)* Καναδός kanaTHos

canal κανάλι n kanalee

cancel, to ακυρώνω akeerono 68

cancer *(disease)* καρκίνος m karkeenos

candle κερί n keree 148

candy καραμέλα f karamela 150

canoe κανώ kano

capital city πρωτεύουσα f protevoosa

captain *(boat)* καπετάνιος kapetaneeos

car αυτοκίνητο n aftokeeneeto 81, 86, 87, 88, 89, 90, 153; **by ~** με το αυτοκίνητο me to aftokeeneeto 95; **~ alarm** συναγερμός αυτοκινήτου m seenayermos aftokeeneetoo; **~ ferry** φέρυ-μπωτ n "ferry" bot; **~ rental** ενοικίαση αυτοκινήτων f eneekeeasee aftokeeneeton 70, 86; **~ park** χώρος στάθμευσης m khoros stathmefsees 87; **~wash** πλύσιμο αυτοκινήτου n pleeseemo aftokeeneetoo

carafe καράφα f karafa 37

caravan *(trailer)* τροχόσπιτο n trokhospeeto 30, 81

cards χαρτιά npl karteea 121

careful: be careful! Πρόσεχε! prosekhe

carpet *(fitted)* μοκέτα f moketa; *(rug)* χαλί n khalee

carry-cot καροτσάκι (μωρού) n karotsakee (moroo)

carton κουτί n kootee 159

cartoon γελοιογραφία f yeleeoghrateea

cash, to εξαργυρώνω eksargheerono 138; **cash desk** ταμείο n tameeo 132, 136

casino καζίνο n "casino" 112

cassette κασέτα f kaseta 157

castle κάστρο(n) kastro 99

casualty dept. τμήμα πρώτων βοηθειών n tmeema proton voeetheeon

cat γάτα f ghata

catch, to *(bus)* παίρνω perno

cathedral καθεδρικός ναός(m) katheTHreekos naos 99

cave σπήλαιο(f) speeleo 107

cent λεπτό n lepto 139

change, to αλλάζω alazo 75

cheap φτηνό fteeno 14

cheese τυρί n teeree 49

check *(bill)* λογαριασμός m logharyazmos 32

check [cheque] *(bank)* επιταγή f epeetaghee 138

chips [crisps] τσιπς n, πατατάκια "chips", patatakeea 160

Christmas Χριστούγεννα khreestooghena 219

clean καθαρό katharo 14

clothing store κατάστημα ρούχων n katasteema rookhon 130

cold *(temperature)* κρύος kreeos 14, 41, 122

cold *(flu)* κρυολόγημα n kreeoloyeema 141, 163

collapse: he's collapsed κατέρρευσε katerefse

collect, to παίρνω perno 151

color χρώμα n khroma 134, 143; **~ film** έγχρωμο φιλμ enkhromo film 151

comb χτένα f khtena 142

come, to έρχομαι erkhome 36; **~ back** *(return)* επιστρέφω epeestrefo 165

commission προμήθεια f promeetheea 138

communion Μετάληψη f metaleepsee

compact disk CD, κόμπακτ ντισκ n "CD", "compact disk" 157

company *(business)* εταιρία f etereea; *(companionship)* παρέα f parea 126
complain: where can I make a complaint? πού μπορώ να παραπονεθώ; poo boro na paraponetho 137
complaints *(restaurant)* παράπονα npl parapona 41
concert συναυλία f seenavleea 108, 111; **~ hall** αίθουσα συναυλιών f ethoosa seenavleeon 111
concession μειωμένο εισιτήριο n meeomeno eeseeteereeo 100
concussion, to have έχω διάσειση ekho THeeaseesee
conditioner γαλάκτωμα για τα μαλλιά n ghalaktoma ya ta maleea 142
condom προφυλακτικό n profeelakteeko 141
conductor διευθυντής ορχήστρας THee-eftheendees orkheestras 111
conference συνέδριο n seeneTHreeo
confirm, to *(reservation)* επιβεβαιώνω epeeveveono 22, 68
congratulations! συγχαρητήρια! seenkhareeteereea
conscious, to be έχω τις αισθήσεις μου ekho tees estheesees moo
constipation δυσκοιλιότητα f THeeskeeleeoteeta
Consul Πρόξενος m proksenos ; **Consulate** Προξενείο n prokseneeo 152
consult, to συμβουλεύομαι seemvoolevome 165
contact, to επικοινωνώ epeekeenono 28
contact lens φακός επαφής m fakos epafees 167; **~ fluid** υγρό για φακούς επαφής n eeghro ya fakoos epafees
contageous μεταδοτικός metaTHoteekos 165
contain, to περιέχω peree-ekho 39, 69, 155
contemporary dance μοντέρνος χορός m mondernos khoros 111
contraceptive αντισυλληπτικό n andeeseeleepteeko
cook book βιβλίο μαγειρικής n veevleeo mayeereekees
cook *(chef)* μάγειρας mayeeras
cook, to μαγειρεύω mayeerevo
cooker κουζίνα f koozeena 28, 29
cookies μπισκότα n beeskota 160
copper χαλκός m khalkos 149
corkscrew τιρμπουσόν n teerbooson 148
corn plaster αυτοκόλλητος επίδεσμος για κάλους m aftokoleetos epeeTHezmos ya kaloos
corner γωνία f ghoneea 95
correct *(see also* **right***)* σωστό sosto
cosmetics καλλυντικά n kaleendeeka
cot παιδικό κρεββάτι n peTHeeko krevatee 22
cotton [wool] βαμβάκι n vamvakee 141
cough βήχας m veekhas 141; **~ syrup** σιρόπι για το βήχα n seeropee ya to veekha 141
cough, to βήχω veekho 164
could I have ...? μπορώ να έχω ...; boro na ekho 18
counter ταμείο n tameeo
country *(nation)* χώρα f khora
countryside εξοχή f eksokhee 119
couple *(pair)* ζευγάρι n zevgharee
courier *(guide)* κούριερ "courier"
course *(meal)* πιάτο n piato
court house δικαστήριο n THeekasteereeo
cousin ξάδελφος m ksaTHelfos
cramp κράμπα f kramba
crêche βρεφονηπιακός σταθμός m vrefoneepeeakos stathmos
credit card πιστωτική κάρτα f peestoteekee karta 42, 109, 136
crib παιδικό κρεββάτι n peTHeeko krevatee 22

crisps τσιπς n, πατατάκια "chips", patatakeea 160
crockery πιατικά npl piateeka 29, 148
crossroad σταυροδρόμι n stavroTHromee 95
crowded έχει πολύ κόσμο ekhee polee kozmo 31
crown *(dental)* κορώνα f korona 168
cruise κρουαζιέρα f krooazyera
crutches δεκανίκια n THekaneekeea
crystal κρύσταλλο n kreestalo 149
cuisine κουζίνα f koozeena 119
cup φλυτζάνι n fleetzanee 39
cupboard ντουλάπα f doolapa
curlers μπικουτί n beekootee
currency νόμισμα n nomeezma 67; **~ exchange** συνάλλαγμα(n) seenalaghma 70; **~ exchange office** γραφείο συναλλάγματος n ghrafeeo seenalaghmatos 138
curtains κουρτίνες f koorteenes
cushion μαξιλάρι n makseelaree
customs τελωνείο n teloneeo 67, 157; **~ declaration** τελωνειακή δήλωση f teloneeakee THeelosee 155
cut *(wound)* κόψιμο n kopseemo 162
cut and blow-dry κούρεμα και πιστολάκι n koorema ke peestolakee 147
cut glass σκαλιστό γυαλί n skaleesto yalee 149
cutlery μαχαιροπήρουνα npl makheropeeroona 29, 148
cycle helmet κράνος (ποδηλατιστού) n kranos (poTHeelateestoo)
cycling ποδηλασία f poTHeelaseea 114
cyclist ποδηλατιστής poTHeelateestees
Cypriot *(n)* Κύπριος keepreeos
Cyprus Κύπρος f keepros 119
cystitis κυστίτιδα f keesteeteeTHa 165

D

daily καθημερινά katheemereena 13
damage ζημιά f zeemeea
damaged χαλασμένος khalazmenos 28
dance *(performance)* παράσταση χορού f parastasee khoroo 111
dancing, to go πάω για χορό pao ya khoro 124
dangerous επικίνδυνος epeekeenTHeenos
dark *(color)* σκούρος skooros 14, 134; *(room)* σκοτεινό skoteeno 24
daughter κόρη f koree 120, 162
dawn ξημερώματα npl kseemeromata 221
day ημέρα/μέρα f eemera/mera 97; **~ trip** ημερήσια εκδρομή eemereeseea ekTHromee
deaf, to be είμαι κουφός eeme koofos 163
December Δεκέμβριος m THekemvreeos 218
decide: we haven't decided yet δεν έχουμε αποφασίσει ακόμη THen ekhoome apofaseesee akomee
deck *(ship)* κατάστρωμα n katastroma; **~ chair** σεζ-λονγκ f sez-long 116
declare, to δηλώνω THeelono 67
deduct, to *(money)* αφαιρώ afero
defrost, to ξεπαγώνω ksepaghono
degrees *(temperature)* βαθμοί mpl vathmee
delay καθυστέρηση f katheestereesee 70
delicatessen τυριά-αλλαντικά teerya-alandeeka 130, 158
delicious νόστιμο nosteemo 14
deliver, to παραδίδω paraTHeeTHo
dental floss κλωστή f klostee

A-Z

dentist οδοντίατρος oTHondeeatros 131, 168
dentures τεχνητή οδοντοστοιχία f tekhneetee oTHondosteekheea 168
deodorant αποσμητικό n apozmeeteeko 142
department *(in store)* τμήμα n tmeema 132; **~ store** πολυκατάστημα n poleekatasteema 130
departure *(train/airplane)* αναχώρηση (τραίνου) f anakhoreesee (trenoo) 76; **~ lounge** αίθουσα αναχωρήσεων f ethoosa anakhoreeseon
depend: it depends on εξαρτάται eksartate
deposit προκαταβολή f prokatavolee 24, 115
describe, to περιγράφω pereeghrafo 152
designer σχεδιαστής skheTHeeastees
desserts επιδόρπια npl epeeTHorpeea 49
detergent απορρυπαντικό n aporeepandeeko
develop, to *(photos)* εμφανίζω emfaneezo 151
diabetes διαβήτης m THeeaveetees
diabetic διαβητικός/-ή THeeaveeteekos/-ee 39, 163
diagnosis διάγνωση f THeeaghnosee 164
dialling code κωδικός m koTHeekos 127
diamond διαμάντι n THyamandee 149
diamonds *(cards)* καρώ karo
diapers πάνες μωρού f panes moroo 142
diarrhoea διάρροια f THeeareea 141; **to have ~** έχω διάρροια ekho THeeareea 163
dice ζάρια npl zarya
dictionary λεξικό n lekseeko 150
diesel ντήζελ "diesel" 87
diet: I'm on a κάνω δίαιτα kano THee-eta
difficult δύσκολο THeeskolo 14
dining car εστιατόριο στο τραίνο n esteeatoreeo sto treno 75, 77
dining room τραπεζαρία f trapezareea 26, 29
dinner βραδυνό n vraTHeeno 124; **~ jacket** βραδυνό κοστούμι n vraTHeeno kostoomee
direct κατευθείαν kateftheean 75; **~-dial telephone** απευθείας κλήση apeftheeas kleesee
direct, to κατευθύνω kateftheeno 18
direction of, in the στην/προς την κατεύθυνση steen/pros teen kateftheensee 95
directions κατεύθυνση f kateftheensee 95
director *(film)* σκηνοθέτης skeenothetees; *(of company)* διευθυντής THee-eftheendees
directory *(telephone)* τηλεφωνικός κατάλογος m teelefoneekos kataloghos
dirty βρώμικος vromeekos 14, 28
disabled *(npl)* άτομα με ειδικές ανάγκες npl atoma me eeTHeekes ananges 22, 100
discotheque ντισκοτέκ f "discotheque" 112
dish *(meal)* πιάτο n piato 37; **~ cloth** πανί για τα πιάτα n panee ya ta piata 148
dishwashing detergent υγρό πιάτων n eeghro piaton 148
dislocated, to be είναι εξαρθρωμένος eene eksarthromenos 164
display case/cabinet βιτρίνα f veetreena 134, 149
disposable camera μιας χρήσεως φωτογραφική μηχανή f mias khreeseos fotoghrafeekee meekhanee 151
distilled water απεσταγμένο νερό n apestaghmeno nero

district περιφέρεια f pereeferееa
disturb: don't disturb μην ενοχλείτε meen enokhleete
diving equipment εξοπλισμός για υποβρύχιο κολύμπι m eksopleezmos ya eepovreekheeo koleembee 116
divorced, to be διαζευγμένος THeeazevghmenos 120
dizzy, to feel έχω ζαλάδες ekho zalaTHes 163
do: do you accept ...? δέχεστε ...; THekheste 136; **do you have ...?** έχετε ...; ekhete...? 37; **things to do** κάτι να κάνουμε katee na kanoome 123
dock προκυμαία f prokeemea
doctor γιατρός yatros 131, 161, 167
dog σκύλος m skeelos
doll κούκλα f kookla 157
dollar δολλάριο n THolareeo 67, 138
door πόρτα f porta 25
dosage δοσολογία f THosoloyeea 140
double διπλός THeeplos 81; **~ bed** διπλό κρεββάτι THeeplo krevatee 21; **~ room** διπλό δωμάτιο THeeplo THomateeo 21
downtown area κέντρο της πόλης n kendro tees polees 99
dozen ντουζίνα f doozeena 217
drain υπόνομος m eeponomos
dress φόρεμα n forema 144
drink(s) *(n)* ποτό n poto 41, 70, 124, 125, 126; **alcoholic ~** οινοπνευματώδη npl eenopnevmatoTHee 50, 51
drinking water πόσιμο νερό n poseemo nero 30
drip: the faucet [tap] drips η βρύση στάζει ee vreesee stazee
drive, to οδηγώ oTHeegho 93
drop off, to *(children)* αφήνω afeeno 113
drowning: someone is drowning κάποιος πνίγεται kapeeos pneeyete
drugstore φαρμακείο n farmakeeo 130
drunk μεθυσμένος metheezmenos
dry cleaner καθαριστήριο n kathareesteereeo 131
dry cut κούρεμα n koorema 147
dry clean στεγνό καθάρισμα steghno khathareesma 147
dubbed, to be μεταγλωττισμένος metaghloteezmenos 110
dummy *(pacifier)* πιπίλα f peepeela
dustbins τενεκέδες mpl teneкеTHes 30
dusty σκονισμένος skoneezmenos
duty: to pay ~ πληρώνω φόρο pleerono foro 67; **~-free goods** αφορολόγητα είδη npl aforoloyeeta eeTHee ; **~-free shop** κατάστημα αφορολόγητων ειδών n katasteema aforoloyeeton eeTHon ; **~-free shopping** αγορά αφορολόγητων ειδών f aghora aforoloyeeton eeTHon 67
duvet πάπλωμα n paploma

E

each: how much each? πόσο το καθένα; poso to kathena
ear αυτί n aftee 166; **~ drops** σταγόνες για τα αυτιά staghones ya ta afteea; **~ache** πόνος στο αυτί m ponos sto aftee 163
early νωρίς norees 14, 221; **earlier** νωρίτερα noreetera 125, 147
east ανατολικά anatoleeka 95
Easter Πάσχα n paskha 219
easy εύκολο efkolo 14
eat, to τρώω tro-o 41; **places to ~** μέρη για φαγητό meree ya fayeeto 123; **we've already eaten** έχουμε ήδη φάει ekhoome eeTHee faee
economical οικονομικός eekonomeekos
economy class τουριστική θέση tooreesteekee thesee 68
egg αυγό n avgho 44
eight οχτώ okhto 216
eighteen δεκαοκτώ THekaokto 216

eighty ογδόντα oghTHonda 217
elastic *(adj)* ελαστικός elasteekos
electric: ~ blanket ηλεκτρική κουβέρτα f eelektreekee kooverta; **~ fire** αερόθερμο n aerothermo; **~ shaver** ξυριστική μηχανή f kseereesteekee meekhanee
electricity meter ρολόι ηλεκτρικού ρεύματος n roloee eelektreekoo revmatos 28
electronic game ηλεκτρονικό παιχνίδι n eelektroneeko pekhneeTHee 157
elevator ασανσέρ n asanser 26, 132
eleven έντεκα endeka 216
embark, to *(boat)* επιβιβάζομαι epeeveevazome
embassy πρεσβεία f prezveea
emerald σμαράγδι n zmaraghTHee
emergency επείγον epeeghon 127; **~ exit** έξοδος κινδύνου f eksoTHos keenTHeenoo; **it's an emergency** είναι έκτακτη ανάγκη eene ektaktee anangee
empty άδειο aTHyo 14
end, to τελειώνω teleeono 109
engine μηχανή f meekhanee 88
engineer μηχανικός meekhaneekos
England Αγγλία f angleea 119
English Αγγλικά angleeka 11, 67, 110, 150, 152, 161; **~-speaking** Αγγλόφωνος anglofonos 98, 152
enjoy, to ευχαριστιέμαι efkhareestee-eme 110; μου αρέσει moo aresee 121; περνάω καλά pernao kala 123
enlarge, to *(photos)* μεγενθύνω meghentheeno 151
enough αρκετά arketa 15, 42, 136
ensuite bathroom μπάνιο σουίτα n baneeo sooeeta
entertainment guide οδηγός θεαμάτων m oTHeeghos theamaton
entrance fee είσοδος f eesoTHos 100
entry visa βίζα f veeza
epileptic είμαι επιληπτικός/-ια eeme epeeleepteekos/-eea 163
equally εξίσου ekseesoo 17
error λάθος n lathos
escalator κυλιόμενες σκάλες fpl keeleeomenes skales 132
essential απαραίτητα apareteeta 89
estate agent κτηματομεσίτης m kteematomeseetees
EU Ευρωπαϊκή Ένωση f evropaeekee enosee
euro ευρώ n evro 139
evening: in the ~ το βράδυ to vraTHee 221; **~ dress** βραδυνό ένδυμα n vraTHeeno enTHeema 112
every week κάθε εβδομάδα kathe evTHomaTHa 13
examination *(medical)* ιατρική εξέταση f eeatreekee eksetasee
example, for για παράδειγμα ya paraTHeeghma
excess baggage υπέρβαρο n eepervaro 69
exchange, to *(money)* αλλάζω alazo 138; **~ rate** τιμή συναλλάγματος teemee seenalaghmatos 138
excluding meals χωρίς γεύματα khorees ghevmata 24
excursion εκδρομή f ekTHromee 97, 98
excuse me *(apology)* συγγνώμη seeghnomee 10; *(attention)* παρακαλώ parakalo 10, 94
exhausted, to be είμαι ξεθεωμένος eeme ksetheomenos 106
exhibition έκθεση f ekthesee
exit έξοδος f eksoTHos 70; **at the ~** στην έξοδο steen eksoTHo
expensive ακριβός akreevos 14, 134
expiration [expiry] date ημερομηνία λήξεως eemeromeeneea leekseos 109
exposure *(photos)* στάση f stasee 151
express *(mail)* εξπρές, επείγον "express", epeeghon 155

extension *(number)* εσωτερική γραμμή esotereekee ghramee 128
extra *(additional)* άλλο ένα, ένα ακόμη allo ena, ena akomee 23
extracted *(tooth)* βγάζω (δόντι) vghazo (THondee) 168
eye μάτι n matee 166; **~liner** μολύβι ματιών n moleevee mateeon; **~shadow** σκιά ματιών f skeea mateeon

F

face πρόσωπο n prosopo 166
facial καθαρισμός προσώπου m kathareezmos prosopoo 147
facilities εξυπηρέτηση, διευκόλυνση ekseepeereteesee, THee-efkoleensee 22, 30
faint, to feel έχω λιποθυμίες ekho leepotheemee-es 163
fall: he's had a fall έπεσε epese
fall *(autumn)* φθινόπωρο n ftheenoporo 219
family οικογένεια f eekoyeneea 66, 74, 120
famous φημισμένος feemeesmenos
fan ανεμιστήρας m anemeesteeras 25
far μακριά makreea 95; **how far is it?** πόσο απέχει; poso apekhee 73
fare: how much is the fare? πόσο κάνει το εισιτήριο; poso kanee to eeseeteereeo 79
farm φάρμα f farma 107
fast γρήγορα ghreeghora 35; **~ food** φαστ φουντ "fast food" 40; **~ food restaurant** φαστ φουντ n "fast food" 35; **you were driving too ~** οδηγούσατε πολύ γρήγορα oTHeeghoosatee polee ghreeghora
fat λίπος n leepos 39
father πατέρας m pateras 120
faucet βρύση f vreesee 25
fault: it's my/your ~ ήταν λάθος μου/σας eetan lathos moo/sas
faulty ελαττωματικό elatomateeko 137
favorite αγαπημένος aghapeemenos
fax φαξ n "fax" 155; **~ facilities** υπηρεσία φαξ f eepeereseea "fax" 22
February Φεβρουάριος m fevrooareeos 218
feed, to ταΐζω taeezo 39; **feeding bottle** μπιμπερό n beembero
feel ill/sick δεν αισθάνομαι καλά THen esthanome kala 98, 163
female γυναίκα yeeneka 152
fence φράχτης m frakhtees
ferry φέρυ-μπωτ n "ferry" bot 81
festival φεστιβάλ n festeeval
feverish, to feel αισθάνομαι σαν να έχω πυρετό esthanome san na ekho peereto 163
few λίγο leegho 15
fiancé(e) αρραβωνιαστικός/-ιά aravoneeasteekos/ eea
field χωράφι f khorafee 107
fifteen δεκαπέντε THekapende 216
fifth πέμπτος pemptos 217
fifty πενήντα peneenda 217
filling *(dental)* σφράγισμα n sfragheezma 168
film *(camera)* φιλμ n "film" 151; *(movie)* ταινία f teneea 108, 110
filter φίλτρο n feeltro 151; **~ paper (for coffee)** φίλτρο (καφέ) n feeltro (kafe)
find out: could you find out ...? μπορείτε να βρείτε boreete na vreete
fine *(penalty)* πρόστιμο prosteemo 93
fine *(well)* καλά kala 118
finger δάχτυλο n THakhteelo 166
fire: ~ alarm συναγερμός πυρκαγιάς m seenaghermos peerkayas; **~ brigade** πυροσβεστική f peerozvesteekee 92; **~ escape** έξοδος κινδύνου f eksoTHos keenTHeenoo; **~ extinguisher** πυροσβεστήρας m peerozvesteeras; **~place** τζάκι n tzakee; **~wood** καυσόξυλα npl kafsokseela; **there's a fire!** Φωτιά! foteea

first πρώτος protos 68, 75, 81, 217; **~ class** πρώτη θέση protee thesee 68, 74
first-aid kit κουτί πρώτων βοηθειών n kootee proton voeetheeon
fish ψάρι n psaree 45, 158; **~ store [fishmonger]** ιχθυοπωλείο n eekhtheeopoleeo 130
fishing: to go ~ πάω για ψάρεμα pao ya psarema; **~ rod** καλάμι ψαρέματος n kalamee psarematos
fit, to *(clothes)* μου κάνει moo kanee 146
five πέντε pende 216
flag σημαία f seemea
flash *(electronic)* (ηλεκτρονικό) φλας n (eelektroneeko) flas 151
flashlight φακός m fakos 31
flat *(puncture)*: **I have a ~** παθαίνω λάστιχο patheno lasteekho 88
flat *(apartment)* διαμέρισμα n THeeamereezma
flea ψύλλος m pseelos
flight πτήση f pteesee 70; **~ number** αριθμός πτήσεως m areethmos pteeseos 68
flip-flops σαγιονάρες fpl sayonares 145
flood πλημμύρα f pleemeera
floor *(storey)* όροφος m orofos 132
floor mop σφουγγαρόπανο n sfoongaropano
floor show ζωντανό σώου n zondano "show" 112
florist ανθοπωλείο n anthopoleeo 130
flower λουλούδι n loolooTHee 106
flu γρίππη f ghreepee 165
flush: the toilet won't flush το καζανάκι δε δουλεύει to kazanakee THen THoolevee
fly *(insect)* μύγα f meegha
foggy, to be έχει ομίχλη ekhee omeekhlee 122
folk: ~ art λαϊκή τέχνη f laeekee tekhnee; **~ dance** δημοτικός/παραδοσιακός χορός m THeemoteekos/paraTHoseeakos khoros 111; **~ music** δημοτική/παραδοσιακή μουσική f THeemoteekee/paraTHoseeakee mooseekee 111
follow, to ακολουθώ akolootho 95
food φαγητό n fayeeto 39, 41; **~ poisoning** τροφική δηλητηρίαση f trofeekee THeeleeteereeasee 165
foot πόδι n poTHee 166
football *(soccer)* ποδόσφαιρο n poTHosfero 114
footpath μονοπάτι f monopatee 107
for: for a day για μια ημέρα ya mia mera 86; **for a week** για μια εβδομάδα ya mia evTHhomaTHa 86
forecast πρόβλεψη provlepsee 122
foreign ξένος ksenos; **~ currency** ξένο συνάλλαγμα n kseno seenalaghma 138
forest δάσος f THasos 107
forget, to ξεχνώ ksekhno 41; **I forgot** ξέχασα ksekhasa 42
fork πηρούνι n peeroonee 39, 41, 148; *(in the road)* διασταύρωση f THeeastavrosee
form έντυπο n endeepo 153, 168
formal evening dress βραδυνό ένδυμα n vraTHeeno enTHeema 111
forms έντυπα n endeepa 23
fortnight δεκαπενθήμερο n THekapentheemero
fortunately ευτυχώς efteekhos 19
forty σαράντα saranda 217
forward: please forward my mail παρακαλώ διαβιβάστε την αλληλογραφία μου parakalo THeeaveevaste teen aleeloghrafeea moo
fountain συντριβάνι n seendreevanee 99

four τέσσερις, τέσσερα teserees, tesera 216; **~-door car** τετράπορτο αυτοκίνητο n tetraporto aftokeeneeto 86; **~-wheel drive** τετρακινητήριο tetrakeeneeteereeo 86
fourteen δεκατέσσερα THekatesera 216
fourth τέταρτος tetartos 217
frame *(glasses)* σκελετός (γυαλιών) m skeletos (yaleeon)
free *(available)* ελεύθερος eleftheros 36, 77, 124
freezer κατάψυξη f katapseeksee 29
frequent: how frequent? πόσο συχνά; poso seekhna 76; **frequently** συχνά seekhna 13
fresh φρέσκος freskos 14, 41
Friday Παρασκευή f paraskevee 218
fridge ψυγείο n pseeyeeo 29
fried τηγανητός teeghaneetos
friend φίλος/-η feelos/-ee 162; **friendly** φιλικός feeleekos
fries πατάτες τηγανητές fpl patates teeghaneetes 38, 40
frightened, to be είμαι φοβισμένος eeme foveezmenos
from από apo 12; **from ... to** *(time)* από ... (έ)ως apo ... (e)os 13
frosty, to be έχει παγετό ekhee payeto 122
fruit φρούτο n frooto 48, 158; **~ juice** χυμός φρούτων m kheemos frooton 40
frying pan τηγάνι n teeghanee 29
fuel *(gasoline)* καύσιμα npl kafseema 86
full γεμάτο yemato 14; **~ board** *(A.P.)* με πλήρη διατροφή me pleeree THeeatrofee 24; **~ insurance** ολική ασφάλεια f oleekee asfaleea 86
fun, to have περνάω καλά pernao kala
furniture έπιπλα npl epeepla
further: how much further to Athens? πόσο απέχει ακόμη η Αθήνα; poso apekhee akomee ee atheena
fuse ασφάλεια f asfaleea 28; **~ box** κουτί με τις ασφάλειες n kootee me tees asfalee-es 28; **~ wire** καλώδειο ασφάλειας n kaloTHeeo asfaleeas

G

gallon γαλλόνι n ghalonee
gambling χαρτοπαιξία f khartopekseea
game *(toy)* παιχνίδι n pekhneeTHee 157
garage γκαράζ n garaz 26; συνεργείο n seeneryeeo 88
garden κήπος m keepos
gardener κηπουρός keepooros
gardening κηπουρική f keepooreekee
gas: ~ bottle μπουκάλα γκαζιού f bookala gazeeoo; **I smell gas!** μυρίζω γκάζι! meereezo gazee
gas station βενζινάδικο n venzeenaTHeeko 87
gasoline βενζίνη venzeenee 87
gastritis γαστρίτιδα f ghastreeteeTHa 165
gate *(airport)* έξοδος f eksoTHos 70
gay club κλαμπ για ομοφυλόφιλους n "club" ya omofeelofeeloos 112
genuine αυθεντικός afthendeekos 134
get off, to *(transport)* κατεβαίνω kateveno 79
get out, to *(of vehicle)* βγαίνω vyeno 83
get to, to φτάνω ftano 77; **how do I get to ...?** πώς πάνε στο ...; pos pane sto ...? 73, 94
gift δώρο n THoro 67, 156; **~ store** κατάστημα με είδη δώρων n katasteema me eeTHee THoron 130
girl κορίτσι n koreetsee 120, 157
girlfriend φίλη f feelee 120
give, to δίνω THeeno
glass ποτήρι n poteeree 37, 39, 148
glasses *(optical)* γυαλιά n yaleea 167
glove γάντι n ghandee

A-Z

go pame; **~ away!** φύγε! feeghe; **~ back** *(turn around)* γυρίζω πίσω/επιστρέφω gheereezo peeso / epeestrefo 95; **~ for a walk** πάω ένα περίπατο pao ena pereepato 124; **~ shopping** πάω για ψώνια pao ya psoneea 124; **let's go!** πάμε!

goggles γυαλιά npl yaleea

gold χρυσός m khreesos 149; **~-plate** επίχρυσο epeekhreeso 149

golf γκόλφ n "golf" 114; **~ course** γήπεδο γκολφ yeepeTHo "golf" 115

good καλός kalos 14, 35; **~ morning** καλημέρα kaleemera 10; **~ afternoon** καλησπέρα kaleespera 10; **~ evening** καλησπέρα kaleespera 10; **~ night** καληνύχτα kaleeneekhta 10; **~ value** καλή τιμή kalee teemee 101

good-bye αντίο, χαίρετε, γειά σας andeeo, kherete, ya sas 10

gram γραμμάριο n ghramareeo 159

grandparents παππούς και γιαγιά papoos ke yaya

grapes σταφύλια n stafeeleea 160

grass γρασίδι n, χόρτο n ghraseeTHee, khorto

gratuity φιλοδώρημα n feeloTHoreema

graze γρατζουνιά f ghratzooneea 162

greasy *(hair, skin)* λιπαρό leeparo

Greece Ελλάδα f elaTHa 119

Greek *(adj)* Ελληνικά eleeneeka; *(n)* 110 Έλλην-ας/-ίδα eleen-as / -eeTHa; *(language)* Ελληνικά eleeneeka 11, 126

green πράσινος praseenos 143

greengrocer οπωροπωλείο n oporopoleeo 130

gray γκρι, γκρίζος gree, greezos 143

grilled στη σχάρα stee skhara

grocery store παντοπωλείο n pandopoleeo 130, 159

ground *(earth)* έδαφος n eTHafos 31; **~cloth [~sheet]** μουσαμάς για το έδαφος m moosamas ya to eTHafos 31

group γκρουπ n "group" 66

guarantee εγγύηση f engee-eesee 135; **is it guaranteed?** έχει εγγύηση; ekhee engee-eesee

guide *(tour)* ξεναγός ksenaghos 98; **~book** τουριστικός οδηγός m tooreesteekos oTHeeghos 150; **guided tour** ξενάγηση f ksenayeesee 100

guitar κιθάρα f keethara

gum *(mouth)* ούλο n oolo

guy rope σκοινί της τέντας n skeenee tees tendas 31

gynaecologist γυναικολόγος yeenekologhos 167

H

hair μαλλιά npl maleea 147; **~ brush** βούρτσα f voortsa 142; **~ dryer** σεσουάρ n sesooar; **~ mousse** αφρός χτενίσματος, μους για τα μαλλιά f afros khteneesmatos, "mousse" ya ta maleea 142; **~ spray** λακ f lak 142; **~cut** κούρεμα n koorema 147; **~dresser** κομμωτήριο n komoteereeo 131, 147

half μισό meeso 217; **~ board** *(M.A.P.)* με ημιδιατροφή me eemeeTHeeatrofee 24; **~ fare** μισό εισιτήριο meeso eeseeteereeo; **~ past** ... και μισή ... ke meesee 220

hammer το σφυρί n sfeeree 31

hand χέρι n kheree 166; **~ cream** γαλάκτωμα χεριών n ghalaktoma kheryon; **~ luggage** αποσκευές χειρός fpl aposkeves kheeros 69; **~ towel** πετσέτα χεριών f petseta kheryon

handbag τσάντα f tsanda 144

handicrafts λαϊκή τέχνη f laeekee tekhnee

handkerchief χαρτομάντηλο n khartomandeelo

handle πόμολο n pomolo

hanger κρεμάστρα f kremastra 27

happen: what happened? τί συνέβη; tee seenevee 93

harbor λιμάνι n leemanee 99; **~ front** προκυμαία f prokeemea 96
hat καπέλλο n kapelo 144
have, to έχω ekho 18, 133
have to: do I have to ... ? χρειάζεται να ... ; khreeazete 75, 79
hayfever αλλεργία σε γύρη f aleryeea se yeeree 141
head κεφάλι n kefalee 166; **~ache** πονοκέφαλος m ponokefalos 163; **~ waiter** αρχισερβιτόρος arkheeserveetoros 41
head, to *(travel)* πηγαίνω προς peeyeno pros 83
health: ~ food store κατάστημα με υγιεινές τροφές katasteema me eeyee-eenes trofes 130; **~ insurance** ασφάλεια υγείας f asfaleea eeyeeas 168
hearing aid ακουστικό βαρυκοΐας n akoosteeko vareekoeeas
heart καρδιά f karTHya 166; **~ attack** καρδιακό έμφραγμα n karTHyako emfraghma; **~ condition** πρόβλημα καρδιάς n provleema karTHeeas 163
hearts *(cards)* κούπα koopa
heat *(n)* θέρμανση f thermansee 25; **~ wave** καύσωνας kafsonas 122
heater *(water)* θερμοσίφωνας m thermoseefonas
heating θέρμανση f thermansee 25
heavy βαρύ varee 14
height ύψος n eepsos 152
helicopter ελικόπτερο n eleekoptero
hello χαίρετε kherete 10, 118
help, to βοηθώ voeetho 18; **can you ~ me?** μπορείτε να με βοηθήσετε; boreete na me voeetheesete 71, 92
her *(her friend)* της tees 16; *(for/to her)* αυτήν, της, την afteen, tees, teen 16;
herbs βότανα npl votana 48
here εδώ eTHO 12, 17
hernia κοίλη f keelee 165
hers δικό της THeeko tees 16; **it's hers** είναι δικό της eene THeeko tees
hi! γειά σας ya sas 10
highlighted *(hair)* ανταύγειες fpl andavyee-es 147
highway Εθνική Οδός f/ αυτοκινητόδρομος m ethneekee oTHOS / aftokeeneetoTHromos 94
hike, to *(walk)* κάνω πεζοπορία kano pezoporeea 106
hiking πεζοπορία f pezoporeea
hill λόφος m lofos 107
him *(for/to him)* αυτόν, του, τον afton, too, ton 16
hindu n ινδουιστής inTHooeestees
hire, to νοικιάζω neekeeazo; **I'd like to hire ...** θα ήθελα να νοικιάσω ... tha eethela na nekeeaso
his *(his name)* του too 16; **it's his** είναι δικό του eene THeeko too
history ιστορία f eestoreea
hitchhiking ώτο-στοπ oto-stop 83
HIV-positive HIV-θετικός HIV-theteekos
hobby *(pastime)* χόμπυ n "hobby" 121
hold on, to περιμένετε pereemenete 128
hole *(in clothes)* τρύπα f treepa
holiday διακοπές fpl THeeakopes 123; **on ~** για διακοπές ya THeeakopes 66; **~ resort** τόπος διακοπών topos THeeakopon
home: I'm going ~ επιστρέφω epeestrefo
homeopathic remedy ομοιοπαθητική θεραπεία omeopatheeteekee therapeea
homosexual *(adj)* ομοφυλόφιλος omofeelofeelos
honeymoon, to be on είμαι στο μήνα του μέλιτος eeme sto meena too meleetos
hopefully ελπίζω να ... elpeezo na 19
horse άλογο n alogho; **~-racing** ιπποδρομίες fpl eepoTHromee-es 114
hospital νοσοκομείο n nosokomeeo 131, 164, 167

A-Z

A-Z

hot *(weather)* ζεστό zesto 14, 122; **~ dog** χοτ-ντογκ n "hot-dog" 110; **~ spring** θερμή πηγή f thermee peeghee; **~ water** ζεστό νερό zesto nero 25; **~ water bottle** θερμοφόρα f thermofora

hotel ξενοδοχείο n ksenoTHokheeo 21

hour ώρα f ora 76, 97

household articles είδη οικιακής χρήσεως npl eeTHee eekeeakees khreeseos 148

housewife (ν)οικοκυρά f (n)eekokeera

how? πώς; pos 17; **how are you?** τι κάνεις (κάνετε *formal*); tee kanees (kanete *formal*) 118; **how far?** πόσο απέχει; poso apekhee 94; **how long?** *(time)* πόση ώρα; posee ora 76, 78, 88, 94, 98; **how many?** πόσοι; posee 15, 80; **how much?** πόσο κάνει; poso kanee 21, 84, 109; **how often?** πόσο συχνά; poso seekhna 140; **how old?** πόσων χρονών; poson khronon 120

hundred εκατό ekato 217

hungry, to be πεινάω peenao

hurt: to be ~ είμαι χτυπημένος eeme khteepeemenos 92; **it hurts** πονάει ponaee 162

husband άντρας m andras 120, 162

hypermarket υπεραγορά f eeperaghora

I

I'd like ... θα ήθελα tha eethela 18, 36, 37, 40

I'll have ... θα πάρω ... tha paro 37

ice πάγος m paghos 38; **~ dispenser** μηχανή πάγου f meekhanee paghoo; **~ lolly** γρανίτα f ghraneeta; **~ rink** παγοδρόμιο n paghoTHromeeo

ice cream παγωτό n paghoto 40, 160; **~ cone** παγωτό χωνάκι n paghoto khonakee

icy, to be έχει πάγο ekhee pagho 122

identification ταυτότητα f taftoteeta 136

illegal: it's illegal είναι παράνομο eene paranomo

illness αρρώστεια f arosteea

imitation απομίμηση f apomeemeesee 134

immediately αμέσως amesos 13

impressive εντυπωσιακό endeeposeako 101

in *(place)* στο(-η) sto (-ee) 12; *(time)* σε se 13

in-law: father/mother-in-law, πεθερ-ός/-ά pether-os/-a

included: is ... included? συμπεριλαμβάνεται το ...; seembereelamvanete to 86, 98

inconvenient: it's inconvenient δεν είναι βολικό THen eene voleeko

indigestion δυσπεψία f deespepseea

indoor εσωτερικός esotereekos; **~ pool** κλειστή πισίνα kleestee peeseena 116

inexpensive φτηνός fteenos 35

infected μολυσμένος moleezmenos 165

inflammation φλεγμονή f fleghmonee 165

informal *(dress)* πρόχειρο prokheero

information πληροφορίες fpl pleeroforee-es 97; **~ office** γραφείο πληροφοριών n ghrafeeo pleeroforeeon 73, 96

injection ένεση f enesee 168

injured, to be είμαι τραυματισμένος eeme travmateezmenos 92, 162

innocent αθώος atho-os

insect bite τσίμπημα από έντομο n tseembeema apo endomo 141, 162

insect repellent/spray εντομοαπωθητικό n, εντομοκτόνο n endomoapotheeteeko, endomoktono 141

inside μέσα mesa 12; **~ lane** εσωτερική λωρίδα f esotereekee loreeTHa

insist: I insist επιμένω epeemeno

insomnia αϋπνία f aeepneea

instant coffee νεσκαφέ m neskafe 160
instead of αντί andee
instructions οδηγίες fpl oTHeeyee-es 135
instructor εκπαιδευτής, δάσκαλος ekpeTHeftees, THaskalos
insulin ινσουλίνη f eensooleenee
insurance certificate πιστοποιητικό της ασφάλειας n peestopee-eeteeko tees asfaleeas 93
insurance ασφάλεια f asfaleea 86, 89, 93, 168; **~ claim** ασφάλεια f asfaleea 153; **~ company** ασφαλιστική εταιρία f asfaleesteekee etereea 93
interest *(hobby)* ενδιαφέρον enTHeeaferon 121
interest rate επιτόκιο n epeetokeeo
interesting ενδιαφέρον enTHeeaferon 101
international διεθνής THee-ethnees; **International Student Card** διεθνής φοιτητική κάρτα f THee-ethnees feeteeteekee karta 29
interpreter διερμηνέας THee-ermeeneas 93, 153
intersection σταυροδρόμι n stavroTHromee 95
interval διάλειμμα n THeealeema
introduce: may I introduce ...? να συστήσω .... na seesteeso 118
introductions συστάσεις seestasees 118
invitation πρόσκληση f proskleesee 124
invite, to καλώ kalo 124
involved, to be είμαι αναμεμειγμένος eeme anamemeeghmenos 93
iodine ιώδειο n eeoTHeeo
Ireland Ιρλανδία f eerlanTHeea 119
Irish n Ιρλανδός eerlanTHos
iron, to σιδερώνω seeTHerono
is there ...? υπάρχει ...; eeparkhee 17
it is ... είναι ... eene 16, 17
Italian *(restaurant)* ιταλικό eetaleeko 35
itemized bill αναλυτικός λογαριασμός m analeeteekos logharyazmos 32

J

jack *(cards)* βαλές vales
jam μαρμελάδα f marmelaTHa 43,159
jammed, to be έχει σφηνώσει ekhee sfeenosee 25
January Ιανουάριος m eeanooareeos 218
jar βάζο n vazo 159
jaw σαγόνι n saghonee 166
jeans μπλου-τζην n bloo-tzeen 144
jellyfish μέδουσα f meTHoosa
jet-ski τζετ-σκι n "jet-ski" 116
jeweller κοσμηματοπωλείο n kozmeematopoleeo 131, 149
jewish *(adj)* εβραϊκός evraeekos
job: what's your job? τί δουλειά κάνετε; tee THooleea kanete
jogging: to go ~ πάω τζόγκιγκ pao ya "jogging"; **~ pants** φόρμα για τζόγκιγκ forma ya "jogging"
join: may we join you? να έρθουμε μαζί σας; na erthoome mazee sas 124
joint passport κοινό διαβατήριο n keeno THeeavateereeo 66
joke ανέκδοτο n anekTHoto
joker *(cards)* μπαλαντέρ m balander
journalist δημοσιογράφος THeemoseeoghrafos
journey ταξίδι n takseeTHee 76, 78, 123
July Ιούλιος m eeooleeos 218
jump leads καλώδια μπαταρίας npl kaloTHeea batareeas
jumper πουλόβερ n poolover 144
junction *(intersection)* κόμβος m, έξοδος f komvos, eksoTHos
June Ιούνιος m eeooneeos 218

K

keep: keep the change! Κρατήστε τα ρέστα! krateeste ta resta
kerosene stove καμινέτο n kameeneto 31

khartofeelakas

key κλειδί n kleeTHee 27, 28, 71, 88; **~ ring** μπρελόκ n brelok 156

kidney νεφρό n nefro 166

kilo(gram) κιλό n keelo 69, 159

kind: what kind of ...? τι είδους ...; tee eeTHoos ...

king *(cards)* ρήγας m reeghas; *(chess)* βασιλιάς m vaseeleeas

kiosk περίπτερο n pereeptero

kiss, to φιλώ feelo 126

kitchen κουζίνα f koozeena 29; **~ paper** χαρτί κουζίνας n khartee koozeenas

kitchenette κουζινούλα f koozeenoola

knapsack σάκκος m sakos 31

knave *(cards)* βαλές vales

knee γόνατο n ghonato 166

knife μαχαίρι n makheree 39, 41, 148

knight *(chess)* ιππότης m eepotees

know: I don't know δεν ξέρω THen ksero 15

L

label ετικέτα f eteeketa

ladder σκάλα f skala

ladies *(toilet)* γυναικών yeenekon

lake λίμνη f leemnee 107

lamp λάμπα f lamba 29

land, to προσγειώνομαι prozyeeonome 70

landlord σπιτονοικοκύρης speetoneekokeerees

language course σειρά μαθημάτων ξένης γλώσσας f seera matheematon ksenees ghlosas

large μεγάλος meghalos 40, 110

last *(adj)* τελευταίος telefteos 68, 75, 80, 81

late αργά argha 14; αργότερα arghotera 221; **it will be late** θα αργήσει argheesee 70; **later** αργότερα arghotera 125, 147

laugh, to γελώ yelo 126

laundry service υπηρεσία πλυντηρίου f eepeereseea pleendeereeoo 22

lavatory μπάνιο n baneeo

lawyer δικηγόρος m THeekeeghoros 152

laxative καθαρτικό n katharteeko

lead, to *(road)* πηγαίνω peeyeno 94

lead-free *(gas [petrol])* αμόλυβδη amoleevTHee 87

leaflet φυλλάδιο n feelaTHeeo 97

leak, to *(roof/pipe)* στάζω stazo

learn, to *(language/sport)* μαθαίνω matheno

leave me alone! αφήστε με ήσυχο/-η afeeste me eeseekho/-ee 126

leave, to *(deposit)* αφήνω afeeno 71, 73, 86; *(depart)* φεύγω fevgo 32, 68, 70, 98, 126

lecturer λέκτωρας lektoras

left: on the ~ στα αριστερά sta areestera 76, 95; **~hand side** στην αριστερή μεριά steen areesteree mereea 95; **~-handed** αριστερόχειρας areesterokheeras

left-luggage office φύλαξη αποσκευών f feelaksee aposkevon 73

leg πόδι n poTHee 166

legal: it's legal είναι νόμιμο eene nomeemo

leggings κολλάν n kolan 144

lemon λεμόνι n lemonee 38

lend: could you lend me ...? μπορείτε να μου δανείσετε ...; boreete na moo THaneesete

length μήκος n meekos

lens φακός m fakos 151, 167; **~ cap** κάλυμμα φακού n kaleema fakoo 151

lesbian club κλαμπ για λεσβίες n "club" ya lezvee-es

less λιγότερο leeghotero 15

letter γράμμα n ghrama 154; **~box** γραμματοκιβώτιο n ghramatokeevoteeo

level *(even)* ομαλό omalo 31

library βιβλιοθήκη f veevleeotheekee 131

lie down, to ξαπλώνω ksaplono

lifebelt σωσίβιο n soseeveeo

lifeboat ναυαγοσωστική λέμβος f navaghososteekee lemvos

lifeguard ναυαγοσώστης navaghosostees 116

lifejacket σωσίβιο n soseeveeo

lift *(elevator)* ασανσέρ n asanser 26, 132; **~ pass** άδεια (σκι) aTHeea "ski" 117

light *(color)* ανοιχτό aneekhto 14, 134; *(not heavy)* ελαφρύ elafree 14, 134; **lighter***(color)* ανοιχτότερος aneekhtoteros 143

light *(electric)* φως (ηλεκτρικό) n fos (eelektreeko) 25; **~ bulb** λάμπα f lamba 148; **lights** *(bicycle)* φώτα (ποδηλάτου) n fota (poTHeelatoo) 83

lighter *(cigarette)* αναπτήρας m anapteeras 150

lighthouse φάρος m faros

lightning αστραπή f astrapee

like *(similar to)*: **~ this** σαν αυτό san afto

like: I'd like (to) ... θα ήθελα ... tha eethela 124, 133

line *(metro)* γραμμή f ghramee 80; *(telephone)*: **an outside line, please** μια εξωτερική γραμμή, παρακαλώ mia eksotereekee ghramee, parakalo

lips χείλη n kheelee; **lipstick** κραγιόν n krayon

liqueur λικέρ m leeker

liter λίτρο n leetro 87, 159

little μικρός meekros

live together, to συζώ seezo 120

liver ήπαρ (medical) n, συκώτι n eepar, seekotee 166

living room σαλόνι n salonee 29

local τοπικός topeekos 35, 37; **~ anaesthetic** τοπικό αναισθητικό n topeeko anestheeteeko 168

lock *(canal)* φράγμα n, υδατοφράκτης m fraghma, eeTHatofraktees

lock *(key)* κλειδαριά f kleeTHarya 25; **it's locked** είναι κλειδωμένο eene kleeTHomeno; **lock oneself out, to** κλειδώνομαι έξω kleeTHonome ekso 27

locker θυρίδα f theereeTHa

London Λονδίνο n lonTHeeno

long μακρύς makrees 146; **~-distance bus** υπεραστικό λεωφορείο n eeperasteeko leoforeeo 78; **~-distance call** υπεραστικό τηλεφώνημα n eeperasteeko teelefoneema; **~-sighted** πρεσβύωπας prezveeopas 167; **how long?** πόσο καιρό; poso kero 164; **how much longer?** πόση ώρα ακόμη; posee ora akomee 41

look: I'm just looking απλώς κοιτάω aplos keetao; **~ for** ψάχνω psakhno 18; **~ forward: I'm looking forward to it** Το περιμένω με χαρά to pereemeno me khara; **to have a ~** ρίχνω μια ματιά reekhno mia mateea 89

loose *(fitting)* φαρδύς farTHees 117, 146

lorry φορτηγό n forteegho

lose, to χάνω khano 28; **I've lost ...** έχασα ... ekhasa 153; **it's lost ...** χάθηκε khatheeke 71

loss απώλεια f apoleea 71

lost-and-found [lost property] office γραφείο απωλεσθέντων αντικειμένων n ghrafeeo apolesthendon andeekeemenon 73

lotion λοσιόν f loseeon

lots πολύ polee

loud: it's too loud έχει πολύ θόρυβο ekhee polee thoreevo; **louder** πιο δυνατά peeo THeenata 128

love: I love Greek food μου αρέσει το ελληνικό φαγητό moo aresee to eleeneeko fayeeto; **I love you** σε αγαπώ se aghapo

low-fat χαμηλό σε λιπαρά khameelo se leepara
lower *(berth)* κάτω (κουκέτα) kato (kooketa) 74
lubricant λιπαντικό n leepandeeko
luck: good luck! καλή επιτυχία! kalee epeeteekheea 219
luggage αποσκευές fpl aposkeves; **~ locker** θυρίδα f theereeTHa 71; **~ carts (trolleys)** καροτσάκια αποσκευών n karotsakeea aposkevon 71
lump σβώλος m svolos 162
lunch μεσημεριανό n meseemeryano 98
lung πνεύμονας m pnevmonas
luxury πολυτέλεια f poleeteleea

M

magazine περιοδικό n pereeoTHeeko 150
magnificent μεγαλοπρεπές meghaloprepes 101
maid καμαριέρα f kamaryera 27
maiden name πατρικό όνομα n patreeko onoma
mail αλληλογραφία f aleeloghrafeea 27; **by ~** με επιστολή me epeestolee 22; **~box** ταχυδρομικό κουτί n takheeTHromeeko kootee 154
main κύριος keereeos 130; **~ rail station** κεντρικός σιδηροδρομικός σταθμός m kendreekos seeTHeeroTHromeekos stathmos 73; **~ street** κύριος δρόμος keereeos THromos 95
mains κεντρικός διακόπτης m kendreekos THeeakoptees
make *(brand)* μάρκα f marka
make an appointment, to κλείνω ένα ραντεβού kleeno ena randevoo 161
make-up μακιγιάζ n makeeyaz
male άνδρας anTHras 152
mallet κόπανος m kopanos 31
man *(male)* άνδρας anTHras; *(mankind)* άνθρωπος anthropos
manager διευθυντής THee-eftheendees 25, 137
manicure μανικιούρ n maneekeeoor 147
manual *(car)* χειροκίνητος kheerokeeneetos
map χάρτης m khartees 94, 106, 150
March Μάρτιος m marteeos 218
market αγορά f aghora 99, 131; **~ day** ημέρα λαϊκής αγοράς eemera laeekees aghoras
married, to be είμαι παντρεμένος eeme pandremenos 120
mask *(diving)* μάσκα f maska
mass λειτουργία f leetooryeea 105
massage μασάζ n "massage" 147
match *(game)* αγώνας m /παιχνίδι n aghonas/pekhneeTHee 114
matches σπίρτα npl speerta 31, 148, 150
material *(cloth)* ύφασμα n eefasma
matinée απογευματινή παράσταση apoyevmateenee parastasee 109
matter: it doesn't matter δεν πειράζει THen peerazee; **what's the matter?** τι πρόβλημα υπάρχει; tee provleema eeparkhee
mattress *(air)* στρώμα (αέρα) n stroma (aera) 31
May Μάιος m maeeos 218
may I ...? μπορώ ...; boro ...? 18, 37
maybe ίσως eesos
me *(for/to me)* εμένα, μου, με emena, moo, me 16
meal γεύμα n yevma 42, 125; φαγητό n fayeeto 38
mean, to σημαίνω seemeno 11
measles ιλαρά f eelara 165
measure, to μετρώ metro 146
measurement μέτρηση f metreesee
meat κρέας n kreas 41, 46, 158
medication φάρμακα npl farmaka 164, 165
medium *(adj)* κανονικός kanoneekos 40

medium *(steak)* μέτρια ψημένο metreea pseemeno
meet, to συναντώ seenando 106, 125; **pleased to meet you** χαίρω πολύ khero polee 118
member *(of club)* μέλος n (του κλαμπ) melos (too "club") 112, 115
memorial μνημείο n mneemeeo 99
men *(toilets)* ανδρών anTHron
mend, to διορθώνω THeeorthono 137
mention: don't mention it παρακαλώ, τίποτα parakalo, teepota 10
message μήνυμα n meeneema 27, 128
metal μέταλλο n metalo
metro *(subway)* μετρό n (υπόγειος σιδηρόδρομος, ηλεκτρικός m "metro" (eepoyeeos seeTHeeroTHromos, eelektreekos) 80; **~ station** σταθμός μετρό m stathmos "metro" 80
microwave *(oven)* (φούρνος) μικροκυμάτων (foornos) meekrokeematon
midday μεσημέρι n meseemeree
midnight μεσάνυχτα npl mesaneekhta 220
migraine ημικρανία f eemeekraneea
mileage τα χιλιόμετρα ta kheeleeometra 86
milk γάλα n ghala 13, 160; **with ~** με γάλα me ghala 40
milk of magnesia γάλα μαγνησίας n ghala maghneeseeas
million εκατομμύριο ekatomeereeo 217
mind: do you mind? σας πειράζει; sas peerazee 77, 126
mine δικό μου THeeko moo 16
mine: it's mine είναι δικό μου eene THeeko moo
mineral water εμφιαλωμένο νερό n emfeealomeno nero 40
mini-bar μίνι-μπαρ n "mini-bar" 32
minimart παντοπωλείο n pandopoleeo 158
minimum n ελάχιστο elakheesto
minister πάστορας pastoras
minor road δευτερεύων δρόμος m THeftereyon THromos
minute λεπτό n lepto 76
mirror καθρέφτης m kathreftees
missing, to be λείπω leepo 137, 152
mistake λάθος n lathos 32, 41, 42
misunderstanding: there's been a ~ έγινε κάποια παρεξήγηση eyeene kapia parekseeyeesee
modern art σύγχρονη τέχνη f seenkhronee tekhnee
modern μοντέρνο monderno 14
moisturizer *(cream)* υδατικό γαλάκτωμα n eeTHateeko ghalaktoma
monastery μοναστήρι, η μονή *(on road signs)* monasteeree/monee 99
Monday Δευτέρα f THeftera 218
money order ταχυδρομική επιταγή f takheeTHromeekee epeetayee
money χρήματα npl khreemata 42
money-belt ζώνη για χρήματα f zonee ya khreemata
month μήνας m meenas 218
monument μνημείο n mneemeeo 99
moped μοτοποδήλατο n motopoTHeelato 83
more παραπάνω parapano 15; **I'd like some more** θα ήθελα λίγο ακόμη tha eethela leegho akomee 39
morning, in the το πρωί to proee 221
morning-after pill χάπι της "επομένης" n khapee tees epomenees 167
Moslem *(adj)* μωαμεθανός moamethanos
mosquito κουνούπι n koonoopee; **~ bite** τσίμπημα κουνουπιού n tseembeema koonoopeeoo
mother μητέρα f meetera 120
motorbike μοτοσυκλέτα f motoseekleta 83
motorboat εξωλέμβιο f eksolemveeo 116

A-Z

motorway Εθνική Οδός f/ αυτοκινητόδρομος m ethneekee oTHos/ aftokeeneetoTHromos 94
mountain βουνό, όρος (on maps) n voono, oros 107; **~ pass** ορεινό πέρασμα f oreeno perazma 107
mountaineering ορειβασία f oreevaseea
mousetrap φάκα f faka
moustache μουστάκι n moostakee
mouth στόμα n stoma 166; **~ ulcer** αύτρ(ι)α f aftr(ee)a
move, to *(room)* μετακομίζω metakomeezo 25; **don't move him!** μην τον μετακινήσετε! meen ton metakeeneesete 92
movie theatre κινηματογράφος m keeneematoghrafos
Mr. κύριος keereeos
Mrs. κυρία keereea
much πολύ polee 15
multiple journey *(ticket)* (εισιτήριο για) πολλαπλά ταξίδια (eeseeteereeo ya) polapla takseeTHeea 79
muscle μυς m mees 166
museum μουσείο n mooseeo 99
music μουσική f mooseekee 111; **~ box** μουσικό κουτί n mooseeko kootee
musician μουσικός mooseekos
must: I must πρέπει prepee
mustard μουστάρδα f moostarTHa 38
my μου moo 16

N

nail: ~ polish βερνίκι νυχιών n verneekee neekheeon; **~ scissors** ψαλιδάκι νυχιών n psaleeTHakee neekheeon
name όνομα n onoma 22, 36, 93; **my name is** λέγομαι leghome 118; **what's your name?** πώς λέγεστε; pos leyeste 118
napkin πετσέτα f petseta 39
nappies πάνες μωρού f panes moroo 142
narrow στενό steno 14
national εθνικός ethneekos
nationality υπηκοότητα f eepeeko-oteeta
nature: ~ reserve εθνικός δρυμός m ethneekos THreemos 107; **~ trail** μονοπάτι f monopatee 107
nausea ναυτία f nafteea
near κοντά konda 12; **nearby** εδώ κοντά eTHo konda 21; **nearest** κοντινότερος kondeenoteros 80, 88, 92, 130, 140
necessary απαραίτητα apareteeta 89
neck *(part of body)* αυχένας m afkhenas 166; *(clothing)* λαιμόκοψη f lemokopsee 144
need: do we need to ...? χρειάζεται να ...; khreeazete na 112; **I need to ...** χρειάζομαι ... khreeazome 18
neighbor γείτονας yeetonas
nephew ανηψιός aneepseeos
nerve νεύρο n nevro
never ποτέ pote 13; **~ mind** δεν πειράζει THen peerazee 10
New Zealand Νέα Ζηλανδία f nea zeelanTHeea
new καινούργιο kenooryo 14; **New year** Καινούριος Χρόνος m kenooryos khronos 219
newsdealer [newsagent] περίπτερο n pereeptero 150
newspaper εφημερίδα f efeemereeTHa 150
next επόμενος epomenos 68, 75, 78, 80, 81, 87; **~ stop!** η επόμενη στάση! ee epomenee stasee 79
next to δίπλα THeepla 12, 95
niece ανηψιά aneepseea
night: at ~ τη νύχτα tee neekhta 221; **~club** νυχτερινό κέντρο n neekhtereeno kendro 112
nightdress νυχτικό n neekhteeko
nine εννέα enea 216
nineteen δεκαεννέα THekaenea 216

ninety ενενήντα eneneenda 217
no όχι okhee 10
noisy θορυβώδες thoreevoTHes 14, 24
non-smoking μη καπνίζοντες mee kapneezondes 36; **non-smoking (area)** (περιοχή για) μή καπνίζοντες (pereeokhee ya) mee kapneezondes 69
none, no one κανένας, καμμία, κανένα kanenas/kameea/kanena 15, 16
noon μεσημέρι n meseemeree 220
normal allowance επιτρεπόμενα όρια npl epeetrepomena oreea 67
north βόρεια voreea 95
Northern Ireland Βόρεια Ιρλανδία voreea eerlanTHeea
nose μύτη f meetee 166; **~bleed** αιμορραγία μύτης f emorayeea meetees
not yet όχι ακόμη okhee akomee 13
nothing else τίποτε άλλο teepote alo 15
November Νοέμβριος m noemvreeos 218
now τώρα tora 13, 84
nudist beach παραλία γυμνιστών f paraleea yeemneeston
number *(telephone)* τηλέφωνο n teelefono 84
nurse νοσοκόμα f nosokoma
nut *(for bolt)* παξιμάδι n pakseemaTHee

O

o'clock: it's ... ~ είναι ... η ώρα eene ... ee ora 220
occupied κατειλημένο kateeleemeno 14
October Οκτώβριος m oktovreeos 218
of course βεβαίως veveos 19
office γραφείο n ghrafeeo
often συχνά seekhna 13
okay εντάξει endaksee 10, 19
old *(not new)* παλιό paleeo 14; *(not young)* γέρος yeros 14; **~ town** παλιά πόλη f paleea polee 96, 99; **~-fashioned** ντεμοντέ demonde 14
olive oil ελαιόλαδο n eleolaTHo
omelet ομελέττα f omeleta 40
on *(date)* στις stees 13; *(day)* την teen 13; **~ board** *(transport)* μέσα στο τραίνο mesa sto treno 74; **~ foot** με τα πόδια me ta poTHya 17, 95; **~ the left** στα αριστερά sta areestera 12; **~ the right** στά δεξιά sta THekseea 12; **~ the other side of** από την άλλη μεριά apo teen alee merya 95
once μία φορά mia fora 217
one ένας, μια, ένα enas, mia, ena 216; **~-way ticket** απλό εισιτήριο n aplo eeseeteereeo 68, 79
open *(adj)* ανοιχτό aneekhto 14; **~ to the public** ανοιχτό στο κοινό aneekhto sto keeno 100; **~-air pool** ανοιχτή πισίνα aneekhtee peeseena 116
open, to ανοίγω aneegho 132, 140
opening hours ώρες λειτουργίας fpl ores leetooryeeas 100
opera όπερα f opera 108, 111; **~ house** όπερα f opera 99, 111
opposite απέναντι apenandee 12
optician οφθαλμίατρος ofthalmeeatros 131, 167
or ή ee 19
orange πορτοκάλι n portokalee 143, 160
orchestra ορχήστρα f orkheestra 111
order, to παραγγέλνω paragelno 37, 89, 135; **I ordered** παρήγγειλα pareegeela 41; **to ~ a taxi** καλώ ένα ταξί kalo ena taksee 32
organized οργανωμένος orghanomenos 106
others άλλα ala 134
our μας mas 16
ours δικό μας THeeko mas 16
out: he's out είναι έξω eene ekso
outdoor εξωτερικός eksotereekos
outside lane εξωτερική λωρίδα f eksotereekee loreeTHa
outside έξω ekso 12, 36

A-Z

oval οβάλ oval 134
oven φούρνος m foornos
over: ~ there εκεί ekee 76; **~ the road** απέναντι apenandee 12
overdone *(adj)* πολύ ψημένο polee pseemeno 41
overnight ένα βράδυ n ena vraTHee 23
owe: how much do I owe you? πόσο σας χρωστώ; poso sas khrosto
own: on my ~ μόνος/-η μου monos/-ee moo 65
owner κάτοχος katokhos

P

p.m. μ.μ. meta meseemvreeas
pacifier πιπίλα f peepeela
pack of cards τράπουλα f trapoola
pack, to *(baggage)* φτιάχνω τις βαλίτσες fteeakhno tees valeetses 69
packet of cigarettes πακέτο τσιγάρα n paketo tseeghara 150
paddling pool ρηχή πισίνα f reekhee peeseena 113
padlock λουκέτο n looketo
pain, to be in πονάω ponao 167
painkiller παυσίπονο n pafseepono 141, 165
paint, to ζωγραφίζω zoghrafeezo 104; **painter** ζωγράφος zoghrafos 104
pair of ένα ζευγάρι n ena zevgharee 217
pajamas πιτζάμες f peetzames
palace ανάκτορα npl anaktora 99
panorama πανόραμα f panorama 107
pants *(trousers)* παντελόνι n pandelonee 144
panty hose καλτσόν n kaltson 144
paper χαρτί n khartee 150; **~ napkin** χαρτοπετσέτα f khartopetseta 148
paraffin παραφινέλαιο n parafeeneleo 31
paralysis παραλυσία f paraleeseea
parcel πακέτο n, δέμα n paketo, THema 155
pardon? ορίστε; oreeste 11
parents γονείς mpl ghonees 120
park πάρκο n parko 96, 99, 107; **~ ranger** δασοφύλακας THasofeelakas
parking χώρος στάθμευσης m khoros stathmefsees 87; **~ meter** παρκόμετρο n parkometro 87; **~ lot** χώρος στάθμευσης m khoros stathmefsees 87
parliament building Βουλή f voolee 99
partner *(boyfriend/girlfriend)* σύντροφος seendrofos
parts *(components)* ανταλλακτικά n andalakteeka 89
party *(social)* πάρτυ n "party" 124
pass, to περνώ perno 77; **~ through** περνώ perno 66
passenger επιβάτης epeevatees
passport διαβατήριο n THeeavateereeo 66, 69
pastry store ζαχαροπλαστείο n zakharoplasteeo 131
path μονοπάτι f monopatee 107
pay, to πληρώνω pleerono 42, 136; **~ a fine** πληρώνω πρόστιμο pleerono prosteemo 93
paying πληρωμή f pleeromee 42, 136
peak κορυφή f koreefee 107
pearl μαργαριτάρι n marghareetaree 149
pebbly *(beach)* με χαλίκια me khaleekeea 116
pedestrian: ~ crossing διάβαση πεζών f THeeavasee pezon 96; **~ zone** ο πεζόδρομος(m) o pezoTHromos 96
pen στυλό n steelo 150
penfriend φίλος μέσω αλληλογραφίας feelos meso aleeloghrafeeas
penknife σουγιάς m sooyas
pensioner συνταξιούχος seendakseeookhos 100
pepper *(seasoning)* πιπέρι n peeperee 38

per: ~ day την ημέρα teen eemera 30, 83, 86, 87, 115; **~ hour** την ώρα teen ora 87, 115; **~ night** τη βραδιά tee vraTHya 21; **~ week** την εβδομάδα teen evTHomaTHa 83, 86
perhaps ίσως eesos 19
period *(menstrual)* περίοδος f pereeoTHos 167; **~ pains** πόνοι περιόδου m ponee pereeoTHoo 167
period *(of time)* περίοδος f pereeoTHos 104
perm περμανάντ f permanand
permed περμανάντ f permanand 147
permit άδεια f aTHeea
petrol βενζίνη f venzeenee 87, 88; **~ station** βενζινάδικο n venzeenaTHeeko 87
pewter κασσίτερος m kaseeteros 149
phone *(see also* **telephone***)*: **~ call** τηλεφώνημα n teelefoneema 152; **~ card** τηλεκάρτα f teelekarta 127, 155
photo φωτογραφία f fotoghrafeea; **passport-size ~** φωτογραφία διαβατηρίου fotoghrafeea THeeavateereeoo 115
photo, to take a φωτογραφίζω fotoghrafeezo
photocopier φωτοτυπικό n fototeepeeko 155
phrase φράση f frasee 11
pick up, to παίρνω perno 28, 113
pickup truck ημιφορτηγό n eemeeforteegho
picnic area περιοχή για πικνίκ f pereeokhee ya "picnic" 107
piece τεμάχιο n temakheeo 69; **a piece of ...** ένα κομμάτι ... ena komatee 40
Pill *(contraceptive)*: **to be on the ~** παίρνω το αντισυλληπτικό χάπι perno to andeeseeleepteeko khapee 167
pillow μαξιλάρι n makseelaree 27; **~ case** μαξιλαροθήκη f makseelarotheekee
pilot light φλόγιστρο n floyeestro
pink ροζ roz 143
pipe *(smoking)* πίπα f peepa; **~ cleaners** καθαριστής πίπας m kathareestees peepas; **~ tobacco** καπνός πίπας m kapnos peepas
pity: it's a pity κρίμα kreema
pizzeria πιτσαρία f peetsareea 35
place *(space)* θέση f thesee 29
place a bet, to βάζω στοίχημα vazo steekheema 114
plain *(not patterned)* απλό aplo
plane αεροπλάνο n aeroplano 68
plans σχέδια npl skheTHeea 124
plant φυτό n feeto
plastic bag πλαστική σακούλα f plasteekee sakoola
plate πιάτο n piato 39, 148
platform αποβάθρα f apovathra 73, 76, 77
platinum πλατίνα f plateena 149
play, to παίζω pezo 110, 121; *(music)* παίζω (μουσική) pezo (mooseekee) 111; **~ground** παιδική χαρά f peTHeekee khara 113; **~group** παιδικός σταθμός m peTHeekos stathmos 113
playing field γήπεδο yeepeTHo 115
playwright δραματουργός THramatoorghos 110
pleasant ευχάριστο efkhareesto 14
please παρακαλώ parakalo 10
plug πρίζα f preeza 148
plumber υδραυλικός eeTHravleekos
pneumonia πνευμονία f pnevmoneea 165
point: Point! δείξτε! THeekste 11
poison δηλητήριο n THeeleetereeo 140
poisonous δηλητηριώδης THeeleetereeoTHees
police αστυνομία f asteenomeea 92, 152; **~ certificate** πιστοποιητικό αστυνομίας n peestopee-eeteeko asteenomeeas 153; **~ station** αστυνομικό τμήμα n asteenomeeko tmeema 96, 131, 152

A-Z

pond λιμνούλα f leemnoola 107
popcorn ποπ-κορν "popcorn" 110
popular δημοφιλής THeemofeelees 157
porter αχθοφόρος akhthoforos 71
portion μερίδα f mereeTHa 40
possible: as soon as possible όσο το δυνατόν πιο σύντομα oso to THeenaton peeo seendoma
post *(mail)*: **~ office** ταχυδρομείο n takheeTHromeeo 96, 131, 154; **~box** ταχυδρομικό κουτί n takheeTHromeeko kootee 154; **~card** κάρτα f karta 150, 154, 156
potatoes πατάτες fpl patates 38
pottery αγγειοπλαστική f angeeoplasteekee
poultry πουλερικά poolereeka 46, 158
pound *(sterling)* λίρα (στερλίνα) f leera (sterleena) 67, 138
power cut διακοπή ρεύματος f THeeakopee revmatos
pregnant, to be είμαι έγκυος eeme engeeos 163
prescribe, to γράφω συνταγή ghrafo seendayee 165
prescription συνταγή γιατρού f seendayee yatroo 140, 141
present *(gift)* δώρο n THoro
press, to σιδερώνω seeTHerono 137
pretty όμορφο omorfo 101
priest ιερέας ee-ereas
prison φυλακή f feelakee
private bathroom ιδιωτικό μπάνιο n eeTHeeoteeko baneeo
problem πρόβλημα n provleema 88
program πρόγραμμα n proghrama 109; **~ of events** οδηγός θεαμάτων oTHeeghos theamaton 108
prohibited: is it prohibited? απαγορεύεται; apaghorevete
promenade deck κατάστρωμα n katastroma
pronounce, to προφέρω profero 11
Protestant Διαμαρτυρόμενος THeeamarteeromenos
public: ~ building δημόσιο κτίριο n THeemoseeo kteereeo 96; **~ holiday** δημόσια αργία f THeemoseea aryeea 219
pullover πουλόβερ n poolover 144
pump τρόμπα, αεραντλία f tromba, aerandleea 83
puncture *(flat)*: **I have a ~** παθαίνω λάστιχο patheno lasteekho 88
purple μωβ mov 143
purpose σκοπός m skopos 66
put: where can I put ...? Πού να βάλω ...; poo na valo

Q

quality ποιότητα f peeoteeta 134
quantity ποσότητα f posoteeta 134
quarantine καραντίνα f karandeena
quarter, a ένα τέταρτο ena tetarto 217; **~ past ...** ... και τέταρτο ... ke tetarto 220; **~ to ...** ... παρά τέταρτο ... para tetarto 220
quay προβλήτα, αποβάθρα f provleeta, apovathra
queen *(cards)* ντάμα f dama; *(chess)* βασίλισσα f vaseeleesa
question ερώτηση f eroteesee
queue ουρά f oora
queue, to περιμένω στην ουρά pereemeno steen oora 112
quick γρήγορο ghreeghoro 14; **quickly** γρήγορα ghreeghora 17
quiet ήσυχο eeseekho 14; **quieter** πιο ήσυχο peeo eeseekho 24, 126

R

rabbi ραββίνος m raveenos
race track [race course] ιπποδρόμιο n eepoTHromeeo 114

racket *(tennis, squash)* ρακέτα f raketa 115
radio ραδιόφωνο n raTHeeofono 25
rail station σιδηροδρομικός σταθμός m seeTHeeroTHromeekos stathmos 73
rain, to βρέχει vrekhee 122
raincoat αδιάβροχο n aTHeeavrokho 145
rapids ρεύμα ποταμού f revma potamoo 107
rare *(steak)* με το αίμα του, σενιάν me to ema too, seneean; *(unusual)* σπάνιος spaneeos
rash εξάνθημα n eksantheema 162
ravine ρεματιά f remateea 107
razor blades ξυραφάκια n kseerafakeea 142
razor ξυραφάκι n kseerafakee
ready έτοιμος eteemos 89, 151; **it's ready** είναι έτοιμο eene eteemo 137; **are you ready?** Είστε έτοιμος; eeste eteemos
real *(genuine)* αληθινός aleetheenos 149
really? αλήθεια; aleetheea 19
receipt απόδειξη f apoTHeeksee 32, 89, 136, 137, 151
reception *(hotel)* ρεσεψιόν f resepseeon
reclaim tag ετικέτα παραλαβής αποσκευών eteeketa paralavees aposkevon 71
recommend, to συστήνω seesteeno 21, 35; **can you recommend?** μπορείτε να συστήσετε; boreete na seesteesete 97, **what do you recommend?** τι συστήνετε; tee seesteenete? 37
record *(lp)* δίσκος m THeeskos 157; **~ store** δισκάδικο n THeeskaTHeeko 131
red κόκκινος kokeenos 143; **~ wine** κόκκινο κρασί n kokeeno krasee 40
reduction μειωμένο εισιτήριο n meeomeno eeseeteereeo 74, 100
refund επιστροφή χρημάτων f epeestrofee khreematon 137
refuse bag σακκούλα σκουπιδιών f sakoola skoopeeTHeeon 148
refuse tip σκουπιδότοπος m skoopeeTHotopos
region περιοχή f pereeokhee 106
registration number αριθμός κυκλοφορίας m areethmos keekloforeeas 88, 93
registration plates πινακίδες fpl peenakeeTHes 87
regular *(gas [petrol])* απλή aplee 87; *(size of drink)* μέτριο metreeo 110
religion θρησκεία f threeskeea
remember: I don't remember Δεν θυμάμαι THen theemame
rent, to νοικιάζω neekeeazo 29, 86; **I'd like to rent ...** θα ήθελα να νοικιάσω ... tha eethela na nekeeaso
repair, to επισκευάζω epeeskevazo 89; διορθώνω THeeorthono 137
repairs επισκευές fpl epeeskeves 89, 137
repeat, to επαναλαμβάνω epanalamvano 94, 128; **please repeat that** παρακαλώ επαναλάβετέ το parakalo epanalavete to 11
replacement part ανταλλακτικό n andalakteeko 137
report, to αναφέρω anafero 152
require: it is required χρειάζεται khreeazete 111
reservation κράτηση f krateesee 22, 68, 77, 112
reserve, to κλείνω kleeno 21, 36, 109, **I'd like to reserve ...** θα ήθελα να κλείσω ... tha eethela na kleeso 74
restaurant εστιατόριο n esteeatoreeo 35
retired, to be συνταξιούχος seendakseeookhos 121
return, to επιστρέφω epeestrefo 75, 81, 98; **~ ticket** εισιτήριο με επιστροφή eeseeteereeo me epeestrofee 68, 74, 79
reverse the charges με χρέωση του παραλήπτη me khreosee too paraleeptee 127

revolting αηδιαστικό aeeTHeeasteeko 14
rheumatism ρευματισμοί mpl revmateezmee
rib πλευρό n plevro 166
right *(correct)* σωστός sostos 14, 77, 79, 80, 94; **that's right** σωστά sosta
right *(not left)*: **on the ~** στα δεξιά sta THekseea 76, 95; **~handed** δεξιόχειρας THekseeokheeras
right of way προτεραιότητα f protereoteeta 93, 106
rip-off n κλεψιά klepseea 101
river ποταμός m potamos 107
road δρόμος m THromos 94; **~ assistance** οδική βοήθεια f oTHeekee voeetheea 88; **~ sign** πινακίδα f, σήμα n peenakeeTHa seema 93
roasted ψητός pseetos
robbery ληστεία f leesteea
rock climbing αναρρίχηση f anareekheesee
rocks βράχια npl vrakheea
rolls ψωμάκια n psomakeea 43; **is this the road for ...** Αυτός είναι ο δρόμος για ...; aftos eene o THromos ya
romantic ρομαντικό romandeeko 101
roof *(house/car)* σκεπή f, στέγη f skepee, steyee; **~-rack** σχάρα αυτοκινήτου f skhara aftokeeneetoo
rook *(chess)* πύργος m peerghos
room δωμάτιο n THomateeo 21; **~ service** υπηρεσία δωματίου f eepeereseea THomateeoo 26
rope σχοινί n skheenee
round *(adj)* στρογγυλός strongeelos 134
round *(of golf)* παιχνίδι n pekhneeTHee 115
roundtrip *(ticket)* εισιτήριο με επιστροφή eeseeteereeo me epeestrofee 68, 74, 79
route διαδρομή f THeeaTHromee 106
rowing κωπηλασία f kopeelaseea
rubbish σκουπίδια npl skoopeeTHya 28
rucksack σακκίδιο n sakeeTHeeo 145
rude, to be είμαι αγενής eeme ayenees
run: ~ out *(fuel)* μένω από meno apo 88; **~ into: I ran into ...** χτύπησα ... khteepeesa 93
rush hour ώρα αιχμής f ora ekhmees

S

safe *(lock-up)* θυρίδα f theereeTHa 27
safe *(not dangerous)* ασφαλής asfalees 116; **to feel ~** αισθάνομαι ασφαλής esthanome asfalees 65
sailing boat ιστιοπλοϊκό n eesteeoploeeko 116
salad σαλάτα f salata
sales rep αντιπρόσωπος πωλήσεων andeeprosopos poleeseon
sales tax ΦΠΑ fee pee a 24
salt αλάτι n alatee 38, 39, 160
salty αλμυρό almeero
same ίδιος eeTHeeos 75; **the same again please** το ίδιο παρακαλώ to eeTHeeo parakalo
sand άμμος f amos; **sandy** *(beach)* με άμμο me amo 116
sandals πέδιλα npl peTHeela 145
sandwich σάντουιτς n "sandwich" 40
sanitary towels σερβιέττες f servee-etes 142
satellite TV δορυφορική τηλεόραση f THoreeforeekee teeleorasee 22
satin σατέν n saten
sattelite TV δορυφορική τηλεόραση f THoreeforeekee teeleorasee
Saturday Σάββατο n savato 218
sauce σάλτσα f saltsa 38
saucepan κατσαρόλα f katsarola 29
sauna σάουνα f saoona
sausages λουκάνικα npl lookaneeka 40
saw *(tool)* πριόνι n preeonee
say: how do you say ...? Πώς λέγεται ...; pos leyete; **what did he say?** Τί είπε; tee eepe
scarf κασκώλ n kaskol 144

scenic route γραφική διαδρομή ghrafeekee THeeaTHromee 106
scheduled flight προγραμματισμένη πτήση f proghramateezmenee pteesee
sciatica ισχυαλγία f eeskheealyeea 165
scientist επιστήμονας epeesteemonas
scissors ψαλίδι n psaleeTHee 148
Scotland Σκωτία f skoteea 119
Scottish n Σκωτσέζος skotsezos
screw βίδα f veeTHa
screwdriver κατσαβίδι n katsaveeTHee 148
sea θάλασσα f thalassa 107; **~food** θαλασσινά thalaseena 45
seafront προκυμαία f prokeemea
seasoning αλατοπίπερο n alatopeepero 38
seat θέση f thesee 74, 77, 109
second δεύτερος THefteros 217; **~ class** δεύτερη θέση THefteree thesee 74; **~-hand shop** κατάστημα μεταχειρισμένων ειδών n katasteema metakheereezmenon eeTHon 131
secretary γραμματέας ghramateas
security guard φύλακας m feelakas
sedative ηρεμιστικό n eeremeesteeko
see, to βλέπω vlepo 34, 37; **~ again** ξαναβλέπω ksanavlepo 126
self-employed, to be ελεύθερος επαγγελματίας eleftheros epangelmateeas 121
self-service σελφ-σέρβις n "self-service" 87
send, to στέλνω stelno 88, 155
senior citizen συνταξιούχος seendakseeookhos 74
separately ξεχωριστά ksekhoreesta 42
September Σεπτέμβριος m septemvreeos 218
service λειτουργία f leetooryeea 105; **is ~ included?** συμπεριλαμβάνεται η υπηρεσία; seembereelamvanete ee eepeereseea 42; **~ charge** ποσοστό υπηρεσίας n pososto eepeereseeas
set menu μενού α λα καρτ n menoo ala kart 37
seven επτά epta 216
seventeen δεκαεπτά THekaepta 216
seventy εβδομήντα evTHomeenda 217
sex *(act)* σεξ n "sex"
shade απόχρωση f apokhrosee 143; **shady** έχει σκιά ekhee skeea 31
shampoo σαμπουάν n sampooan 142; **~ and set** σαμπουάν και χτένισμα n sampooan ke khteneezma 147
shape σχήμα n skheema 134
shaving brush βούρτσα ξυρίσματος f voortsa kseereezmatos
shaving cream κρέμα ξυρίσματος f krema kseereezmatos
sheet *(bedding)* σεντόνι n sendonee 28
shelf ράφι n rafee
ship πλοίο n pleeo
shirt πουκάμισο n pookameeso 144
shock *(electric)* ηλεκτρικό σοκ n eelektreeko sok
shoe: shoes παπούτσια npl papootseea 145; **~ store** κατάστημα υποδημάτων n katasteema eepoTHeematon 130; **~ laces** κορδόνια παπουτσιών npl korTHoneea papootseeon; **~ polish** λούστρο παπουτσιών n loostro papootseeon; **~ repair** διόρθωση παπουτσιών f THeeorthosee papootseeon
shop *(store)* κατάστημα n katasteema 130
shopping: to go ~ πάω ψώνια pao psoneea; **~ area** εμπορική περιοχή f emboreekee pereeokhee 99; **~ mall [centre]** εμπορική περιοχή f emboreekee pereeokhee 130
shore *(sea/lake)* ακτή f aktee
short κοντό kondo 14, 146; **~-sighted** μύωπας meeopas 167
shorts σόρτς n "shorts" 144

shoulder ώμος m omos 166
show, to: show! δείξετε! THeeksete 18; **can you show me?** μπορείτε να μου δείξετε; boreete na moo THeeksete 94, 106, 133
shower gel αφρόλουτρο για ντουζ n afrolootro ya dooz
shower το ντουζ n to dooz 26, 30
shut *(adj)* κλειστό kleesto 14
shut: when do you shut? Πότε κλείνετε; pote kleenete
shutter παραθυρόφυλλο n paratheerofeelo 25
sick, to feel αισθάνομαι άρρωστος esthanome arostos 163
sick: I'm going to be θα κάνω εμετό tha kano emeto
side *(of road)* μεριά f merya 95; **~ street** παράδρομος m paraTHromos 95
sights αξιοθέατα npl akseeotheata
sightseeing tour ξενάγηση στα αξιοθέατα ksenayeesee sta akseeotheata 97
sign *(road)* σήμα n seema 95
signpost σήμα τροχαίας n seema trokheas
silk μετάξι n metaksee
silver ασήμι n aseemee 149; **~-plate** επάργυρο eparyeero 149
singer τραγουδιστής (τραγουδίστρια) traghooTHeestees (traghooTHeestreea) 157
single μονός monos 81; **~ room** μονό δωμάτιο mono THomateeo 21; **to be ~** *(unmarried)* είμαι ελεύθερος eeme eleftheros 120; **~ ticket** απλό εισιτήριο n aplo eeseeteereeo 68, 79
sink *(bathroom)* νιπτήρας m neepteeras 25
sister αδελφή f aTHelfee 120
sit, to κάθομαι kathome 36, 77, 126
six έξι eksee 216
sixteen δεκαέξι THekaeksee 216
sixty εξήντα ekseenda 217
size μέγεθος n meyethos 115, 146
skates παγοπέδιλα npl paghopeTHeela 117
skating rink παγοδρόμιο n paghoTHromeeo
ski σκι n "ski" 117; **~ boots** μπότες του σκι fpl botes too "ski" 117; **~ poles** μπαστούνια του σκι bastooneea too "ski" 117; **~-lift** τελεφερίκ n telefereek 117; **~-school** σχολή σκι f skholee too "ski" 117; **skiing** σκι n "ski" 117
skin δέρμα n THerma 166
skirt φούστα f foosta 144
sledge έλκηθρο n elkeethro
sleep, to κοιμάμαι keemame 167; **sleeping bag** υπνόσακκος m eepnosakos 31; **sleeping car** βαγκόν-λι n vagon-lee 77; **sleeping pill** υπνωτικό χάπι n eepnoteeko khapee
slice φέτα f feta 159
slippers παντόφλες fpl pandofles 145
slope *(ski)* πλαγιά f playa 117
slow αργό argho 14; **slowly** αργά argha 11, 17, 94; **slow down!** Κόψτε ταχύτητα! kopste takheeteeta
SLR camera μονοοπτική ρεφλέξ φωτογραφική μηχανή f mono-opteekee refleks fotoghrafeekee meekhanee 151
small μικρός meekros 14, 24, 40, 110, 117, 134; **~ change** ψιλά npl pseela 136
smell: there's a bad smell Μυρίζει άσχημα meereezee askheema
smoke, to καπνίζω kapneezo 126; **I don't smoke** Δεν καπνίζω THen kapneezo; **it's too smoky** Έχει πολύ καπνίλα ekhee polee kapneela; **smoking** καπνίζοντες kapneezondes 36; **smoking area** περιοχή για καπνίζοντες pereeokhee ya kapneezondes 69

snack bar κυλικείο n keeleekeeo 73
sneakers αθλητικά παπούτσια npl athleeteeka papootseea
snorkel αναπνευστήρας m anapnefsteeras
snow, to χιονίζει kheeoneezee 122
snowed in, to be έχω κλειστεί από το χιόνι ekho kleestee apo to kheeonee
snowplow χιονοκαθαριστήρας m kheeonokathareesteeras
soap powder απορρυπαντικό n aporeepandeeko
soap σαπούνι sapoonee 27, 142
soccer ποδόσφαιρο n poTHosfero 114
socket πρίζα f preeza
socks κάλτσες fpl kaltses 144
soda [soft drink] αναψυκτικό n anapseekteeko 110, 160
sofa καναπές m kanapes; **~-bed** καναπές-κρεββάτι m kanapes-krevatee
sole *(shoes)* σόλα f sola
something κάτι katee 14
sometimes μερικές φορές mereekes fores 13
son γιος m yos 120, 162
soon σύντομα seendoma 13; **as soon as possible** όσο το δυνατόν πιο σύντομα oso to THeenaton peeo seendoma 161
sore: it's ~ πονάει ponaee; **~ throat** πονόλαιμος m ponolemos 141, 163
sorry! συγγνώμη seeghnomee 10
sort είδος n eeTHos 134
soup σούπα f soopa 44
sour ξυνός kseenos 41
South Africa Νότια Αφρική f noteea afreekee
South African n Νοτιοαφρικανός noteeoafreekanos
south νότεια noteea 95
souvenir σουβενίρ n "souvenir" 98, 156; **~ store** κατάστημα σουβενίρ n katasteema "souvenir" 131
souvlaki/gyros stand σουβλατζίδικο n soovlatzeeTHeeko 35
spa ιαματικά λουτρά npl eeamateeka lootra 107
space χώρος m khoros 30
spade *(shovel)* φτυαράκι n fteearakee 157
spades *(cards)* μπαστούνι n bastoonee
spare *(extra)* επιπλέον, έξτρα epeepleon, "extra"
speak, to μιλώ meelo 11, 18, 41, 67, 128; **do you speak English?** μιλάτε Αγγλικά; meelate angleeka? 11
special requirements ειδικές ανάγκες f eeTHeekes ananges 39
specialist ειδικός eeTHeekos 164
specimen δείγμα n THeeghma 164
spectacles γυαλιά n yaleea
speed, to τρέχω trekho 93
spell: it is spelled γράφεται ghrafete 11
spend, to ξοδεύω ksoTHevo
spices μπαχαρικά npl bakhareeka 48
spicy καυτό kafto
spin-dryer στεγνωτήριο n steghnoteereeo
spine σπονδυλική στήλη f sponTHeeleekee steelee 166
spoon κουτάλι n kootalee 39, 41, 148
sport αθλητισμός athleeteezmos 114; **sports club** αθλητικός όμιλος athleeteekos omeelos 115; **sports ground** (αθλητικό) στάδιο n (athleeteeko) staTHeeo 96; **sporting goods store** κατάστημα αθλητικών n katasteema athleeteekon 131
spring άνοιξη f aneeksee 219
square τετράγωνος tetraghonos 134
stadium στάδιο n staTHeeo 96
stain λεκές m lekes
stairs σκάλες f skales
stale μπαγιάτικο bayateeko 14
stamp γραμματόσημο n ghramatoseemo 150, 154

start, to αρχίζω arkheezo 98, 112
statement *(legal)* δήλωση (νομική) f THeelosee (nomeekee) 93
station σταθμός m stathmos 73, 96
statue άγαλμα n aghalma 99
stay, to μένω meno 23, 65, 123
sterilizing solution αποστειρωτικό διάλυμα n aposteeroteeko THeealeema 142
stern *(ship)* πρύμνη f preemnee
sting τσίμπημα n tseembeema 162
stolen, to be κλάπηκε klapeeke 71
stomach στομάχι n stomakhee 166; **~ache** στομαχόπονος m stomakhoponos 163
stop *(bus/tram)* στάση f stasee 79, 80
stop, to σταματώ stamato 77, 98; **~ at** σταματώ στο/στη stamato sto/stee 76, 78
store *(shop)* κατάστημα n katasteema 130; **~ guide** οδηγός καταστήματος m oTHeeghos katasteematos 132
stove κουζίνα f koozeena 28, 29
straight ahead ευθεία/ίσια eftheea/eeseea 95
strange παράξενο parakseno 101
straw *(drinking)* καλαμάκι n kalamakee
stream ρυάκι f reeakee 107
string σπάγγος m spagos
striped *(patterned)* ριγέ reeye
student φοιτητής (φοιτήτρια) feeteetees (feeteetreea) 74, 100
study, to σπουδάζω spooTHazo 121
style ρυθμός m reethmos 104
subtitled, to be με υπότιτλους me eepoteetloos 110
subway *(metro)* μετρό n (υπόγειος σιδηρόδρομος, ηλεκτρικός) m "metro" (eepoyeeos seeTHeeroTHromos, eelektreekos) 80; **~ station** σταθμός μετρό m stathmos "metro" 80, 96
suede σουέτ sooet
sugar ζάχαρη f zakharee 38, 39, 160
suggest, to προτείνω proteeno 123
suit *(men's)* κουστούμι n koostoomee 144; *(women's)* ταγιέρ n tayer 144
suitable κατάλληλος kataleelos 117, 140
summer καλοκαίρι n kalokeree 219
sun: ~glasses γυαλιά ήλιου n yaleea eeleeoo 144; **~-tan cream/lotion** κρέμα/λάδι ήλιου krema/laTHee eeleeoo 142; **~burn** έγκαυμα ηλίου n engavma eeleeoo 141; **~shade** ομπρέλλα f ombrela 116; **~stroke** ηλίαση f eeleeasee 163; **to be sunny** έχει ήλιο ekhee eeleeo 122
Sunday Κυριακή f keereeakee 218
superb έξοχο eksokho 101
supermarket σουπερμάρκετ n "supermarket" 131, 158
supervision επίβλεψη f epeevlepsee 113
supplement επιβάρυνση f epeevareensee 74
suppositories υπόθετα n eepotheta 165
sure: are you sure? Είστε σίγουρος; eeste seeghooros
surname επίθετο n epeetheto
sweatshirt αθλητική μπλούζα f athleeteekee blooza 144
sweet *(taste)* γλυκός ghleekos
sweets *(candy)* καραμέλες fpl karameles 150
swelling πρήξιμο n preekseemo 162
swimming κολύμβηση f koleemveesee 114; **~ pool** πισίνα f peeseena 22, 26, 116; **~ trunks** μαγιώ n mayo 144
swimsuit ολόσωμο μαγιώ n olosomo mayo 144
switch on/off, to ανοίγω/κλείνω aneegho/kleeno
swollen πρησμένος preezmenos
symptoms συμπτώματα npl seemptomata 163
synagogue συναγωγή f seenaghoyee

T

T-shirt μπλουζάκι n bloozakee 144, 156

table τραπέζι n trapezee 36, 112; **~ cloth** τραπεζομάντηλο n trapezomandeelo; **~ tennis** πινγκ-πονγκ n peeng-pong

tablet χάπι n khapee 140

take, to παίρνω perno 24, 78, 165; **I'll take it** θα το πάρω tha to paro 24, 135; **~ away** παίρνω (σπίτι) perno speetee 40; **~ photographs** παίρνω φωτογραφίες perno fotoghrafee-es 98; **how long does it take?** πόσο διαρκεί; poso THeearkee 78; **it takes time** παίρνει ώρα/κάνει ώρα pernee ora / kanee ora 84

taken *(occupied)* πιασμένος piazmenos 77

talk, to μιλώ meelo

tall ψηλό pseelo 14

tampons ταμπόν n tambon 142

tan μαύρισμα n mavreezma

tap *(water)* βρύση f vreesee 25

taxi ταξί n taksee 70, 71, 84; **~ rank** πιάτσα ταξί f piatsa taksee 96; **~ driver** ταξιτζής m takseetzees

tea τσάι n tsaee 40; **~ bags** φακελλάκια τσαγιού n fakelakeea tsayoo 160; **~ spoon** κουταλάκι n kootalakee 148

teacher δάσκαλος THaskalos

team ομάδα f omaTHa 114

teat *(for baby bottle)* ρώγα f rogha

teddy bear αρκουδάκι n arkooTHakee 157

teenager έφηβος efeevos

telephone τηλέφωνο n teelefono 22, 70, 73, 92, 127; **~ bill** λογαριασμός τηλεφώνου m logharyazmos teelefonoo 32; **~ booth** τηλεφωνικός θάλαμος m teelefoneekos thalamos 127; **~ directory** τηλεφωνικός κατάλογος m teelefoneekos kataloghos 127; **~ number** αριθμός τηλεφώνου m areethmos teelefonoo 127

tell: tell me! πείτε μου!/ πέστε μου peete moo / peste moo 79

temperature *(body)* θερμοκρασία f thermokraseea 164

temple ναός naos 99

temporarily προσωρινά prosoreena 89

temporary προσωρινός prosoreenos

ten δέκα THeka 216

tennis τέννις n "tennis" 114; **~ court** γήπεδο τέννις n yeepeTHo "tennis" 115

tent σκηνή f skeenee 30, 31; **~ pegs** παλούκι n palookee 31; **~ pole** στύλος της σκηνής m steelos tees skeenees 31

terrible φοβερό fovero 101

tetanus τέτανος m tetanos 164

thank you ευχαριστώ efkhareesto 10; **thanks for your help** ευχαριστώ για τη βοήθειά σας efkhareesto ya tee voeetheea sas 94

that one εκείνο ekeeno 16, 134

theater θέατρο n theatro 96, 110; *(ancient)* (αρχαίο) θέατρο n (arkheo) theatro 99

theft κλοπή f klopee 71, 153

their τους toos 16

theirs δικό τους THeeko toos 16

them αυτούς aftoos 16

then *(time)* τότε tote 13

there εκεί ekee 12, 17; **there is ...** υπάρχει ... eeparkhee 17

thermometer θερμόμετρο n thermometro

thermos flask θερμός n thermos

these αυτά afta 134

thick χοντρό khondro 14

thief κλέφτης kleftees

thin λεπτό lepto 14

think: I think νομίζω nomeezo 42, 77; **~ about it** το σκέφτομαι to skeftome 135

third *(adj.)* τρίτος treetos 217; *(n)* ένα τρίτο ena treeto 217

A-Z

thirsty διψάω THeepsao
thirteen δεκατρία THekatreea 216
thirty τριάντα treeanda 216
this one αυτό afto 16, 134
those εκείνα ekeena 134
thousand χίλια kheeleea 217
three τρεις, τρία trees, treea 216
throat λαιμός m lemos 166
thrombosis θρόμβωση f thromvosee
thumb αντίχειρας m andeekheeras 166
thundery, to be έχει καταιγίδες ekhee kateyeeTHes 122
Thursday Πέμπτη f pemptee 218
ticket εισιτήριο n eeseeteereeo 68, 69, 75, 77, 79, 80, 100, 114; **~ office** γραφείο εισιτήριων n ghrafeeo eeseeteereeon 73
tie γραβάτα f ghravata 144
tight στενός stenos 117
tights καλτσόν n kaltson 144
till receipt απόδειξη f apoTHeeksee
time: on ~ στην ώρα του steen ora too 76; **free ~** ελεύθερος χρόνος m eleftheros khronos 98; **~table** δρομολόγιο n THromologheeo 75
tin opener ανοιχτήρι n aneekhteeree 148
tire *(on wheel)* λάστιχο n lasteekho 83
tired, to be είμαι κουρασμένος eeme koorazmenos
tissues χαρτομάντηλα n khartomandeela 142
to *(place)* στο(-η) sto(-ee) 12
toaster τοστιέρα f tostee-era
tobacco καπνός m kapnos 150; **tobacconist** καπνοπωλείο n kapnopoleeo 131
today σήμερα seemera 124, 218
toe δάχτυλο ποδιού n THakhteelo poTHyoo 166
toilet(s) τουαλέττα f tooaleta 25, 26, 29, 73, 96, 98; **toilet paper** χαρτί υγείας n khartee eeyeeas 25, 29, 142
toiletries καλλυντικά n kaleendeeka 142
tomorrow αύριο avreeo 84, 124, 218
tongue γλώσσα f ghlosa 166
tonight απόψε apopse 110, 124
tonsillitis αμυγδαλίτιδα f ameeghTHaleeteeTHa
tonsils αμυγδαλές fpl ameeghTHales
too *(extreme)* πολύ polee 17, 93; **~ much** πάρα πολύ para polee 15
tooth δόντι n THondee 168; **~brush** οδοντόβουρτσα f oTHondovoortsa 142; **~paste** οδοντόπαστα f oTHondopasta 142; **~ache** πονόδοντος m ponoTHondos
top πάνω pano; **~ floor** ο επάνω όροφος m o epano orofos
torch φακός m fakos 31
torn, to be *(muscle)* είναι σχισμένος eene skheezmenos 164
tough *(food)* σκληρός skleeros 41
tour guide ξεναγός ksenaghos
tour ξενάγηση f ksenayeesee 97
tourist τουρίστας tooreestas
tow rope σχοινί για ρυμούλκηση n skheenee ya reemoolkeesee
towards προς pros 12
tower πύργος(m) peerghos 99
town πόλη f polee 70, 94; **~ hall** Δημαρχείο(n) THeemarkheeo 99
toy παιχνίδι n pekhneeTHee 157
traditional παραδοσιακός paraTHoseeakos 35
traffic κίνηση f keeneesee
trailer τροχόσπιτο n trokhospeeto 30, 81
train τραίνο n treno 75, 76, 77, 80; **~ times** δρομολόγιο τραίνου n THromoloyeeo trenoo 75
training shoes αθλητικά παπούτσια npl athleeteeka papootseea 145
transfer, to μεταφέρω metafero
transit, in στην μεταφορά stee metafora 71

translate, to μεταφράζω metafrazo 11
translation μετάφραση f metafrasee
translator μεταφραστής metafrastees
trash σκουπίδια npl skoopeeTHya 28; **~cans** τενεκέδες mpl tenekeTHes 30
travel: ~ agency ταξιδιωτικό γραφείο n takseeTHeeoteeko ghrafeeo 131; **~ sickness** ναυτία f nafteea 141
traveler's check [traveller's cheque] ταξιδιωτικές επιταγές takseeTHeeoteekes epeetayes 136, 138
tray δίσκος m THeeskos
tree δέντρο n THendro 106
trim διόρθωμα n THeeorthoma 147
trolley *(cart)* καροτσάκι n karotsakee 158
trolley-bus τρόλλεϋ n "trolley" 78, 79
trousers παντελόνι n pandelonee 144; **trouser press** σιδερωτήριο n seeTHeroteereeo
true: that's not true Αυτό δεν είναι αλήθεια afto THen eene aleetheea
try on, to δοκιμάζω THokeemazo 146
Tuesday Τρίτη f treetee 218
tumor όγκος m ongos 165
tunnel τούνελ n toonel
Turkey Τουρκία f toorkeea
turn; turn! στρίψτε! streepste 95; **~ off** σβήνω sveeno 25; **~ on** ανάβω anavo 25; **~ down** *(volume, heat)* χαμηλώνω khameelono; **~ up** *(volume, heat)* ανεβάζω anevazo
turning στενό n steno 95
TV τηλεόραση f teeleorasee 22, 25
twelve δώδεκα THoTHeka 216
twenty είκοσι eekosee 216
twice δύο φορές THeeo fores 217
twin beds δύο κρεββάτια (pl.) THeeo krevateea 21
two δύο THeeo 216; **~-door car** δίπορτο αυτοκίνητο n THeeporto aftokeeneeto 86
typical τυπικός teepeekos 37
tyre λάστιχο n lasteekho 83

U

U.K. Ηνωμένο Βασίλειο n eenomeno vaseeleeo
U.S. Ηνωμένες Πολιτείες fpl eenomenes poleetee-es 119
ugly άσχημο askheemo 14, 101
ulcer έλκος n elkos
uncle θείος m theeos 120
unconscious αναίσθητος anestheetos 92
underdone όχι καλά ψημένο okhee kala pseemeno 41
underpass υπόγεια διάβαση f eepoyeea THeeavasee 76, 96
understand, to καταλαβαίνω katalaveno 11; **do you understand?** καταλαβαίνετε; katalavenete 11; **I don't understand** δεν καταλαβαίνω THen katalaveno 11, 67
uneven *(ground)* ανώμαλος anomalo 31
unfortunately δυστυχώς THeesteekhos 19
uniform στολή f stolee
unit μονάδα f monaTHa 155
United States Ηνωμένες Πολιτείες fpl eenomenes poleetee-es
university Πανεπιστήμιο n panepeesteemeeo
unleaded petrol αμόλυβδη βενζίνη f amoleevTHee venzeenee
unlimited mileage απεριόριστα χιλιόμετρα apereeoreesta kheeleeometra
unpleasant δυσάρεστο THeesaresto 14
until ως, μέχρι os, mekhree 221
upper *(berth)* πάνω (κουκέτα) pano (kooketa) 74
upset stomach στομαχόπονος m stomakhoponos 141
upstairs επάνω epano 12
urgent επείγον epeeghon 161
urine ούρα npl oora 164

A-Z

use, to χρησιμοποιώ khreeseemopeeo 139
useful χρήσιμος khreeseemos

V

vacancy ελεύθερο δωμάτιο n eleftheroTHomateeo 21
vacant ελεύθερο elefthero 14
vacate, to αδειάζω aTHyazo 32
vacation διακοπές fpl THeeakopes 123; **on ~** για διακοπές ya THeeakopes 66; **~ resort** τόπος διακοπών topos THeeakopon
vaccinated against έχω κάνει εμβόλιο για ... ekho kanee emvoleeo ya 164
vaccination εμβόλιο n emvoleeo
valid ισχύει eeskhee-ee 75
valley κοιλάδα f keelaTHa 107
valuable πολύτιμος poleeteemos
value αξία f akseea 155
vanilla *(flavor)* βανίλλια vaneeleea 40
VAT ΦΠΑ fee pee a 24
vegetable λαχανικό n lakhaneeko 47, 158
vegetarian χορτοφάγος khortofaghos 39
vein φλέβα f fleva 166
velvet βελούδο n velooTHo
venereal disease αφροδισιακό νόσημα n afroTHeeseeako noseema 165
very πολύ polee 17
video ταινία βίντεο f teneea "video"; **~ game** παιχνίδι βίντεο n pekhneeTHee "video"; **~ recorder (VCR)** βίντεο n "video"
village χωριό f khoryo 107
vineyard αμπελώνας m ambelonas 107
visit επίσκεψη f epeeskepsee 119; **visiting hours** ώρες επισκεπτηρίου f ores epeeskepteereeoo 167
vitamin tablets βιταμίνες fpl veetameenes 141
volleyball βόλεϋ n "volley" 114
vomit, to κάνω εμετό kano emeto 163

W

wait, to περιμένω pereemeno 76, 89, 140; **wait!** περιμένετε! pereemenete 98
waiter! Γκαρσόν! garson 37
waitress! Δεσποινίς! THespeenees 37
wake to: wake (me)! ξυπνήσετε! kseepneesete 27
Wales Ουαλλία f ooaleea 119
walk περπατώ perpato 65; **walking boots** μπότες πεζοπορίας fpl botes pezoporeeas 145
wall τοίχος m teekhos
wallet πορτοφόλι n portofolee 42
want, to θέλω thelo 18
ward *(hospital)* πτέρυγα f ptereegha 167
warm χλιαρό khleearo 14; *(weather)* ζεστός zestos 122
washing machine πλυντήριο n pleendeereeo 29
washing powder απορρυπαντικό n aporeepandeeko 148
washing-up liquid υγρό πιάτων n eeghro piaton 148
wasp σφήκα f sfeeka
watch ρολόι n roloee; **~ strap** λουρί ρολογιού n looree roloyoo
water νερό n nero 87; **~ heater** θερμοσίφωνας m thermoseefonas 28; **~-skis** θαλάσσια σκί npl thalaseea "ski" 116; **~skiing** θαλάσσιο σκι n thalaseeo" ski"; **~proof** αδιάβροχο n aTHeeavrokho
waterfall καταρράχτης m katarakhtees 107
wave κύμα n keema
waxing χαλάουα f khalaooa 147
way: I've lost my way έχασα το δρόμο μου ekhsasa to THromo moo 94
we εμείς emees
weak: I feel weak αισθάνομαι αδύναμος esthanome aTHeenamos
wear: he/she was wearing φορούσε forοose 152

weather καιρός keros 122; **~ forecast** πρόβλεψη καιρού provlepsee keroo 122
wedding γάμος m ghamos; **~ ring** δακτυλίδι γάμου n THakteeleeTHee ghamoo
Wednesday Τετάρτη f tetartee 218
week εβδομάδα f evTHomaTHa 23, 218
well-done *(steak)* καλοψημένο kalopseemeno
Welsh *(adj)* ουαλλέζικος ooalezeekos; *(n)* Ουαλλός ooalos
west δυτικά THeeteeka 95
wetsuit στολή δύτη f stolee THeetee
what? τι; tee 18; **what time ...?** τί ώρα ...; tee ora 68, 76, 78, 81; **what's the time?** τί ώρα είναι; tee ora eene 220; **what kind of ...?** τί είδους ...; tee eeTHoos ... 37; **what sort of ...?** τί είδους ...; tee eeTHoos 106
wheelchair αναπηρική καρέκλα f anapeereekee karekla
when? πότε; pote? 13
where? πού; poo 12; **where is ...?** πού είναι ...; poo eene 99; **where are you from?** από πού είσαι/είστε *(formal)*; apo poo eese/eeste *(formal)* 119
which? ποιό; peeo 16; **which stop?** ποιά στάση; pia stasee 80
white άσπρος aspros 143; **~ wine** άσπρο κρασί n aspro krasee 40
who? ποιός peeos 16
whose? ποιανού/-ής; peeanoo/-ees 16
why? γιατί; yatee 15
wide φαρδύ farTHee 14
wife γυναίκα f yeeneka 120, 162
window παράθυρο n paratheero 25, 77; *(in shop)* βιτρίνα f veetreena 134, 149; **~ seat** θέση στο παράθυρο f thesee sto paratheero 74
wine κρασί n krasee 40
winery οινοποιεία f eenopee-eea 107
winter χειμώνας m kheemonas 219
with με me 17
withdraw, to κάνω ανάληψη kano analeepsee 139
without χωρίς khorees 17
witness μάρτυρας marteeras 93
wood *(material)* ξύλο n kseelo
wood δάσος f THasos 107
work, to δουλεύω THoolevo 83, 89, 121; **it doesn't work** δεν δουλεύει THen THoolevee 25
worry: I'm worried ανησυχώ aneeseekho
worse χειρότερο kheerotero 14
worst ο χειρότερος o kheeroteros
wound *(cut)* πληγή f pleeyee 162
write (down), to γράφω ghrafo 136
writing pad μπλοκ n blok 150
wrong λάθος lathos 14, 136; **~ number** λάθος νούμερο lathos noomero 128

X YZ

x-ray ακτινογραφία f akteenoghrafeea 164
yacht γιωτ n "yacht"
year χρόνος m khronos 218
yellow κίτρινος keetreenos 143
yes ναι ne 10
yesterday χτες khtes 218
yogurt γιαούρτι n yaoortee 43, 160
you *(informal sing)* εσύ esee; *(plural or formal sing)* εσείς esees
young νέος neos 14
your *(sing/plur)* σου/σας soo/sas
yours: it's yours *(informal/formal)* είναι δικό σου/σας eene THeeko soo/sas
youth hostel ξενώνας νεότητος m ksenonas neoteetas 29
zebra crossing διάβαση πεζών f THeeavasee pezon
zero μηδέν meeTHen
zipper [zip] φερμουάρ n fermooar
zoo ζωολογικός κήπος m zo-oloyeekos keepos 113
zoology ζωολογία f zo-oloyeea

Glossary
Greek - English

The Greek-English glossary covers all the areas where you may need to decode written Greek: hotels, public buildings, restaurants, stores, ticket offices, airports, and stations. The Greek is written in large type to help you identify the character(s) from the signs you see around you.

General ΓΕΝΙΚΑ

ΑΡΙΣΤΕΡΑ	*areestera*	LEFT
ΔΕΞΙΑ	*THekseea*	RIGHT
ΕΙΣΟΔΟΣ	*eesoTHos*	ENTRANCE
ΕΞΟΔΟΣ	*eksoTHos*	EXIT
ΤΟΥΑΛΕΤΕΣ	*tooaletes*	TOILETS
ΑΝΔΡΩΝ	*anTHron*	MEN (TOILETS)
ΓΥΝΑΙΚΩΝ	*gheenekon*	WOMEN (TOILETS)
ΑΠΑΓΟΡΕΥΕΤΑΙ ΤΟ ΚΑΠΝΙΣΜΑ	*apaghorevete to kapneesma*	NO SMOKING
ΚΙΝΔΥΝΟΣ	*keenTHeenos*	DANGER
ΑΠΑΓΟΡΕΥΤΑΙ Η ΕΙΣΟΔΟΣ	*apaghorevete ee eesoTHos*	NO ENTRY
ΕΛΞΑΤΕ	*elksate*	PULL
ΩΘΗΣΑΤΕ	*ootheesate*	PUSH
ΕΠΙΤΡΕΠΕΤΑΙ	*epeetrepete*	ALLOWED
ΑΠΑΓΟΡΕΥΕΤΑΙ	*apaghorevete*	FORBIDDEN

General (Continued)

ΤΜΗΜΑ ΑΠΟΛΕΣΘΕΝΤΩΝ ΑΝΤΙΚΕΙΜΕΝΩΝ	*tmeema apolesthendon andeekeemenon*	LOST PROPERTY
ΑΠΑΓΟΡΕΥΕΤΑΙ Η ΚΟΛΥΜΒΗΣΗ	*apaghorevete ee koleemveesee*	NO SWIMMING
ΠΟΣΙΜΟ ΝΕΡΟ	*poseemo nero*	DRINKING WATER
ΙΔΙΩΤΙΚΟΣ ΧΩΡΟΣ	*eeTHeeoteekos khoros*	PRIVATE
ΜΗΝ ΠΕΤΑΤΕ ΣΚΟΥΠΙΔΙΑ	*meen petate skoopeeTHya*	NO LITTER
ΠΡΟΣΟΧΗ ΣΚΥΛΟΣ	*prosokhee skeelos*	BEWARE OF THE DOG
ΥΠΟΓΕΙΑ ΔΙΑΒΑΣΗ	*eepogheea THeeavasee*	UNDERPASS / SUBWAY
ΠΡΟΣΕΞΤΕ ΤΟ ΣΚΑΛΟΠΑΤΙ	*proseksete to skalopatee*	MIND THE STEP
ΦΡΕΣΚΟ-ΒΑΜΜΕΝΟ	*freskovameno*	WET PAINT
ΠΡΩΤΗ ΘΕΣΗ	*protee thesee*	FIRST CLASS
ΔΕΥΤΕΡΗ ΘΕΣΗ	*THefteree thesee*	SECOND CLASS

Road Signs
ΟΔΙΚΕΣ ΠΙΝΑΚΙΔΕΣ

ΕΞΟΔΟΣ ΟΧΗΜΑΤΩΝ	*eksoTHos okheematon*	EXIT IN USE
ΚΡΑΤΑΤΕ ΤΗ ΔΕΞΙΑ	*kratate tee THekseea*	KEEP RIGHT
ΚΡΑΤΑΤΕ ΤΗΝ ΑΡΙΣΤΕΡΑ	*kratate teen areestera*	KEEP LEFT
ΜΟΝΟΔΡΟΜΟΣ	*monoTHromos*	ONE WAY
ΑΠΑΓΟΡΕΥΕΤΑΙ Η ΠΡΟΣΠΕΡΑΣΗ	*apaghorevete ee prosperasee*	NO PASSING
ΑΠΑΓΟΡΕΥΕΤΑΙ Η ΣΤΑΘΜΕΥΣΗ/ ΤΟ ΠΑΡΚΑΡΙΣΜΑ	*apaghorevete ee stathmefsee/ to parkareesma*	NO PARKING
ΕΘΝΙΚΗ ΟΔΟΣ	*ethneekee oTHos*	FREEWAY [MOTORWAY]
ΔΙΟΔΙΑ	*THeeoTHeea*	TOLL
ΚΟΜΒΟΣ	*komvos*	JUNCTION
ΠΑΡΑΚΑΜΠΤΗΡΙΟΣ	*parakampteereeos*	DETOUR
ΠΡΟΣ ΛΙΜΕΝΑ	*pros leemena*	TO PORT
ΠΡΟΣ ΚΕΝΤΡΟ	*pros kendro*	DOWNTOWN

Airport/Station
ΑΕΡΟΔΡΟΜΙΟ/ ΣΙΔΗΡΟΔΡΟΜΙΚΟΣ ΣΤΑΘΜΟΣ

ΠΛΗΡΟΦΟΡΙΕΣ	*pleeroforee-es*	INFORMATION
ΠΛΑΤΦΟΡΜΑ 1	*platforma 1*	PLATFORM 1
ΕΞΟΔΟΣ/ΠΥΛΗ 1	*eksoTHos/peelee 1*	GATE 1
ΤΕΛΩΝΕΙΟ	*teloneeo*	CUSTOMS
ΤΜΗΜΑ ΑΛΛΟΔΑΠΩΝ	*tmeema alloTHapon*	IMMIGRATION
ΑΦΙΞΕΙΣ	*afeeksees*	ARRIVALS
ΑΝΑΧΩΡΗΣΕΙΣ	*anakhoreesees*	DEPARTURES
ΠΑΡΑΛΑΒΗ ΑΠΟΣΚΕΥΩΝ	*paralavee aposkevon*	LUGGAGE RECLAIM
ΛΕΩΦΟΡΕΙΟ/ ΤΡΕΝΟ	*leoforeeo/ treno*	BUS/TRAIN
ΕΝΟΙΚΙΑΣΗ ΑΥΤΟΚΙΝΗΤΩΝ	*eneekeeasee aftokeeneeton*	CAR RENTAL
ΠΡΟΣ ΗΛΕΚΤΡΙΚΟΝ/ ΜΕΤΡΟ	*pros eelektreekon/ metro*	SUBWAY [METRO]
ΕΛΕΓΧΟΣ ΔΙΑΒΑΤΗΡΙΩΝ	*eelenkhos THeeavateereeon*	PASSPORT CONTROL

Hotel / Restaurant
ΞΕΝΟΔΟΧΕΙΟ/ ΕΣΤΙΑΤΟΡΙΟ

ΠΛΗΡΟΦΟΡΙΕΣ	*pleeroforee-es*	INFORMATION
ΡΕΣΕΨΙΟΝ/ ΥΠΟΔΟΧΗ	*resepseeon/ eepoTHokhee*	RECEPTION
ΚΛΕΙΣΜΕΝΟ	*kleesmeno*	RESERVED
ΕΞΟΔΟΣ ΚΙΝΔΥΝΟΥ	*eksoTHos keenTHeenoo*	EMERGENCY / FIRE EXIT
ΖΕΣΤΟ (ΝΕΡΟ)	*zesto (nero)*	HOT (WATER)
ΚΡΥΟ (ΝΕΡΟ)	*kreeo (nero)*	COLD (WATER)
ΜΟΝΟ ΓΙΑ ΠΡΟΣΩΠΙΚΟ	*mono ya prosopeeko*	STAFF ONLY
ΒΕΣΤΙΑΡΙΟ	*vesteeareeo*	COATCHECK [CLOAKROOM]
ΤΑΡΑΤΣΑ/ΚΗΠΟΣ	*taratsa/keepos*	TERRACE / GARDEN
ΜΠΑΡ	*"bar"*	BAR
ΖΑΧΑΡΟ-ΠΛΑΣΤΕΙΟ	*zakharoplasteeo*	CAKE SHOP

Stores ΚΑΤΑΣΤΗΜΑΤΑ

ΑΝΟΙΧΤΟ	*aneekhto*	OPEN
ΚΛΕΙΣΤΟ	*kleesto*	CLOSED
ΤΜΗΜΑ	*tmeema*	DEPARTMENT
ΟΡΟΦΟΣ	*orofos*	FLOOR
ΥΠΟΓΕΙΟ	*eepogheeo*	BASEMENT
ΑΣΑΝΣΕΡ/ ΑΝΕΛΚΥΣΤΗΡΑΣ	*asanser/ anelkeesteeras*	ELEVATOR [LIFT]
ΚΥΛΙΟΜΕΝΕΣ ΣΚΑΛΕΣ	*keeleeomenes skales*	ESCALATOR
ΤΑΜΕΙΟ	*tameeo*	CASHIER
ΕΚΠΤΩΣΕΙΣ	*ekptosees*	DISCOUNT
ΟΡΟΦΟΣ	*orofos*	FLOOR
ΗΜΙΟΡΟΦΟΣ/ ΜΕΣΟΠΑΤΩΜΑ	*eemeeorofos/ mesopatoma*	MEZZANINE
ΠΩΛΕΙΤΑΙ	*poleete*	FOR SALE

Sightseeing ΑΞΙΟΘΕΑΤΑ

ΕΛΕΥΘΕΡΑ ΕΙΣΟΔΟΣ/Η ΕΙΣΟΔΟΣ ΔΩΡΕΑΝ	*eleftherα eesoTHos/ ee eesoTHos THorean*	ADMISSION FREE
ΕΝΗΛΙΚΕΣ	*eneeleekes*	ADULTS
ΠΑΙΔΙΑ (ΑΚΑΤΑΛΛΗΛΟ ΓΙΑ ΠΑΙΔΙΑ)	*peTHya (akataleelo ya peTHya)*	CHILDREN (CHILDREN NOT ALLOWED)
ΦΟΙΤΗΤΙΚΑ/ ΜΑΘΗΤΙΚΑ	*feeteeteeka/ matheeteeka*	CONCESSIONS (students/ pupils)
ΣΟΥΒΕΝΙΡ/ ΕΙΔΗ ΔΩΡΩΝ	*sooveneer/ eeTHee THoron*	SOUVENIRS/ GIFTS
ΚΥΛΙΚΕΙΟ/ ΑΝΑΨΥΚΤΙΚΑ• ΚΑΦΕΣ	*keeleekeeo/ anapseekteeka•kafes*	REFRESHMENTS
ΜΗΝ ΑΓΓΙΖΕΤΕ	*meen angeezete*	DO NOT TOUCH
ΑΠΑΓΟΡΕΥΕΤΑΙ Η ΦΩΤΟΓΡΑΦΗΣΗ	*apaghorevete ee fotoghrafeesee*	NO PHOTOGRAPHY
ΗΣΥΧΙΑ!	*eeseekheea*	SILENCE
ΑΠΑΓΟΡΕΥΕΤΑΙ Η ΠΡΟΣΒΑΣΗ	*apaghorevete ee prosvasee*	NO ACCESS
ΕΚΔΟΣΗ ΕΙΣΙΤΗΡΙΩΝ	*ekTHosee eeseeteereeon*	TICKETS

Public Buildings
ΔΗΜΟΣΙΑ ΚΤΙΡΙΑ

ΝΟΣΟΚΟΜΕΙΟ	*nosokomeeo*	HOSPITAL
ΙΑΤΡΟΣ/ΙΑΤΡΕΙΟ	*eeatros/eeatreeo*	DOCTOR
ΟΔΟΝΤΙΑΤΡΟΣ/ ΟΔΟΝΤΙΑΤΡΕΙΟ	*oTHondeeatros/ oTHondeeatreeo*	DENTIST
ΑΣΤΥΝΟΜΙΑ	*asteenomeea*	POLICE
ΤΡΑΠΕΖΑ	*trapeza*	BANK
ΤΑΧΥΔΡΟΜΕΙΟ	*takheeTHromeeo*	POST OFFICE
ΚΟΛΥΜΒΗΤΗΡΙΟ/ ΠΙΣΙΝΑ	*koleemveeteereeo/ peeseena*	SWIMMING POOL
ΔΗΜΑΡΧΕΙΟ	*THeemarkheeo*	TOWN HALL
ΤΑΞΙ	*taksee*	TAXI STAND
ΜΟΥΣΕΙΟ	*mooseeo*	MUSEUM
ΝΟΜΑΡΧΕΙΑ	*nomarkheea*	COUNTY HALL
ΚΙΝΗΜΑΤΟ-ΓΡΑΦΟΣ	*keenematoghrafos*	MOVIE THEATER [CINEMA]
ΘΕΑΤΡΟ	*theatro*	THEATER
ΛΟΥΝΑ ΠΑΡΚ	*loona park*	FAIR SITE

Reference

Numbers

GRAMMAR

The Greek numbers 1, 3, and 4 – and the corresponding 21, 23, 24, 31, etc. – have different forms depending on the gender of the word that follows. Number 1 has three forms, while 3 and 4 have two forms. These are shown in parentheses below.

0	μηδέν	*meeTHen*
1	ένας (μια, ένα)	*enas (meea/mia, ena)*
2	δύο	*THeeo*
3	τρεις (τρία)	*trees (treea)*
4	τέσσερις (τέσσερα)	*teserees (tesera)*
5	πέντε	*pende*
6	έξι	*eksee*
7	επτά	*epta*
8	οκτώ	*okhto*
9	εννέα	*enea*
10	δέκα	*THeka*
11	έντεκα	*endeka*
12	δώδεκα	*THOTHeka*
13	δεκατρία	*THekatreea*
14	δεκατέσσερα	*THekatesera*
15	δεκαπέντε	*THekapende*
16	δεκαέξι	*THekaeksee*
17	δεκαεπτά	*THekaepta*
18	δεκαοκτώ	*THekaokto*
19	δεκαεννέα	*THekaenea*
20	είκοσι	*eekosee*
21	είκοσι ένα	*eekosee ena*
22	είκοσι δύο	*eekosee THeeo*
23	είκοσι τρία	*eekosee treea*
24	είκοσι τέσσερα	*eekosee tesera*
25	είκοσι πέντε	*eekosee pende*
26	είκοσι έξι	*eekosee eksee*
27	είκοσι επτά	*eekosee epta*
28	είκοσι οκτώ	*eekosee okto*
29	είκοσι εννέα	*eekosee enea*
30	τριάντα	*treeanda*
31	τριάντα ένα	*treeanda ena*

32	τριάντα δύο *treeanda THeeo*
40	σαράντα *saranda*
50	πενήντα *peneenda*
60	εξήντα *ekseenda*
70	εβδομήντα *evTHomeenda*
80	ογδόντα *oghTHonda*
90	ενενήντα *eneneenda*
100	εκατό *ekato*
101	εκατόν ένα *ekaton ena*
102	εκατόν δύο *ekaton THeeo*
200	διακόσια *THeeakoseea*
300	τριακόσια *treeakoseea*
400	τετρακόσια *tetrakoseea*
500	πεντακόσια *pendakoseea*
600	εξακόσια *eksakoseea*
700	εφτακόσια *eftakoseea*
800	οχτακόσια *okhtakoseea*
900	εννιακόσια *eneeakoseea*
1,000	χίλια *kheeleea*
10,000	δέκα χιλιάδες *THeka kheeleeaTHes*
1,000,000	ένα εκατομμύριο *ena ekatomeereeo*
first	πρώτος *protos*

second	δεύτερος *THefteros*
third	τρίτος *treetos*
fourth	τέταρτος *tetartos*
fifth	πέμπτος *pemtos*
once	μια φορά *mia fora*
twice	δύο φορές *THeeo fores*
three times	τρείς φορές *trees fores*
a half	μισό *meeso*
half an hour	μισή ώρα *meesee ora*
half a tank	μισό ντεπόζιτο *meeso depozeeto*
a quarter	ένα τέταρτο *ena tetarto*
a third	ένα τρίτο *ena treeto*
a pair of …	ένα ζευγάρι … *ena zevgharee*
a dozen …	μια ντουζίνα *mia doozeena*
1999	χίλια εννιακόσια ενενήντα εννέα *kheeleea eneeakoseea eneneenda enea*
2003	δύο χιλιάδες τρία *THeeo kheeleeaTHes treea*

Days Ημέρες

Monday	Δευτέρα *THeftera*
Tuesday	Τρίτη *treetee*
Wednesday	Τετάρτη *tetartee*
Thursday	Πέμπτη *pemtee*
Friday	Παρασκευή *paraskevee*
Saturday	Σάββατο *savato*
Sunday	Κυριακή *keeyakee*

Months Μήνες

January	Ιανουάριος *eeanooareeos*
February	Φεβρουάριος *fevrooareeos*
March	Μάρτιος *marteeos*
April	Απρίλιος *apreeleeos*
May	Μάιος *maeeos*
June	Ιούνιος *eeooneeos*
July	Ιούλιος *eeooleeos*
August	Αύγουστος *avghoostos*
September	Σεπτέμβριος *septemvreeos*
October	Οκτώβριος *oktovreeos*
November	Νοέμβριος *noemvreeos*
December	Δεκέμβριος *THekemvreeos*

Dates Ημερομηνίες

It's ...	Είναι ... *eene*
July 10	δέκα Ιουλίου *THeka eeooleeoo*
yesterday	χτες *khtes*
today	σήμερα *seemera*
tomorrow	αύριο *avreeo*
this ...	αυτό τον/αυτή την ... *afto ton/aftee teen*
last ...	τον προηγούμενο/την προηγούμενη ... *ton proeeghoomeno/* *teen proeeghoomenee*
next ...	τον επόμενο/την επόμενη ... *ton epomeno/teen epomenee*
week/month/year	εβδομάδα/μήνα/χρόνο *evTHomaTHa/meena/khrono*

Seasons Εποχές

spring	η άνοιξη *ee aneeksee*
summer	το καλοκαίρι *to kalokeree*
fall [autumn]	το φθινόπωρο *to ftheenoporo*
winter	ο χειμώνας *o kheemonas*
in spring	την άνοιξη *teen aneeksee*
during the summer	κατά τη διάρκεια του καλοκαιριού *kata tee THeearkeea too kalokeryoo*

Greetings Χαιρετισμοί

Happy birthday!	Να τα εκατοστήσετε! *na ta ekatosteesete*
Best wishes! (on namedays)	Χρόνια πολλά! *khroneea pola*
Merry Christmas!	Καλά Χριστούγεννα! *kala khreestooyena*
Happy New Year!	Ευτυχισμένος ο Καινούριος Χρόνος! *efteekheezmenos o kenooryos khronos*
Congratulations!	Συγχαρητήρια *seenkhareeteereea*
Good luck! / All the best!	Καλή επιτυχία! *kalee epeeteekheea*

Public holidays Δημόσιες αργίες

1 January	Πρωτοχρονιά *protokhroneea*	New Year's Day
6 January	Θεοφάνεια *theofaneea*	Epiphany
25 March	Ευαγγελισμός/Εθνική εορτή *evangeleesmos/ethneekee eortee*	Annunciation / Anniversary of start of Greek War of Independence
2nd Mon. in May	Πρωτομαγιά *protomaya*	May Day
15 August	Κοίμηση της Θεοτόκου *keemeesee tees theotokoo*	Assumption
28 October	Εθνική εορτή *ethneekee eortee*	Anniversary of Greece's rejection of Mussolini's ultimatum and entry into WW2
25 December	Χριστούγεννα *khreestooyena*	Christmas Day
26 December	Αγίου Στεφάνου *agheeoo stefanoo*	St Stephen's Day

Movable feasts:

Easter Πάσχα *paskha* ; First day of Lent Καθαρή Δευτέρα *katharee THeftera;*
50 days after Easter Sunday Αγίου Πνεύματος *ayeeou pnevmatos;*
Each city or town has a patron saint. Their name day is a local public holiday.

Time Η ώρα

Excuse me. Can you tell me the time?	Συγγνώμη. Τι ώρα είναι; *seeghnomee. tee ora eene*
It's …	Είναι … *eene*
five past one	μία και πέντε *mia ke pende*
ten past two	δύο και δέκα *THeeo ke THeka*
a quarter past three	τρεις και τέταρτο *trees ke tetarto*
twenty past four	τέσσερις και είκοσι *teserees ke eekosee*
twenty-five past five	πέντε και είκοσι πέντε *pende ke eekosee pende*
half past six	έξι και μισή *eksee ke meesee*
twenty-five to seven	επτά παρά είκοσι πέντε *epta para eekosee pende*
twenty to eight	οκτώ παρά είκοσι *okhto para eekosee*
a quarter to nine	εννέα παρά τέταρτο *enea para tetarto*
ten to ten	δέκα παρά δέκα *THeka para THeka*
five to eleven	έντεκα παρά πέντε *endeka para pende*
twelve o'clock	δώδεκα η ώρα *THoTHeka ee ora*
noon/midnight	μεσημέρι/μεσάνυχτα *meseemeree/mesaneekhta*

at dawn	τα ξημερώματα *ta kseemeromata*
in the morning	το πρωί *to proee*
during the day	κατά τη διάρκεια της ημέρας *kata tee THeearkeea tees eemeras*
before lunch	πριν το μεσημεριανό *preen to meseemeryano*
after lunch	μετά το μεσημεριανό *meta to meseemeryano*
in the afternoon	το απόγευμα *to apoyevma*
in the evening	το βράδυ *to vraTHee*
at night	τη νύχτα *tee neekhta*
I'll be ready in five minutes.	Θα είμαι έτοιμος/-η σε πέντε λεπτά. *tha eeme eteemos/-ee se pende lepta*
He'll be back in 15 minutes.	Θα επιστρέψει σε ένα τέταρτο της ώρας. *tha epeestrepsee se ena tetarto tees oras*
She arrived half an hour ago.	Έφτασε πριν από μισή ώρα. *eftase preen apo meesee ora*
The train leaves at …	Το τραίνο φεύγει … *to treno fevyee*
13:04	στις δεκατρείς και τέσσερα λεπτά *stees THekatrees ke tesera lepta*
0:40	σαράντα λεπτά μετά τα μεσάνυχτα *saranda lepta meta ta mesaneekhta*
10 minutes late/early	δέκα λεπτά αργότερα/νωρίτερα *THeka lepta arghotera/noreetera*
from 9:00 to 5:00	από τις εννέα ως τις πέντε *apo tees enea os tees pende*
between 8:00 and 2:00	μεταξύ οκτώ και δύο
I'll be leaving by …	Θα φύγω στις … *tha feevgho stees*
Will you be back before … ?	Θα επιστρέψετε πριν τις … ; *tha epeestrepsete preen tees*
We'll be here until …	Θα είμαστε εδώ ως τις … *tha eemaste eTHo os tees*

Bulgaria
Macedonia
Albania
Turkey
Kavala
Alexandroupoli
Thessaloniki
Thasos
Veroia
Limnos
Ioannina
AEGEAN SEA
Trikala
Volos
Greece
Skopelos
Lesbos
Skyros
Agrinio
Evvoia
Chios
Kefallonia
Athens
Samos
Patra
Andros
Corinth
Zante
Tripoli
Kea
Mykonos
Patmos
Ydra
Naxos
Sparti
Kos
Pylos
Milos
Ios
Santorini
Rhodes
Kythira
IONIAN
SEA
Karpathos
Crete